Journal of Pentecostal Theology
Supplement Series
17

Editors
John Christopher Thomas
Rickie D. Moore
Steven J. Land

Sheffield Academic Press
Sheffield

Rites in the Spirit

A Ritual Approach to

Pentecostal/ Charismatic

Spirituality

Daniel E. Albrecht

Sheffield Academic Press

Copyright © 1999 Sheffield Academic Press

Published by
Sheffield Academic Press Ltd
Mansion House
19 Kingfield Road
Sheffield S11 9AS
England

Typeset by Sheffield Academic Press
and
Printed on acid-free paper in Great Britain
by Cromwell Press
Trowbridge, Wiltshire

British Library Cataloguing in Publication Data

A catalogue record for this book is available
from the British Library

ISBN 1-84127-017-2

CONTENTS

PREFACE

Spirituality, Ritual and Pentecostal Experience

This is a book about spirituality, about a particular type of spirituality—
Pentecostal. It presents a study of Pentecostal experience and the rites
and rituals that express, shape, nurture, transform and authenticate the
spirituality of Pentecostals. This volume engages the academic discipline of Christian Spirituality, aiming to produce a careful analysis and
interpretation of Pentecostal/Charismatic (Pent/Char) spirituality.[1]

Rites in the Spirit seeks to engage those who are interested in spirituality—not only those interested in its academic study, but also those
interested in spirituality as a first-hand lived (religious) experience. The
specific focus—Pent/Char spirituality as understood and manifested in
rituals and rites—should interest students of ritual studies and those
curious about Pentecostalism. Other readers' interest may be piqued by
the topics of spiritual experiences, phenomena and expressions that
mark a contemporary, sometimes exotic movement. *Rites in the Spirit*
represents my attempt to engage a variety of interested people in a
'conversation' about some things that I believe really matter.

This is a book about and for Pentecostals. I trust, however, that those
who do not consider themselves a part of Pent/Char Christianity will
find much of interest in this volume. I think that the following interpretation will make Pentecostalism more accessible and understandable to
those with little experience but some interest in the topic. Pentecostals
themselves, I hope, will find many places of identification, experience

---

1.   I often use the term 'Pentecostal/Charismatic' (Pent/Char) synonymously
with Pentecostal. See Chapter 1. I understand the classical Pentecostal movement
rooted in the turn of the twentieth-century revival and the neo-Pentecostal or Charismatic (renewal) movement of the second half the century to be two 'waves' within
one larger movement. The main churches studied within this book represent both
Classical and Charismatic impulses often in the same church. Thus, at times I will
use the generic 'Pentecostal' as inclusive of both, while at other times I will use
Pent/Char to include both.

moments of insight and move toward a deeper understanding of their own native spirituality.

Orientations and Motivations

When embarking on a project that requires much time and energy, such as this one, it is wise to consider one's motivations and aspirations. So, I did. I have discovered that I work best when an issue deeply interests me and engages my affections and concern. This study meets these criteria for me. I am profoundly interested in and moved by this topic. Its complex issues have long intrigued me. However, other factors too have not only motivated but have also helped to orient me as I have proceeded.

Fundamental motivation emerged from two orienting influences in my life—my specific academic discipline and my personal spiritual heritage. In the mid-1980s I became aware of a doctoral program in Christian Spirituality that was a part of Berkeley's Graduate Theological Union (GTU)—Area VIII, 'History and Phenomenology of Religions'. Through a series of events I was invited to participate in a newly established seminar designed for faculty (from GTU and UC Berkeley) and doctoral students pursuing their interests in spirituality. The seminar focused particularly on how the emerging scholarly field of study in spirituality interacted with other more established academic specialties, especially those in religious studies and the human sciences. During that year I encountered some of the finest scholars in their respective fields. I was overwhelmed by the possibilities that lay before me. It seemed clear that the potential for serious study within the burgeoning field of Christian Spirituality was far beyond what I had previously envisioned.

Subsequently I entered the doctoral program in Area VIII. My Berkeley studies broadened, deepened, oriented and motivated my interest in spirituality. Even before I completed my degree, I began to teach in the area of Christian Spirituality. I planned and developed a series of courses that took seriously the contemporary scholarship as well as the richness of the tradition. In the years that followed, my academic orientation and interest in this field within the academy has continued to grow. But my concern for those not directly a part of the academy has also increased. The vast resources of the Christian tradition, now nearly 2000 years old, and the various streams of spiritualities within the larger tradition continue to excite and challenge me. I hope to speak not only with academics but to engage pastors and parishioners as well. This impulse is rooted in the second orienting influence, my personal spiritual heritage.

Cheryl Bridges-Johns speaks for me when she says, 'I bring to this task my heritage'.[2] Let me explain. As a child growing up in a Pentecostal home, integrally a part of a Pentecostal church—its ethos, worship and community—I could not have imagined that I would one day write a book about rituals, rites and spirituality. No true Pentecostal would write such a book. Such terms as 'ritual', 'rites' or even 'spirituality' were not indigenous to our shared Pentecostal vocabulary.

Clearly, I have been influenced by the recent notoriety of the emerging global Pent/Char force, now claiming nearly half a billion adherents, and by the recognition granted by notable scholars in a variety of academic fields, who have begun to notice the presence and actions of Pentecostals. But my reasons for writing are not greatly impacted by the size of the movement, nor by the recent interest in it. I was interested in spirituality before learning to employ the term. And I was serious about a better understanding of my instinctive Pentecostal faith—its expressions, symbols, acts, actions, practices and foundational experiences—long before I understood the concept of symbolic-expressive behavior or before I studied practices designated as ritual and rites.

My Pentecostal culture has affected (at times focused) my orientation; Pentecostal ethos early provided a nascent motivation to study and better understand the spirituality of a people, my people. I am a Pentecostal by birth and (I think) by choice. As such, I was nurtured by people who lived out their everyday lives in light of their experience of and commitment to God. Their experience could not be confined within the walls of a Pentecostal tabernacle, though it was supported, guided, stimulated, challenged, corrected and critiqued weekly within those walls. I came to believe that quite often our shared practices—including the worship rites and ritual—expressed a deep reality for those whom I knew intimately in my early years. They could not abide 'dead ritual', but they did esteem vital, expressive acts that symbolized and gave vent

2. See Cheryl Bridges-Johns, *Pentecostal Formation: A Pedagogy among the Oppressed* (JPTSup, 2; Sheffield: Sheffield Academic Press, 1993), p. 8. I believe that my Pentecostal heritage has provided a fundamental orientation to and motivation for both my academic discipline, in general, and it has functioned as an orienting and motivation force for this present study, in particular.

to the truth of what they often encountered—the unspeakably real and vibrant experience of God. For them, it was an experience that transformed and made sense of their lives.

Even as a questioning young person, I recognized that those who nurtured me spiritually lived in the real world. They were often extremely pragmatic, but they also believed in and experienced another realm— the kingdom of God.[3] Participation in this realm transmuted their lives. At times, the mundane became miraculous, their jobs became opportunities for service, their conversations chances to share God's goodness, 'their trials' the arena in which God revealed loving concern and sovereign power. While yet young, I perceived an authentic faith even amid certain excesses and inauthenticities. This perception encouraged my own spiritual life during key developmental stages of my childhood, adolescence and even early adulthood.

Admittedly, I did not always appreciate my Pentecostal ethos. Being a part of a 'peculiar people' can be exasperating (not to mention embarrassing), but I always wondered about my tradition and sympathetically critiqued its sometimes strange behavior patterns. In fact, I was taught by the Pentecostal folks around me to 'test the spirits' and not gullibly to accept all 'manifestations' or words as authentic, significant or edifying. Now, as a mature adult, I have sought to heed their exhortation, even if by unforseen methods. As I guessed when young, not all Pentecostal expressions ring true. During my investigation, however, so many have rung true that I have gained a new appreciation for my heritage. Thus, my interest in presenting the following interpretation of Pent/Char spirituality arises (in no small part) from within my native subculture. I think that my Pentecostal instinct—that seeks not only to test for authenticity but also to plumb the depths of an experience for significance and meaning—and my academic training have combined to orient and motivate the following study.

An Approach to Spirituality

As a result of personal research and experimentation with several approaches to critical study of spirituality over the past decade, I have come increasingly to see that quality academic study of spirituality

---

3.   On Pentecostals and the kingdom of God, see Steven J. Land, *Pentecostal Spirituality: A Passion for the Kingdom* (JPTSup, 1; Sheffield: Sheffield Academic Press, 1993).

(Pentecostal spirituality included) can yield important data. Such data assist in a more informed interpretation of a particular spirituality. While critical analysis and scholarly interpretation are no substitute for participation within a spiritual community and tradition, neither are scholarly studies and faith-filled participation necessarily opposed or mutually antagonistic. I have discovered that scholarship and faith experience and practices can each provide data and insight in two distinct ways, and as a result, they can ultimately function cooperatively, complementing (even while potentially critiquing, correcting and informing) each other. Such complementarity, I believe, is particularly important within Pentecostal studies.[4] Pentecostals need the assistance that scholarly studies of our spirituality can provide. Such studies, among other things, can help inform and give perspective, a critical dimension within our spirituality. This scholarly role could function analogously to the more intuitive 'testing of spirits'. Let me then state an important presupposition that in part inspires the present study: quality scholarship aimed at investigating and understanding Pentecostal spirituality can both contribute to the academy and help to enrich Pentecostals.

With this twofold intention in mind, a fundamental issue for any serious study in Christian spirituality arises, that is, the choice of a method or an approach to the particular topic. The goal is to employ an approach appropriate to the topic, one that helps make available the data essential to the interpretive process. In general, my approach in this study can be characterized as fundamentally hermeneutical. By that I mean, I have sought to interpret Pent/Char spirituality hoping to make it more understandable and meaningful to interested readers—whether

---

4. I would not argue that all studies in spirituality or in Pentecostal studies must link these two elements. Certainly, there are quality studies, for example, done by scholars who make no faith claim. On the other hand, some studies have revealed a dismissive attitude toward Pentecostals and their spirituality and as a result have 'missed' much of the substance of Pentecostalism. Perhaps some understanding of or sympathy for Pentecostal faith may have served better to inform such studies.

During the research for this volume, I did at times use participatory observation as a means to data gathering. Yet, in the research and the writing, I have attempted to keep a certain distance from the topic, endeavoring to maintain the perspective of a observer. I have taken my cue from Paul Ricoeur's understanding of 'distanciation'. See his essay 'The Hermeneutical Function of Distanciation', in *idem*, *Hermeneutics and the Human Sciences* (ed. and trans. John B. Thompson; Cambridge: Cambridge University Press, 1981), pp. 131-44.

scholar, or lay person, Pentecostal or not. My general approach moves in three somewhat overlapping modes—a 'thick' descriptive mode, a critical analysis and a constructive interpretation.[5] Each of these within the study seeks to disclose something of the substance that we call Pent/Char Spirituality.

While there are numerous specific approaches and methods that hold promise for accessing and interpreting the formal object—Pentecostal (spiritual) experience as experience—I believe, because of the nature of human religious experience, that an 'interdisciplinarity of method' is required. Such interdisciplinarity marks many successful contemporary studies in spirituality.[6] Spirituality as a discipline does not have *one* standard method. Rather, depending on the particular object of a study, methods are chosen for their appropriateness.

Sandra Schneiders, one of the foremost theorists in the field of Spirituality, has articulated a helpful model which envisions spirituality as an 'interdisciplinary academic discipline'. She argues that Christian

> spirituality as an academic discipline is intrinsically and irreducibly interdisciplinary because the object it studies, transformative Christian experience as such, is multi-faceted. Every topic of study in this field requires that several disciplines be used together in a reciprocally interactive and not merely juxtaposed way throughout the process of investigation.[7]

Schneiders recognizes two layers of interdisciplinarity active in research projects in the area of Christian spirituality—what she calls 'constitutive disciplines' and 'problematic disciplines'. On the one hand, the *constitutive* disciplines (Scripture, history of Christianity and sometimes theology) function in relation to the topic because they help supply both the data of the Christian religious experience and the hermeneutical context. On the other hand, *problematic* disciplines are necessarily incorporated in a particular study because of the problematic of the phenomenon under investigation. Problematic disciplines include among others anthropology, sociology, psychology, literature, natural science and any other disciplines that function better to access the experiential aspect of the object of study. The present work reflects Schneider's suggestive approach and categories.

---

5.   See Sandra Schneiders, 'The Study of Christian Spirituality', *CSB* 6.1 (1998), pp. 1-12, for a description of this general approach.
6.   Schneiders, 'Study of Christian Spirituality', p. 3.
7.   Schneiders, 'Study of Christian Spirituality', p. 3.

The leading *problematic discipline* in my analysis is ritual studies. *Ritual studies*, or *ritology* as some prefer, is a discipline that focuses on a broad variety of ritualizations. It includes in its studies all types of rituals, religious and non-religious. Ritology focuses most directly on enactment or performance, that is, it gives priority to the acts, the actions and the gestural activities of people. In a secondary manner, it may focus on written texts and spoken words, but will do so in the context of the people's actions. Ritology seeks to interpret words and other culturally symbolic objects in light of the enactments of a people.[8] As a result an engagement in fieldwork and methods of participatory observation are typical.

Why use ritual studies as the leading problematic discipline for an assessment and interpretation of Pent/Char spirituality? In part, the answer lies in the nature of Pentecostal spirituality itself. Given the characteristic rich expressions of worship, the propensity for a full and various array of expressive behaviors, it seemed to me early on in my investigation that ritology might be an appropriate discipline to employ in Pentecostal studies. My assumptions about Pentecostal worship expressions also moved me toward the utilization of ritology. After some initial experimentation, my hunch was confirmed.

I assume that the Pentecostal worship rites are—at least to some extent—manifestations of a lived faith, of a religious or spiritual experience. If the rites do in fact reflect the inherent spirituality of the Pentecostal worshipers then it seems reasonable to engage methods of ritual studies to access the experiences of Pentecostals in the midst of their worship ritual. For, as noted above, ritual studies focus on the symbolic-expressive behavior of a people, particularly as they engage in fundamental practices—enactments and rites—that characterize and in some ways define them as a people.

The deeper I became involved in this study in applying categories

---

8.   For example, Ronald Grimes, a leading scholar in the field of ritual studies, uses the term 'ritology' to describe the academic discipline. See his *Ritual Criticism: Case Studies in its Practice, Essays on its Theory* (Columbia, SC: University of South Carolina Press, 1990); and *Beginnings in Ritual Studies* (Lanham, MD: University Press of America, 1982), for description of the field. This study draws upon the work of Grimes and his characterization of ritology. He points out that academically the discipline of ritology is both akin to and draws upon the disciplines of symbolic anthropology, liturgiology, kinesics and performance studies (*Ritual Criticism*, p. 9).

and approaches from ritology, the more convinced I became that authentic ritual expressions are not peripheral actions for Pentecostals but represent fundamental elements of an authentic Pentecostal spirituality. Thus, to study Pentecostal rites with the best approach possible promises access to experience that is primary to Pent/Char spirituality. My research among Pentecostals utilizing ritual studies categories has, I believe, yielded important data.

Let me summarize my approach to this present study. In the following pages I examine Pentecostal ritual as integral to, an expression of and an efficacious dynamic within Pent/Char spirituality. I take Christian spirituality to mean *the lived religious experience of the Christian faith*. My aim is to understand Pent/Char spirituality—a particular type of Christian spirituality—by describing, analyzing and constructively interpreting it through the lens of a ritual study. My task originally involved ethnographic field work, including the methods of participant observation and ethnographic interviewing. Consequently, the following interpretation draws on data collected from the central Pentecostal ritual, the Sunday worship service, in three Northern California congregations over a period of more than two years. It evokes the categories and symbols indigenous to Pentecostals and to some extent selects helpful categories suggested by social scientists, theologians and others who study ritual, religious movements or Pentecostalism in particular.[9]

Our Moment: Opportunities and Challenges

Why this study at this time? The Pent/Char movement has arrived at an extraordinary moment in history. On the one hand, this moment presents unprecedented opportunities for Pentecostalism, while on the other hand it represents serious challenges for the movement.

Presently, scholars and church leaders are beginning to recognize the Pent/Char movement as a potent force. I believe that Pentecostals have much to offer the Church and the world, and that current opportunities are extraordinary. Pent/Char contributions include: a significant influence for spiritual renewal within the churches; expressive forms of prayer and worship that have fostered a deepening spirituality for many

---

9.   Noted in the pages below, for example, anthropologists Victor Turner and Mary Douglas, sociologists Robert Bellah and Robert Wuthnow, philosopher Paul Ricoeur, theologians Donald Gelpi and Tom Driver among others have each provided categories that facilitated the following interpretation.

Christians; innovative and energetic evangelization; effective missions; care for hurting people; an ecumenical impulse; and an understanding and experience of Christianity that often transcends the boundaries of traditional, modern, Western Christianity.

The growing interest in Pent/Char spirituality is also related to what it may offer to the religious world of the future—its unrealized potential. Noted Harvard theologian Harvey Cox, an interested, sympathetic observer, is one of the religious scholars who has recently recognized the potential opportunities for Pentecostals. Cox believes that in Pentecostalism observers may glimpse the trajectories of Christianity for the twenty-first century. Pent/Char influences could very well reshape religion during the century that lies before us. Werner Hoerschelmann, another astute observer, states it simply and boldly: '*Pentecostal spirituality is the future.*'[10]

It does seem a remarkable moment for a movement merely one century old. Yet, even in 100 years certain natural developments occur. The processes of maturation within the Pent/Char movement combined with an era of rapid changes throughout the world have produced several significant challenges for the Pentecostal tradition. We find ourselves at a crossroads. For example, calls for renewed self-understanding and a re-visioning the movement have emerged within the movement. These impulses imply a need both to affirm the Pentecostal heritage and to re-appropriate the treasured symbols, the legacy of Pentecostals within changed contexts. Such re-appropriating and re-visioning has begun—Steven Land's work is a prime example—but the challenge largely remains unmet.[11]

Aims and Purposes

With such challenges and opportunities characterizing our moment, I hope to make a modest contribution to the growing conversation con-

10. Cox and Hoerschelmann quoted in Walter Hollenweger, *Pentecostalism: Origins and Developments Worldwide* (Peabody, MA: Hendrickson, 1997), pp. 2-3.

11. Some other examples of challenges to Pentecostalism at this juncture in our history are noted by Walter Hollenweger: the need for a 'critical historiography, for social and political analysis, for a more differentiated treatment of the work of the Spirit, for a spirituality which does not blend out critical thinking, for a new appraisal of pre-Christian cultures in their own Third World sister churches, for ecumenical openness and dialogue'. See Hollenweger, *Pentecostalism*, p. 1.

cerning Pentecostalism, its spirituality and its role in our times. In the
above sections I have implied some of the aims and purpose of this volume. Here let me note a few more hopes for the following chapters.
Rites in the Spirit intends a serious study, a careful interpretation of
Pent/Char spirituality. My aim throughout has been to make Pent/Char
spirituality accessible and understandable to scholars and lay readers, to
Pentecostals and non-Pentecostals alike. For those whose academic
interests center on or intersect with spirituality, Pentecostalism or ritual
studies, this volume seeks to present an analysis and interpretation that
will contribute not only to the larger body of research in these areas, but
will make Pentecostalism more understandable. For those readers whose
concerns focus on praxis, applicational or pastoral issues in spirituality,
I believe that the following study may provide much to ponder and, I
hope, will help point toward some relevant applications.

In addition, I have sought to respond to calls of Pentecostal scholars
and others who study current Pentecostalism. I hope that the following
study will function as a response to the calls for thoughtful assessments.
Rites in the Spirit will, I hope, provide a deeper and more critical
insight into the Pentecostal heritage even for insiders. If so, the book
could assist Pentecostals with a contemporary self-understanding and
self-critique and perhaps even give guidance in the midst of strategic
decisions being made at this stage in our development, a crossroads in
our moment in history.

I have however written this work with the interested non-participant
in mind, also. For some, *Rites in the Spirit* will provide an introduction
to a world little encountered. To others, it will give a reasoned account
and analysis to a world little understood. It is my desire to engage non-
Pentecostals in the conversation too. I hope this work will help to make
Pentecostalism more accessible to non-Pentecostals and provide them
with a clearer understanding of Pentecostals and their attending spirituality. Perhaps the subsequent conversation involving Pentecostal and
non-Pentecostals will bring us toward greater mutual appreciation and
respect—two elements I believe are fundamental to ecumenical dialogue.

With *Rites in the Spirit* I have also entered the conversations that
focus on liturgic and ritual studies. I hope that this volume will be read
by those interested in ritology and liturgical studies. This volume represents a case study. It presents a description of a particular ritual and an
analysis and interpretation of how that fundamental Pentecostal ritual—

with its various, associated rites—expresses, nurtures, enlivens and transforms a particular spirituality.

This study is only a beginning. I have by necessity limited its perspective, its use of analytical tools and its number and types of Pent/ Char groups studied. These restrictions seem all the more limiting against the backdrop of the huge, widely diverse, rapidly growing, global Pentecostal–Charismatic movement. As to the generalizability of this study, its specific implications, and its relevance (or irrelevance), I will have to leave these important issues to my readers, to subsequent analysis and, I hope, to further conversation. I do believe, however, that *Rites in the Spirit* will give a glimpse (if only 'through a glass darkly') into the reality of Pentecostals, our liturgical practices, and our life and rites in the Spirit.

ACKNOWLEDGMENTS

I owe a debt of gratitude to my friends and colleagues who have helped me with this project. Perhaps the greatest debt is to those folks (like the Boyces), family (my parents and extended family) and fellow travelers (like the Groffs and Fred Gere), who nurtured me within a heritage that I did not always appreciate or understand but whose lives revealed a reality that I could not deny. Those authentic Christians have helped me to come to say—with appreciation, understanding and experience—'I am a Pentecostal'.

I am grateful for the kindness and openness of the people and pastors of the congregations within which we did our fieldwork, collected data and came to better understand rites in the Spirit. I learned so much from them. Speaking of the field research, I must also acknowledge those who helped with the preliminary fieldwork and interviews: Yvonne Albrecht, James Carlen, Craig Fisher, Paige Glass, Mari Prieto, Wes Sanders, Lisa Schmidt, Douglas Shelton, Eve Snow and Bernard Wagner. They helped to make the research more thorough.

Certainly, words cannot adequately express my gratitude or repay what I owe to all the members of the Bethany College community. They encouraged, supported and prayed for me not only throughout this project but since I arrived in Santa Cruz. This very special community has made a place for me professionally and spiritually. Special thanks to Richard Israel and Thomas Ward, who continually stimulate and challenge my thinking and often listen to my ramblings; to Robert Abplanalp and Michael Stach for reading early versions of the manuscript and for providing helpful suggestions; and to Deans Everett Wilson, Jimmy Brewer and Willie Snow for providing the 'space'— physical, emotional and intellectual—to complete this project. I am particularly indebted to Joyce Stach for her tireless work with the word processing.

Also, I owe much to my former professors in Berkeley, GTU and UCB. Donald Gelpi, SJ, who not only directed my dissertation but has been mentor and friend. Special thanks also to Robert Bellah and Duane Christensen for their encouragement and guidance, especially during the dissertation phase. I also benefited enormously from interaction with my colleagues in the Christian Spirituality program at the Graduate Theological Union. I am particularly grateful for the conveners of the Christian Spirituality seminars, Sandra Schneiders, IHM, and William Short, OFM. Their scholarship and dedication helped direct me toward and continues to inspire me in the study of spirituality.

Certainly, I am grateful for those who helped bring this work to publication. Thanks to Russell Spittler of Fuller Theological Seminary for reading a draft of this work and suggesting that I look to *Journal of Pentecostal Theology*, Supplement Series for publication. The editors of the series have been so helpful not only pertaining to this project but as colleagues in Pentecostal studies. Rickie Moore has challenged my thinking concerning the place of biblical scholarship and Pentecostal spirituality. Steven Land's work has been both a model and stimulus to my own writing. Steve's personal interest in my work helped move me along in my research and thought. Chris Thomas has assisted me not only with his own scholarly work and example but directly in the preparation of this volume. His gentle promptings and prodding help to motivate me and sharpen my focus. I am grateful for these three brothers.

With friends and helpers such as these, I must take responsibility for the inadequacies of what follows.

One final word. Above all, I am deeply thankful for and indebted to my family whose sympathetic support, loving acceptance, and sensitive understanding sustains me. I dedicate this work to Shannon, Sean and Yvonne, with whom I live, move and have my being.

Dan Albrecht
Santa Cruz, California
1 January 1999
98 years after the outpouring in Topeka

ABBREVIATIONS

BSac	*Bibliotheca Sacra*
CSB	*Christian Spirituality Bulletin: Journal of the Society for the Study of Christian Spirituality*
CT	*Christianity Today*
DCA	Daniel G. Reid *et al.*, *Dictionary of Christianity in America* (Downers Grove, IL: InterVarsity Press, 1990)
DPCM	Stanley Burgess, Gary McGee and Patrick Alexander (eds.), *Dictionary of Pentecostal and Charismatic Movements* (Grand Rapids: Zondervan, 1988)
EOR	Mircea Eliade *et al.* (eds.), *Encyclopedia of Religion* (16 vols.; New York: Macmillan, 1987)
HR	*History of Religions*
HTR	*Harvard Theological Review*
IBMR	*International Bulletin of Missionary Research*
JES	*Journal of Ecumenical Studies*
JR	*Journal of Religion*
JSSR	*Journal for the Scientific Study of Religion*
JPT	*Journal of Pentecostal Theology*
JPTSup	*Journal of Pentecostal Theology*, Supplement Series
PE	*Pentecostal Evangel*
Pneuma	*Pneuma: The Journal of the Society for Pentecostal Studies*
RSV	Revised Standard Version

INTRODUCTION

What does 'ritual' have to do with 'Pentecostal spirituality'? Isn't the free-flowing spirituality of the Pentecostals antithetical to the nature of ritual? On the surface, these questions appear rhetorical. However, I have discovered and in this book maintain that ritual functions as a vital component of Pentecostal spirituality. Consequently, a study of Pentecostal ritual can assist the analysis and comprehension of Pentecostal spirituality.[1] One might question whether a ritual study can truly facilitate an understanding of the elements and dynamics of Pentecostal spirituality. After all, traditionally Pentecostals themselves have often objected to or reject the term 'ritual' and its implied conceptualization. To them, ritual represents something 'dead', meaningless or even 'unscriptural' and 'unspiritual', mechanical, religion. At best, many Pentecostals speak of 'ritual' as too restrictive, routine, potentially inhibiting the Spirit's moving and therefore not conducive to the spiritual experiences that they encourage.[2] However, Pentecostals do in fact,

1. Clearly, when I attempt to use general terms such as 'Pentecostals' or 'Pentecostal spirituality' I do a great injustice to the multitudinous forms of Pentecostalism around the world. Likewise, almost any general statement I make about Pentecostal ritual is inaccurate when compared to specific situations. In this study my illustrations and insights are drawn essentially from my field research, and I can only claim accuracy within these congregations. I do, however, use terms that might imply generalization. It remains for the reader to judge the true generalizability of my specific study.

2. Pentecostals are not the only modern Westerners to question the value of ritual. Many view ritual as foreign or pre-modern, something that has been left behind from a previous era, culture or religious tradition. Others see ritual as irrelevant, not really vital, because for them ritual means 'a routinized act', merely an external gesture void of internal engagement and commitment. This view sees all 'ritual' as 'ritualized ritual', a barren symbol of empty conformity. See Mary Douglas, *Natural Symbols: Explorations in Cosmology* (New York: Pantheon Books 1982 [1970]). Such views of ritual are too restrictive, if not wholly inaccurate. For examples of a more adequate perspective on ritual and a distinction between

engage in rituals, though they often call them by other names: 'worship services', 'spiritual practices', 'Pentecostal distinctives', for example.

Ritual has many definitions,[3] but throughout this volume ritual connotes those acts, actions, dramas and performances that a community creates, continues, recognizes and sanctions as ways of behaving that express appropriate attitudes, sensibilities, values, and beliefs within a given situation. In particular, I apply the term *ritual* to the *corporate worship service*.[4] The Pentecostal service lies at the heart of the Pentecostal/Charismatic (Pent/Char) spirituality and with its attending rites and practices constitutes the most central ritual of Pentecostalism.[5] I employ the term *rite* when referring to a portion or phase of the service (e.g. the sermon, the song service), a particular practice or specific act or enactment (e.g. laying on of hands and prayer, taking an offering, receiving water or Spirit baptism) or a set of actions (e.g. various types of altar/responses) recognized by Pentecostals as a legitimate part of their overall ritual.[6]

Ritual by nature dramatizes and effects the life of a people.[7] In particular, the Pentecostal rites both dramatize and vitalize the spirituality

---

'ritualized ritual' and authentic, vital ritual see Douglas, *Natural Symbols*; Tom F. Driver, *The Magic of Ritual: Our Need for Liberating Rites that Transform our Lives and our Communities* (San Francisco: HarperSanFrancisco, 1991); Grimes, *Beginnings*; *idem*, *Ritual Criticism*; Barbara G. Myerhoff, *Number our Days* (New York: Simon & Schuster, 1978); Barbara G. Myerhoff *et al.*, 'Rites of Passage, an Overview', in *EOR*, XII, pp. 380-86; Victor Turner, *The Ritual Process: Structure and Anti-Structure* (Ithaca, NY: Cornell University Press, 1977).

3.   See Grimes, *Beginnings*, pp. 53-69, for a survey of definitions and a refined composite of connotations with a unique contribution toward a definition of (nascent) ritual.

4.   Examples of Pentecostal rituals (service type) other than the normal weekly corporate worship service include prayer meetings, evangelistic meetings, home group meetings, Bible studies, Sunday School, youth and children's services, camp meetings, retreats, conferences. See Appendix A for a more complete list of Pentecostal (macro) rituals.

5.   Robert Mapes Anderson, *Vision of the Disinherited: The Making of American Pentecostalism* (New York: Oxford University Press, 1979), and *idem*, 'Pentecostal and Charismatic Christianity', in *EOR*, XI, pp. 229-35. I use the term *ritual* here to speak of the entire Pentecostal service.

6.   See Appendix B for a categorization and listing of liturgical rites, foundational and microrites in the Pentecostal service.

7.   See Chapter 6 where I deal in more depth with some essential roles of ritual.

of a community.[8] Pentecostals often experience their rites as essential, life-giving and arguably responsible in part for the vitality of their movement, its spread and the spirituality it encourages. And though it is true that Pentecostal spirituality does not confine itself to its rituals, the rites of the Pentecostals form an indispensable component of the spirituality.[9] Thus, I believe that the Pentecostal ritual performance deserves serious consideration. I assert that, by looking through the lens of ritual, the deliberate and sensitive participant-observer can access, assess and comprehend the symbols, qualities, processes, consequences and general ethos of a Pentecostal spirituality. With this presupposition, this work presents a ritual study of Pentecostal spirituality based on field research of the ritual performances of three selected Pent/Char communities.

When I speak of spirituality, I mean lived experience that actualizes a fundamental dimension of the human being, the spiritual dimension, namely 'the whole of one's spiritual or religious experience, one's beliefs, convictions, and patterns of thought, one's emotions and behavior in respect to what is ultimate, or God'.[10] Little distinguishes

---

8. Because Pentecostal ritual embodies a spirituality, ritual performance portrays that spirituality. But ritual performance functions as both expression and 'work'. By ritual work I mean that Pentecostal ritual has efficacious qualities. Rites may induce experiences and rites emerge as experience themselves. Through their rites Pentecostals work out their values and produce a sense of meaning, through their rites they do theology and work out their salvation.

9. In this study, 'Pentecostal spirituality' refers to a specific type of spirituality within the broader category of Christian spirituality. Pentecostal spirituality cannot be utterly unique for it shares in a basic Christian experience. Pentecostal aims, values and other characteristics are not in themselves peculiar. The editors of the *DPCM* have correctly noted that 'each of the [Pentecostal] characteristics...has appeared before in the rich and colorful tapestry of Christian spirituality through the ages. But the *combination is new*' (emphasis mine). Consequently, much of what I say about Pentecostal spirituality and ritual in this work applies to other Christian traditions. I do not claim that my observations are applicable exclusively to Pentecostalism, nonetheless, I center my observations and interpretations around *Pentecostal* spirituality. See Stanley Burgess, Gary McGee and Patrick Alexander (eds.), *Dictionary of Pentecostal and Charismatic Movement* (*DPCM*) (Grand Rapids: Zondervan, 1988), p. 5.

10. Anne E. Carr, *Transforming Grace* (San Francisco: Harper & Row, 1988), pp. 201-202. For an understanding of contemporary use of the term 'spirituality', see Sandra Schneiders, 'Spirituality in the Academy', *Theological Studies* 50 (1989), pp. 676-97. This and three other excellent essays, by Ewert H. Cousins,

Pentecostalism other than its spirituality. Its trademarks include particular religious convictions, sensibilities, practices, social behaviors, emphasis on individual religious experiences and perceptions of the world.[11] As we will see in the following chapters, Pentecostal spirituality fosters a deep, even mystical, piety that emphasizes the immanent sense of the divine. The belief system accentuates an understanding that 'gifts of the Spirit', including the subjective religious experience of 'Spirit baptism' appear and operate as normative in the life of the Church. This conviction informs all of Pentecostal religious experiences and expressions.[12]

In the following study I will consider the ritual and component rites of each of the three congregations as a strategy for understanding of Pentecostal spirituality. Each congregation exhibits its own unique features. I will note them. However, I seek primarily to discover and comprehend the common core of their spirituality. I will pursue this goal in seven chapters. In Chapter 1 I will set the stage for the examination by presenting the context in which the selected churches have emerged. I will begin by sketching the origins and development of the twentieth-century American Pentecostal movement. Then, I will survey three denominational expressions that not only participate in the movement but support our selected churches.

In Chapter 2 I narrow the scope to consider the three specific

Bradley C. Hanson and Carlos M.N. Eire, comprise Part 1, 'What Is Spirituality?', in Bradley C. Hanson (ed.), *Modern Christian Spirituality: Methodological and Historical Essays* (Atlanta: Scholars Press, 1990), pp. 15-61. For a survey of definitions and the development of the term see Jon Alexander, 'What Do Recent Writers Mean by Spirituality?', *Spirituality Today* 32 (1980), pp. 247-57; Sandra Schneiders, 'Theology and Spirituality: Strangers, Rivals, or Partners?', *Horizons* 13 (1986), pp. 253-74; and Philip Sheldrake, *Spirituality and History: Questions of Interpretation and Method* (New York: Crossroad, 1992), pp. 32-56. See also various issues of the *CSB*, the journal of the Society for the Study of Christian Spirituality.

11. See Anderson, 'Pentecostal and Charismatic Christianity', pp. 229-35; Barbara Hargrove, *The Sociology of Religion: Classical and Contemporary Approaches* (Arlington Heights, IL: Harlan Davidson, 1979); Martin E. Marty, *A Nation of Behavers* (Chicago: University of Chicago Press, 1976); Russell P. Spittler, 'Spirituality: Pentecostal and Charismatic', in *DPCM*, pp. 800-809; Grant Wacker, 'America's Pentecostals: Who They Are', *CT* (16 October 1987), pp. 16-21.

12. Fredrick Dale Bruner, *A Theology of the Holy Spirit: The Pentecostal Experience and the New Testament Witness* (Grand Rapids: Eerdmans, 1970).

congregations themselves. I will sketch a portrait of each of the faith communities seeking to present the congregational contexts in which the rituals emerge. With these contexualizations, I will then be ready in Chapter 3 to consider selected elements within the ritual fields of the three congregations, as a way to understand better the Pentecostal ritual dynamics and the Pentecostal spirituality in general. In this third chapter, I focus upon six chosen components of the ritual field. The components of time, space and identity function as defining ritual frameworks. Then I will assess how the components of sight, sounds and movement assist the dynamics of the Pentecostal ritual.

In Chapter 4 I will seek, first, to describe the foundational/processual rites[13] that provide the basic structure of the core Pentecostal ritual (i.e. the liturgy); secondly, I will briefly highlight some of the component rites, which I have called 'microrites' (e.g. sanctioned practices, behaviors, gestures) that are contained by the foundational rites. I will discover how the foundational/processual rites together with their components, the microrites, constitute the complete ritual. As a part of our discussion, I will give special attention to the charismatic rites as a characteristic category of practices traditionally attached to the Pentecostal ritual and to the Pentecostal spirituality in general.

My focus in Chapter 5 centers on Pentecostal ritual modes of sensibility. As *embodied attitudes*, the modes of ritual sensibility help orient and animate each of the various Pentecostal rites, actions and acts, including the charismata, within the Pentecostal ritual. In my investigation of ritual sensibilities, I have conceived of this dimension as integrally related to, though not necessarily contained within, the structure of the rites. I believe that the modes of ritual sensibility interact with the rites; that is, a dynamic affect mediates between the acts and the attitudes, the rites and the sensibilities. My fieldwork and subsequent analysis revealed at least seven modes or ideal types of ritual sensibility, that pervade the Pentecostal service. I will discuss these seven modes. An explication of these can help illuminate some of the features of the Pentecostal ritual and reveal essential dimensions of the spirituality.

---

13. Chapter 4 discusses the processual nature of the foundational rites. I follow anthropologist Anthony F.C. Wallace in his description of 'processual structure'. His analysis of revitalization movements focuses on the 'processes involving... diachronic sequences... [of] events or happenings'. I will consider the fundamental Pent/Char liturgical rites as supported by a 'processual structure'. See Wallace's 'Revitalization Movements', *American Anthropologist* 58 (1956), pp. 264-81.

In Chapter 6 I will consider two primary roles of the Pentecostal ritual liturgy. First, I approach the *expressive* or communicative character of the Pentecostal ritual. I want to reflect upon some of the ways in which the communicative dimension of ritual functions within our Pentecostal communities, ways in which the ritual *expresses* the Pentecostal spirituality. Secondly, I examine the *efficacious* character of Pentecostal ritual. In the second section, I will consider some of the potentially positive consequences of the Pentecostal liturgy that will point to the final chapter. In Chapter 7 I seek to describe the characteristic qualities of Pentecostal spirituality. Throughout this work I implicitly and explicitly draw attention to the characteristics of Pentecostal spirituality, particularly as expressed and experienced in the rituals of the chosen churches. In the concluding chapter I draw together these concepts and themes of Pentecostal spirituality, focusing wholly upon the characteristic qualities of Pentecostal spirituality. In order to explicate the major qualities of the Pentecostal spirituality, I will proceed in two ways. First, I will suggest six selected indigenous ritual symbols, each symbolizing a cluster of qualities, characteristics, concerns and inclinations of Pentecostal spirituality. Secondly, I will present a general outline of the characteristic qualities of Pentecostal spirituality within the organizing symbol of experiencing God. I turn now to Chapter 1 and the development of the Pentecostal movement.

Chapter 1

THE TWENTIETH-CENTURY PENTECOSTAL/
CHARISMATIC MOVEMENT

With the dawn of the twentieth century came a burst of new religious energy, a revival of Pentecost.[1] It came in obscurity, survived in inner city missions, storefront assemblies and rural chapels. But while it developed on the margins of the American society,[2] it has quietly emerged as the largest Christian movement of the twentieth century.[3] No one knows for sure the size of Pentecostalism around the world. However, as the century comes to a close, Pentecostalism has mushroomed to include, by some assessments, in excess of 500 million peo-

1. Because of the two branches of the twentieth-century movement, I have chosen to use the combined term 'Pentecostal/Charismatic' (Pent/Char). However, sometimes I will use the word 'Pentecostal' as collective term for both branches.

2. Pentecostalism moved immediately from America to other countries and grew in them as well.

3. See Wacker, 'America's Pentecostals', p. 16. Many scholars have in recent years recognized the growth of the Pentecostal movement worldwide, for example, Peter Berger claims that 'the great wave of Protestantism sweeping across the Third World today is primarily Pentecostal'. Roger G. Robins suggests Pentecostalism is perhaps 'the single-most-significant development in twentieth-century Christianity'. Russell P. Spittler notes that 'already in 1982... Pentecostals and Charismatics formed the single largest sector of Protestantism', and Peter W. Williams asserts that Pentecostalism is '*the* popular religious movement of the twentieth century, not only in the United States but throughout the entire Western world'. See Peter Berger, 'Foreword', in David Martin, *Tongues of Fire: The Explosion of Protestantism in Latin America* (Oxford: Basil Blackwell, 1990), p. viii; Roger G. Robins, 'Pentecostal Movement', in *DCA*, pp. 885-91 (885); Russell P. Spittler, 'The Pentecostal View', in Donald L. Alexander (ed.), *Christian Spirituality: Five Views of Sanctification* (Downers Grove, IL: InterVarsity Press, 1988), pp. 133-54 (133); Peter W. Williams, *Popular Religion in America: Symbolic Change and the Modernization Process in Historical Perspective* (Urbana, IL: University of Illinois Press, 1989), p. 144.

ple worldwide, with perhaps 40 million in America.[4] Beyond the demographics, some students of the movement claim that the activities and expressions of Pentecostalism have 'changed the face of Christianity around the world and ushered in a new era of Christian spirituality'.[5]

Most religious observers regarded Pentecostalism as a fringe sect until its second stage arrived, the Charismatic renewal of the 1960s.[6] The two stages define the two main categories of the movement, Pentecostal and Charismatic, but these two subdivide into a host of other classifications, such as Protestant, Catholic, Reformed, Wesleyan, Trinitarian, Unitarian, Mainline, Sectarian, White, Black, Hispanic—and the list goes on. Even the boundaries of these classifications blur amid the mélange of beliefs and practices, socio-economic levels, and regional and cultural qualities. But Pentecostalism thrives in diverse environments, it interacts with an array of religious and socio-cultural elements.[7]

In spite of the diverse expressions of Pentecostalism, many scholars and participants agree on an apparent continuity among the Pentecostal 'species', namely, an underlying or core spirituality.[8] This core spiritu-

---

4.   David B. Barrett, 'Annual Statistical Table on Global Mission: 1997', *IBMR* 21.1 (1997), pp. 24-25; and C. Peter Wagner, 'Church Growth', in *DPCM*, pp. 180-95. Also see Spittler, 'The Pentecostal View', p. 133, where he cites David Barrett's statistics and points out that Pentecostalism in its Protestant forms has 'emerged as the new majority Protestant spirituality... And when the total figures are combined for classical Pentecostals along with Charismatics from Anglican, Orthodox, Roman Catholic and mainline Protestant sectors, the sum exceeds the size of Protestantism as a whole' ('The Pentecostal View', pp. 133-34).

5.   Stanley Burgess, Gary McGee and Patrick Alexander, 'Introduction', in *DPCM*, pp. 1-6. The editors of the *DPCM* go on to claim that 'Pentecostalism, in all its forms has...challenged Christians everywhere to address the issues that have been raised', p. 5. The subtitle of Harvey Cox's *Fire from Heaven* (New York: Addison–Wesley, 1995) reflects one of the themes of his interpretation, '*The Rise of Pentecostal Spirituality and the Reshaping of Religion in the Twenty-first Century*'. Cox believes that Pentecostalism is not only reshaping Christianity around the world, but may help usher onto the global stage a new era for religion in general.

6.   Marty, *A Nation of Behavers*.

7.   For an example of variety see Spittler, 'The Pentecostal View', pp. 31-49.

8.   In asserting an underlying spirituality, I understand that each 'species' of Pentecostalism has a particular type of Pentecostal spirituality. However, I do believe that amid the many Pentecostal spiritualities there is a *core* spirituality, an experience in and of the Spirit that unifies the vast variety. The core or underlying spirituality mixes with many theologies, traditions and cultures to produce a wide

ality gives a sense of unity to the conglomerate of classifications within the movement. Early critics of the movement tagged it the 'Tongues Movement', but this reductionist assessment mistakes a distinguishing characteristic for the central feature, the essential nature of the spirituality.[9] Pentecostalism is predicated on the rejection of the theory that the charismata have ceased to operate, which has held sway in the Western Church since Augustine.[10] Essentially, Pentecostals believe in, experience and 'stress the power and presence of the Holy Spirit and the gifts of the Spirit directed toward the proclamation that Jesus Christ is Lord to the glory of God'.[11]

In this chapter, I must set the stage for my examination of Pentecostal ritual and spirituality. Thus, I will consider some of the historical developments of Pentecostalism as a context for understanding the American Pentecostal movement. I will begin by sketching the origins and development of the twentieth-century American Pentecostal movement in two primary stages. Then, I will survey three denominational expressions that have participated in the development of Pentecostalism.[12]

---

range of types of Pent/Char spirituality. I agree with David Barrett's view when he claims 'an underlying unity' for 'the twentieth-century Pentecostal/Charismatic renewal'. His world-wide survey, which includes '11,000 Pentecostal denominations…3,000 independent Charismatic denominations…150 traditional non-Pentecostal ecclesiastical confessions, families, and traditions…in 8,000 ethnolinguistic cultures', maintains that the twentieth-century world-wide Pentecostal/Charismatic movement is 'one single cohesive movement into which a vast proliferation of all kinds of individuals and communities have been drawn in a whole range of different circumstances' (David B. Barrett, 'The Twentieth-Century Pentecostal/Charismatic Renewal in the Holy Spirit', *IBMR* 12 [July 1988], pp. 119-24 [119]).

9. Spittler, 'The Pentecostal View', p. 135.

10. Early Pentecostals intuitively believed that God's gifts could be experienced in contemporary times. Today historical and theological claims seem to support the theological intuition. See Kilian McDonnell and George Montague (eds.), *Christian Initiation and Baptism in the Holy Spirit* (Collegeville, MN: Liturgical Press, 1991).

11. Kilian McDonnell and Arnold Bittlinger, *The Baptism in the Holy Spirit as an Ecumenical Problem* (South Bend, IN: Charismatic Renewal Services, 1972), cited in Vinson Synan, 'Pentecostalism: Varieties and Contributions', *Pneuma* 8 (Fall 1986), pp. 31-49 (32).

12. I will present these particular three Pent/Char denominations, the Assemblies of God, the International Church of the Foursquare Gospel and the Vineyard Christian Fellowship, because they each respectively represent the parent organization for the three selected congregations in which my field study took place. See Chapter 2.

Origins and Development of the Pentecostal Movement

Two events claim the credit for launching twentieth-century Pentecostalism. Initially, neither episode demanded the attention of any
others than those immediately involved. The first incident occurred in
the beginning hours of the new century when a group of Bible school
students claimed to have experienced baptism in the Holy Spirit, evidenced by tongues speech. Five years later, the second incident un-
folded in an African-American mission, where an interracial group of
holiness believers experienced Spirit baptism in a similar fashion.
These two obscure events mark the symbolic and historical beginnings
of the twentieth-century Pentecostal movement.[13]

The late nineteenth century produced mounting religious fervor
among various groups of North American evangelical Protestants.
Many sought renewal for both their personal and ecclesial piety. Fervor
flowed through several streams, which at some points converged. Pentecostalism represents the confluence of several distinct religious
impulses, ideologies and movements from the late nineteenth century
including holiness and higher life ideologies from the American Wesleyan and the British Keswick traditions, a movement of divine and
faith healers, a millenarian impulse rooted in John Darby and the Ply-
mouth Brethren form of dispensational premillennialism, and a strong

---

13. Among the works that describe and analyze the origins and development of
American Pentecostalism, see Anderson, *Vision of the Disinherited*; Frank Bartle-
man, *Azusa Street* (Plainfield, NJ: Logos International, 1980); Nils Bloch-Hoell,
The Pentecostal Movement: Its Origins, Development, and Distinctive Character
(London: Allen & Unwin, 1964); Edith L. Blumhofer, *The Assemblies of God: A
Chapter in the Story of American Pentecostalism* (2 vols.; Springfield, MO: Gospel
Publishing, 1989); and her *Restoring the Faith: The Assemblies of God, Pente-
costalism, and American Culture* (Urbana, IL: University of Illinois Press, 1993);
Charles W. Conn, *Like a Mighty Army Moves the Church of God, 1886–1995*
(Cleveland, TN: Pathway Press, 1996); Cox, *Fire from Heaven*; Donald W. Dayton,
Theological Roots of Pentecostalism (Grand Rapids: Zondervan, 1987); Walter J.
Hollenweger, *The Pentecostals* (ET; London: SCM Press, 1972); William W. Men-
zies, *Anointed to Serve: The Story of the Assemblies of God* (Springfield, MO:
Gospel Publishing, 1971); John T. Nichol, *Pentecostalism* (New York: Harper &
Row, 1966); Vinson Synan, *The Holiness–Pentecostal Movement in the United
States* (Grand Rapids: Eerdmans, 1971); Grant Wacker, 'Pentecostalism', in Charles
H. Lippy and Peter W. Williams (eds.), *The Encyclopedia of American Religious
Experience*, II (New York: Charles Scribner's Sons, 1988), pp. 933-45.

restorationist bent that idealized the primitivism of the church of the New Testament. How could such disparate strands of tradition merge? Each strand shared in a common religious zeal, but the doctrine of the baptism in the Holy Spirit catalytically blended these impulses into one.

Charles Parham and the Topeka Event

By the end of the nineteenth century, numbers of groups, mostly holiness, proclaimed and some members experienced 'the baptism in the Holy Spirit', but questions arose. Mainly believers wondered, 'How will we recognize this baptism?', 'How will we know when we have been baptized in the Holy Spirit?' Some sought for a conclusive evidence or a sign of the much-heralded baptism.[14] One such inquirer, Charles Fox Parham (1873–1929) claimed to have discovered the answer.[15] Late in 1900, Parham, a former Methodist minister, founded a short-term Bible training institute, Bethel Bible College, in Topeka, Kansas. He attracted about 40 students to pray and study the Scriptures with him in preparation for Christian ministry. Both the students and director Parham, after a study of the Lukan texts, identified the evidence of a person's Spirit baptism with speaking in tongues.[16] Agnes N. Ozman (1870–1937) deeply desiring to be baptized in the Spirit, asked her teacher Parham to lay hands upon her and to pray that she might receive. When Ozman, in her words, 'spoke in tongues as is recorded in Acts 19'[17] she apparently became the first Pentecostal in modern history. Agnes Ozman's glossolalia convinced Parham of his 'initial physical evidence' theory.[18] His theory identified Spirit baptism with an initial proof of tongues. Parham's doctrine and Ozman's experience forged a 'vital theological con-

---

14. See Dayton, *Theological Roots of Pentecostalism*, pp. 87-114.

15. For Parham and the Topeka event, see Anderson, *Vision of the Disinherited*, pp. 47-61, and Blumhofer, *Assemblies*, I, pp. 67-96.

16. See Blumhofer, *Assemblies*, I, pp. 83-85; Anderson, *Vision of the Disinherited*, pp. 47-61, for the discrepancies in the reported sequence of the discovery of tongues as sign and the experience of Spirit baptism among the students.

17. Blumhofer cites Ozman's own report (*Assemblies*, I, p. 82).

18. In sorting out myth and history Blumhofer asserts at least 'one certain conclusion: He [Parham] regarded this standard for evaluating Spirit baptism as an enhancement to his Apostolic Faith message rather than as an inconsequential aberrance.' Tongues symbolize for Parham another element of recovery of a dimension of New Testament religion and reality—the baptism in the Holy Spirit (*Assemblies*, I, p. 84).

nection that has remained essential to much of classical Pentecostal-ism'.[19]

In the following days, a dozen others from the Bethel School, including Parham, experienced glossolalic speech. Parham took this as the sign of restoration, God had restored to the church this gift. Evidently, Charles Parham believed that with the Pentecostal baptisms his school of prayer and Bible study had achieved its purpose, he closed the school and proceeded with some of his students to share their new-found Pentecostal faith throughout the region. Parham's evangelistic efforts aimed to herald the 'Apostolic Faith', as he called it, met with mixed responses. But overall the initial impact of the Topeka event remained limited. It is fair to say that the next five years certainly did not produce the widespread acceptance of the Apostolic faith that Parham envisioned. Perhaps, Parham's greatest contribution to the emerging Pentecostal movement, other than establishing the link between Spirit baptism and tongues, lay in influence on an African-American holiness preacher, William J. Seymour.

William Seymour and the Azusa Street Revival
William Seymour was discipled by Parham during one of Parham's Apostolic faith campaigns in Houston. Subsequently, Seymour carried the Pentecostal message from Houston to Los Angles, the city destined to become the site of the Azusa Street revival.[20] A small group of Baptist believers with holiness leanings called Seymour to the fastest-growing city in the nation. Two days after arriving in Los Angeles, 22 February 1906, Seymour preached Parham's message of Spirit baptism with the sign of tongues. He was subsequently locked out of the mission. However, several sympathetic families invited him to stay on in Los Angles and to teach them. For the next six weeks Seymour lead

19. Burgess, McGee and Alexander, 'Introduction', p. 3.
20. See Anderson, *Vision of the Disinherited*, pp. 62-78; Bartleman, *Azusa Street*; Blumhofer, *Assemblies*, I, pp. 97-112; C.M. Robeck, Jr, 'Azusa Street Revival', in *DPCM*, pp. 31-36 (31); Gary B. McGee, 'The Azusa Street Revival and 20th Century Missions', *IBMR* 12 (April 1988), pp. 58-61; Synan, *The Holiness–Pentecostal Movement*, pp. 95-116. The term 'classical Pentecostal' first emerged in the work of Kilian McDonnell about 1970, and it distinguishes the Pentecostals who trace their origins to the beginning of this century from those neo-Pentecostals or Charismatics who appeared during the second half of the century within the mainline Protestant churches, the Roman Catholic Church and independent churches.

Bible study/prayer meetings in the homes of supporters. But on 9 April 1906 the meetings were transformed.

On Monday, 9 April, a group of believers gathered at a family home on 214 North Bonnie Brae Street. As usual the group included African-Americans and whites, mostly working-class people from the area. This evening, the news that Seymour brought to the meeting transformed it. Shortly before arriving at the Bonnie Brae home, Seymour had visited with another supporter, Edward Lee. Lee reported to Seymour a recent vision. In the vision the apostles showed Lee how to speak in tongues. William Seymour prayed with Edward Lee, whereupon Lee erupted in glossolalic prayer. Seymour traveled directly to Bonnie Brae to proclaim the news. Before that night's meeting concluded Seymour and seven other seekers received the Spirit baptism as Seymour had preached it.

News spread rapidly around the neighborhood. Crowds gathered nightly to hear Seymour proclaim the message from the porch of the Bonnie Brae street home. Participants actively recruited others. They shared their good news around town in the churches and in the neighborhoods. And within a week, Seymour discovered and rented an abandoned Methodist episcopal church to hold the burgeoning groups of Pentecostal believers and seekers. The white-washed, frame church at 312 Azusa Street became the home of the Apostolic Mission and the central site of the Azusa Street revival.

Pentecostal historian Cecil M. Robeck, Jr, describes the early meetings at the Mission:

> Services were long, and on the whole they were spontaneous. In its early days music was *a cappella*, although one or two instruments were included at times. There were songs, testimonies given by visitors or read from those who wrote in, prayer, altar calls for salvation or sanctification or for baptism in the Holy Spirit. And there was preaching. Sermons were generally not prepared in advance but were typically spontaneous. W.J. Seymour was clearly in charge, but much freedom was given to visiting preachers. There was also prayer for the sick. Many shouted. Others were 'slain in the Spirit' or ' fell under the power.' There were periods of extended silence and of singing in tongues. No offerings were collected, but there was a receptacle near the door for gifts.[21]

These meetings attracted a certain amount of attention locally in their first months. But outsiders did not immediately recognize that this

21. Robeck, Jr, 'Azusa Street Revival', p. 33.

humble group of believers would soon be swept up in the wave of revival that they had yearned for. Nevertheless, no other event so symbolizes the emergence of the twentieth-century Pentecostal movement as does the Azusa Street meetings. Nor did any other Pentecostal center produce the widespread influence that the mission did.

News of the happenings at Azusa Street spread. Locally, the press published reports of the revival while excited believers announced the news. The events of the Apostolic Faith Mission also gained national and foreign circulation in holiness and other religious periodicals. The news attracted waves of ministers and lay people from numerous traditions and locales around the country. They swarmed upon the mission like bees to a hive; then, convinced of the message, penetrated by the experience and empowered by the Spirit, they dispersed, carrying the Pentecostal gospel around the world.

Thus, the Azusa Street revival sparked much of the early growth of the Pentecostal movement. Around Los Angeles the revival birthed a dozen churches, while established churches found themselves infused with new life. But the influence of revival could not be contained by Los Angeles. Centers for Pentecostalism began to appear as energy from the explosive Apostolic Faith Mission traveled to cities throughout the United States. The mission claimed responsibility for transforming or establishing numerous prominent Pentecostal churches, including the Church of God of Cleveland, Tennessee, the Pentecostal Holiness Church, the Pentecostal Free Will Baptist Church, the Apostolic Faith of Portland, Oregon, the Pentecostal Assemblies of the World of Los Angeles and the Assemblies of God.[22] Together these churches felt the impact and carried the message of Azusa Street.

While the mission revival lasted only a few years (1906–13), the character of the Pentecostal movement took shape at Azusa Street. The revival

> represented an anomaly on the American religious scene. Blacks, whites, and Hispanics worshiped together. Men and women shared leadership responsibilities. The barrier between clergy and laity vanished, since participants believed that the endowment of spiritual power for ministry was

22. See Robeck, Jr, 'Azusa Street Revival', p. 35 who indicates that 'nearly every Pentecostal denomination in the U. S. traces its roots in some way or other to the Apostolic Faith Mission at 312 Azusa Street'. See also Blumhofer, *Assemblies*, I, pp. 113-40, and Synan, *The Holiness–Pentecostal Movement*, pp. 117-39.

intended for all to receive. The gifts of the Holy Spirit (1 Cor. 12), understood by most denominations as having ceased at the end of the first century, had been restored.[23]

While all the marks of the revival did not persist, the shaping influence of Seymour's Apostolic Faith Mission continues in the contemporary churches of the Pentecostal tradition.

The theological themes and traditions that entered the early Pentecostal movement were combined into a new configuration at Azusa Street; we might say they were baptized in the S/spirit of Pentecost before they were carried around the world. The characteristic emphases of the Apostolic Faith Mission—restorationism, revivalism, divine healing, sanctified holy living, or a 'higher life' and millenarianism—marked the movement for the rest of the century.

Pentecostalism maintained a steady growth through the first half of the century. It flowed in numerous and isolated channels. While many Pentecostals recognized an affinity to fundamentalist doctrines, the Fundamentalists would have little to do with the 'tongues speakers'. Thus the Pentecostals had minimal interaction with other churches, including other Pentecostal churches, especially in the first three decades of the movement. However, neither isolation nor proliferation of Pentecostal denominations stunted the growth of the movement. In fact, the sect experience probably served to free Pentecostals to experiment with forms of spirituality. The refined version of such forms ultimately attracted more people.

Following World War II, Pentecostalism produced more 'up scale' versions of itself as many constituents climbed the social economic ladder. Also, after the war, a large portion of Fundamentalism emerged as Evangelicalism. Though conservative, this new configuration proved more tolerant of Pentecostals. The Evangelicals recognized the growth and evangelization efforts of the Pentecostals. As a result, several Pentecostal groups joined with Evangelicals in the National Association of Evangelicals. The most dramatic interaction, however, began in the middle of the century, when mainline Protestants and Roman Catholics discovered among the Pentecostals a resource for renewal.

23. Burgess, McGee and Alexander, 'Introduction', p. 3.

Mid-Century Pentecostalism: Charismatic Renewal

Clearly, Pentecostal Christianity had attracted some immediate attention as it spread. However, most religious observers regarded Pentecostal groups as fringe sects until the second stage of twentieth-century
Pentecostalism emerged.[24] The second stage, called variously Neo-
Pentecostalism, the Charismatic movement, and Charismatic renewal
dawned on the American religious scene in the 1960s.[25] Roman Catholic scholar Peter Hocken defines the Charismatic renewal as

> the occurrence of distinctively Pentecostal blessings and phenomena,
> baptism in the Holy Spirit with the spiritual gifts of 1 Corinthians 12:8-
> 10, outside a denominational and/or confessional Pentecostal frame-
> work...manifestations of Pentecostal-type Christianity that in some way
> differ from classical Pentecostalism in affiliation and/or doctrine.[26]

Such 'manifestations of Pentecostal-type Christianity' outside the
'confessional Pentecostal framework' burst onto the ecclesiastical terrain when, in 1960, Dennis Bennett, an Episcopalian pastor, proclaimed

24. See Marty, *Nation of Behavers*, p. 106.
25. For examples of works relating to the Charismatic renewal see Dennis J.
Bennett, *Nine O'Clock in the Morning* (Plainfield, NJ: Logos International, 1970);
Arnold Bittlinger (ed.), *The Church Is Charismatic* (Geneva: World Council of
Churches, 1981); Donald L. Gelpi, *Pentecostalism: A Theological Viewpoint* (New
York: Paulist Press, 1971); Michael P. Hamilton (ed.), *The Charismatic Movement*
(Grand Rapids: Eerdmans, 1975); Peter D. Hocken, 'Charismatic Movement', in
DPCM, pp. 130-60; *idem, One Lord One Spirit One Body* (Gaitherburg, MD: Word
among Us Press, 1987); Kilian McDonnell, *Charismatic Renewal and the Churches*
(New York: Seabury, 1976); *idem* (ed.), *Presence, Power, Praise: Documents on the
Charismatic Renewal* (3 vols.; Collegeville, MN: Liturgical Press, 1980); McDon-
nell and Montague (eds.), *Christian Initiation*; Edward D. O'Connor, *The Pente-
costal Movement in the Catholic Church* (Notre Dame, IN: Ave Maria Press, 1971);
Richard Quebedeaux, *The New Charismatics*, II (San Francisco: HarperSanFran-
cisco, 1983); Kevin Ranaghan and Dorothy Ranaghan, *Catholic Pentecostals* (New
York: Paulist Press, 1969); Russell P. Spittler (ed.), *Perspectives on the New Pentecostalism* (Grand Rapids: Baker Book House, 1976); Leon Joseph Suenens, *A New
Pentecost?* (New York: Seabury, 1974); Francis A. Sullivan, 'Catholic Charismatic
Renewal', in *DPCM*, pp. 110-26; Vinson Synan, *The Twentieth-Century Pentecostal Explosion* (Altamonte Springs, FL: Creation House, 1987); J. Rodman
Williams, *The Gift of the Holy Spirit Today* (Plainfield, NJ: Logos International,
1980).
26. Hocken, 'Charismatic Movement', p. 130.

to his congregation and to the world that he had been Spirit baptized. Although numbers of Bennett's parishioners from St Mark's in Van Nuys, California, had experienced Spirit baptism with the accompanying sign of tongues by 3 April 1960, when Bennett made his announcement to his three Sunday services, the declaration traumatized the congregation. Subsequently, Bennett resigned under pressure and accepted reassignment in Seattle.[27] But the effects of Bennett's baptism and the subsequent national press coverage of the charismatic events in Van Nuys catapulted emerging Neo-Pentecostalism (or Charismatic renewal) from obscurity into the mainstream of American religious consciousness.[28]

Emergence and Development

While numerous Protestant Charismatics predated Bennett's announcement, none received the notoriety outside of their own circles that Bennett had. Earlier 'stirrings' and charismatic breezes now gathered the energy of full-force winds. By the early 1960s these winds had crossed nearly all Protestant denominational boundaries, affecting virtually every major Protestant tradition. Mixed response came through official denominational channels, but by the end of the decade nearly every one of the main Protestant denominations included a sizable Charismatic constituency.[29]

Charismatic renewal came to the Catholic Church in the wake of the Second Vatican Council. The movement began in two Catholic univer-

27. For Bennett's narrative of the events see Bennett, *Nine O'Clock in the Morning*.

28. The Charismatic renewal spread far beyond the borders of the United States, in fact the greatest growth and impact seems to be in nations other than America. However, I will limit my brief discussion to the American Charismatic renewal.

29. Examples of the denominations that developed both a Charismatic constituency and an organized Charismatic service agency include: Episcopalian, American Lutheran and Lutheran Church of America, Presbyterian (USA), United Methodist, American Baptist, Church of Christ, United Church of Christ and Mennonite. Most of these denominations adopted positions that neither welcomed enthusiastically nor openly rejected the Charismatic renewal. Instead, generally they affirmed the principle of the charismatic experience. However, two denominations represent notable exceptions. Both the Missouri Synod Lutheran Church and the Southern Baptists actively resisted any charismatic activity. See McDonnell (ed.), *Presence, Power, Praise*, for a compilation of the denominational responses to the movement both affirming and critical.

sities, Duquesne and Notre Dame in 1967 but soon spread across the nation.[30] Prayer groups sprouted up throughout the United States, a number of Catholic Charismatic communities emerged, and headquarters opened.[31] 'Catholic Pentecostalism', as it was first named, not only effected its own church, it impacted greatly the Charismatic movement as a whole. As Catholic Pentecostals gathered in annual conferences at Notre Dame, attracting as many as 30,000 in 1976, other Charismatics followed suit. The rapid expansion of the Catholic contingent challenged others to share their charismatic experience actively within their own traditions and to recognize the potential for church renewal through the Holy Spirit's actions.[32]

During this same period of the late 1960s and the 1970s, a dramatic increase in nondenominational, Charismatic churches and organizations occurred. Churches such as Melodyland Christian Center in Anaheim, California, flourished. Many of the present American megachurches developed during this era as non-aligned Charismatic congregations. Charismatic parachurch organizations such as Full Gospel Businessmen also prospered, many of them using the mass media and attracting their own followings, often of the independent type.

By the beginning of the 1980s, much of the Charismatic renewal had moved into the American religious mainstream.[33] But the flow of the

30. Michigan State University also emerged as an early cite of Catholic Pente-costalism (1968). Numerous leaders arose from the revival in Ann Arbor, making it a prominent center for Catholic charismatic activities.

31. Examples of communities and headquarters include: the Pecos Benedictine Abbey, the University of Steubenville, the Southern California Renewal Center, the Word of God community (later called the Sword of the Spirit) in Ann Arbor, Michigan, People of Praise community in South Bend, Indiana, Servants of the Lord in Minneapolis, and Mother of God Community in Gaithersburg, Maryland. See Harold D. Hunter, 'Charismatic Movement', in *DCA*, pp. 241-44 (244).

32. The Catholic Charismatic movement 'enjoyed official encouragement, beginning with the 1969 report by the Committee on Doctrine submitted to the Catholic Bishops of the USA, the response of Pope Paul VI in 1973, and the more recent encouragement of Pope John Paul II'. See Hunter, 'Charismatic Movement', p. 244; also, McDonnell (ed.), *Presence, Power, Praise*.

33. Hocken points to the subtitle of Quebedeaux's work, *New Charismatics II*, 'How a Christian Renewal Movement Became Part of the American Religious Mainstream'. While Hocken argues that the renewal continues to spread, though less sensationally, since the late 1970s, its primary mode appears as 'consolidation'. He also notes a shift. While 'the overall evidence suggests that the number of Spirit-baptized Christians in North America has continued to increase throughout

movement continued to forge new channels. Many of these new expressions emerged outside of the traditional denominational frameworks and the established charismatic patterns. The emerging 'Signs and Wonders' phenomenon represents one such expression. I will look closer at this dramatic new development in charismatic Christianity below (e.g. pp. 60-70). But for now I need to consider the Charismatic and classical Pentecostal movements together.

Comparing the Two Phases of the Movement

When one compares the traits of the classical Pentecostals with those of the Charismatics one discovers both similarities and differences. Pentecostals and Charismatics in general believe that they share a common experience as their most fundamental similarity. Catholic scholar Francis A. Sullivan put it this way,

> the basic identity of the experiences that Catholics have come to share with others in this [Pent/Char] movement, [is] namely the baptism in the Spirit and the charisms that typically follow. The fact that Catholics may prefer a theological interpretation of baptism in the Spirit that differs from the Pentecostal interpretation does not negate the identity of the experience as such. What all participants in the Pentecostal movement have come to know is that in the course of Christian life one can begin to experience the power of the Spirit in a radically new way.[34]

In addition to the fundamental common experience, Charismatics and Pentecostals in general share several essential elements within their respective spiritualities.[35] Here, I can only briefly mention the most prominent. The practices of glossolalia, prophecy and healing continue to express the spiritual life of the classical Pentecostals as well as the Charismatics. These three manifestations suggest a fundamental common belief in the immanent activity of God's Spirit. 'God speaks today,' Pent/Char Christians proclaim, through God's actions and word. Charismatics claim that God's word in the Bible takes on a greater prominence in their lives. Both groups speak of a love for the Scriptures,

---

the 1970s and 1980s…the increase in not equal in every sector'. In fact, the nondenominational or nonaligned Charismatics have produced the fastest growth, during the 1980s, according to Hocken. See his 'Charismatic Movement', pp. 130-60 (144).

34. Sullivan, 'Catholic Charismatic', p. 115.

35. For a list and explanation of 'essential elements' in Charismatic renewal see Hocken, 'Charismatic Movement', pp. 155-56.

though mainline church members seem less susceptible to fundamentalism. Instead, they claim an increasingly central Christology. 'Charismatic renewal is everywhere marked by a focus on Jesus Christ...a
deeper yielding to Jesus, and a fuller acceptance of Jesus as Lord... The
proclamation "Jesus is Lord" has been the most characteristic banner
and slogan in Charismatic renewal.'[36] Perhaps the centrality of this
most basic and ancient creed accounts in part for the rise in grass roots
ecumenism among Charismatics.

The focus on Jesus yields yet two other common traits, praise and
spiritual power. Pentecostal spirituality always manifests a variety of
explicit forms of praise. The Neo-Pentecostals adopted, adapted and
created their own spectrum of praise patterns. Both groups agree that
the coming of God's spirit as experienced in Spirit baptism results in a
flow of praise from believers to God and God's son Jesus Christ. Charismatic–Pentecostals claim a new capacity to glorify God spontaneously and within well-known patterns.

Charismatic Christians of both phases of the movement often link
praise with the sense of spiritual power. Throughout this century, Pentecostals of all types have believed that Spirit baptism results in spiritual power. This power not only facilitates praise and worship, it equips
for ministry and service, it helps in the overcoming of evil and it assists
the believer in daily life, according to those who claim Spirit baptism.

The differences between the adherents of the Charismatic renewal
and of the classical Pentecostals to a large extent reflects the differences
in religious traditions. While Spirit baptism often causes a reshaping
or transforming of one's understanding of their own religious tradition,
the life of the tradition normally continues to sustain the Charismatic
believer. In fact, often Charismatics claim a better appreciation for their
heritage in the wake of their Pentecostal experience. However, as
Sullivan puts it,

> it is in the nature of theology to seek a deeper understanding of one's
> faith experience. And it is appropriate that if it is a question of a new
> faith experience, one will look for an understanding of it that is consis-
> tent with all that one already believes.[37]

This phenomenon seems to explain many of the distinctions among
Charismatic Christians. For example, the holiness and higher life move-

---

36. Hocken, 'Charismatic Movement', pp. 155-56.
37. Sullivan, 'Catholic Charismatic', p. 117.

ments of the later nineteenth century gave birth to the classical Pentecostals, and consequently they emphasize a particular understanding of holy living, of Spirit baptism as an experience subsequent to conversion, of premillenarianism, and of foreign missions. None of these understandings dominate within the Charismatic renewal. On the other hand, Charismatics whose traditions nurture a rich heritage of theology will, in contrast to classical Pentecostals, recognize the need for a well thought-out theological base for their experience. The resulting theologies will likely differ according to the tradition. The same holds true for spirituality. For example, Charismatics who come from traditions that reflect a highly sacramental worship will normally seek to discover an even deeper understanding of the sacraments and consequently enjoy a greater appreciation of sacramental worship. While Charismatics and Pentecostals have significant differences in their understanding and practice of Christianity, they share a common openness to the work of the Spirit in their lives and in their communities. Ultimately, they share in a common religious movement, the twentieth-century Pentecostal movement.

Having considered the two main branches of the Pent/Char movement, I now can turn to three particular denominational expressions of the movement: Assemblies of God, International Church of the Foursquare Gospel and the Vineyard Christian Fellowship. These three denominations do not reflect the diversity of the movement, not even in the United States. However, they do represent the three national organizations to which the three selected congregations belong.[38] First, I will consider the Assemblies of God.

The Assemblies of God

In April 1914 about 300 persons answered the call to come to Hot Springs, Arkansas, for an organizing convention. During the ten-day gathering, believers prayed for, discussed and planned for a new religious entity, the Assemblies of God [AG]. The new 'co-operative fellowship' founded at the Hot Springs Grand Opera House emerged in the decades to follow as 'the largest, strongest and most affluent white Pentecostal denomination' in the world.[39]

---

38. See Chapter 2 for a sketch of each of the three selected congregations.

39. Edith L. Blumhofer, 'Assemblies of God', in *DPCM*, pp. 23-28 (23). For histories and analysis of the Assemblies of God, see Blumhofer, *Assemblies*; *idem*,

Origins and Early Development

While numerous nascent denominations of the Wesleyan-holiness sort arose in the decade following the Topeka and Los Angeles events, other more independently minded baptistic-type Pentecostal groups avoided organizing beyond the congregational level. However, by 1914 many of the anti-organizational ilk began to suspect that some type of loose-knit structure might be necessary to avoid some of the contemporary Pentecostal confusion and to achieve shared objectives.

The strong restorationist bent of the Pentecostal revival led many to resist denominationalism. To their minds the New Testament only supported the local congregational model. But the anti-structural experiment yielded some undesired results. As 'individuals [and leaders] followed their own inclinations...local groups were sometimes in a state of confusion.'[40] With little emphasis on ministerial training and formal ordination, doctrinal problems proliferated, as did gospel 'rip offs'. Trusting Pentecostals provided a lucrative living for unscrupulous 'preachers'. Also, partisanship, poor-quality and often misguided publications multiplied.[41] Many Pentecostal leaders recognized forms of emotionalism within the ranks as unbalanced and even dangerous. These and other disagreeable consequences spread a sense of chaos throughout the movement. Thus 'increasing numbers of Pentecostals felt both a need to repudiate error and a desire to affirm their distinctive emphases in ways that were best facilitated by cooperation'.[42]

So, *Word and Witness*, a popular Pentecostal magazine, together with other similar periodicals, issued a call for an exploratory convention.[43] The convention aimed toward unity among constituents amid 'so many

Restoring the Faith; Carl Brumback, *Suddenly...from Heaven: A History of the Assemblies of God* (Springfield, MO: Gospel Publishing, 1961); Klaude Kendrick, *The Promise Fulfilled: A History of the Modern Pentecostal Movement* (Springfield, MO: Gospel Publishing, 1961); Menzies, *Anointed to Serve*.

40. Kendrick, *Promise*, p. 73.

41. See Menzies, *Anointed to Serve*, pp. 80-85; Kendrick, *Promise*, pp. 73-75; Blumhofer, *Assemblies*, I, pp. 198-202.

42. Blumhofer, *Assemblies*, I, p. 198.

43. Five very important Pentecostal leaders attached their names to the call in *Word and Witness* (E.N. Bell's publication): M.M. Pinson, A.P. Collins, H.A. Goss, D.C.O. Opperman and E.N. Bell. These men had worked 'behind the scenes' to bring about a cooperative loose-knit organization. See Menzies, *Anointed to Serve*, pp. 92-93; also see Blumhofer, *Assemblies*, I, p. 200, for a brief description of these men.

divisions'.[44] Convention organizers sought to conserve the authentic Pentecostal impulse amid the 'chaotic conditions'. They proposed to coordinate foreign missions efforts, to move toward 'chartering the churches...on [a] legal basis', and to establish 'a general Bible Training School'.[45]

Although the call to a convention met mixed responses, in April some 300 representatives from states around the nation gathered for the first General Council of the Assemblies of God.[46] The delegates spent several days in prayer and typical Pentecostal-style worship services before they commenced their business meetings. Common participation in their Pentecostal rites 'helped allay the reservations of some who feared organization... They discovered unity "in the Spirit".'[47] The first Council did not adopt a constitution nor a doctrinal statement. It did, however, ratify a document titled, 'Preamble and Resolution on Constitution'. This Preamble proclaimed principles of equality, unity and cooperation while assuring the sovereignty of every local church that affiliated with the council. It envisioned a 'cooperative fellowship'.[48] With this action the Council created the A/G.

From Sect Isolation to Evangelical and Ecumenical Leadership
The first decades of the denomination posed problems but provided progressive growth.[49] The A/G resulted from the amalgamation of sev-

---

44. *Word and Witness*, 20 March 1914, quoted in Kendrick, *Promise*, p. 82.

45. Kendrick, *Promise*, p. 82.

46. While the number of representatives from the South and Midwest dominated, delegates came from the West, the Northwest and the East coast as well. From the beginning, the A/G emerged with a nationwide constituency.

47. Blumhofer, *Assemblies*, I, p. 201.

48. Kendrick, *Promise*, p. 84.

49. Pentecostal historian Edith Blumhofer offers a helpful sketch of the Pentecostal process of acculturation (e.g. modes of managing modernity). She suggests a four-stage process by which Pentecostals manage modernity, a process by which they have orientated themselves to the religious and secular cultures. According to Blumhofer: first, restorationism dominated the early ethos. Secondly, the perception of affinities with evangelicals (earlier, fundamentalists) led to the second stage in the 1920s. Thirdly, following World War II the Charismatic renewal offered Pentecostals a role as a 'Third Force', or a renewal movement parallel to Catholicism and Protestantism but distinct from each. Fourthly, the latest stage, since the 1970s, reveals a predilection for popular culture. A stage does not necessarily terminate the preceding stage. Rather, the process allowed successive stages to co-exist with the

eral Pentecostal groups.[50] The consequent diversity and loose knit organization produced severe challenges in the first years of the A/G. General Council meetings between 1914 and 1918 would be forced to define doctrine while attempting to secure unity.[51] But following the stormy doctrinal feuds, the A/G discovered a more stabilized direction and pattern of growth. In the 1920s the 'cooperative fellowship' adopted a constitution and bylaws, established its headquarters in Springfield,

earlier ones. As a result, contemporary Pentecostal denominations, local congregations and even individuals may embody elements of restorationism, evangelicalism, Third Force ecumenism and pop components. See Blumhofer, *Restoring the Faith*, especially her 'Introduction'.

50. Grant Wacker explains the amalgamation of the four distinct groups that laid the foundation of the early A/G: 'The most substantial was the core of Parham's followers in southeastern Texas known as the Apostolic Faith. A second cluster, which called itself the Church of God, grew up in Alabama between 1907 and 1910. These bodies struck an alliance in 1912 and received permission from C.H. Mason's Church of God in Christ to use its name... The third group in the amalgamation was centered in northern Illinois. Parham's disciples had penetrated [John Alexander] Dowie's stronghold in Zion City in 1904. And by 1906 many of the latter's followers had converted to Pentecostalism. The message soon spread to Chicago, where it was heralded by two extraordinary preachers, William H. Durham at North Avenue Mission and William H. Piper at the Stone Church... The fourth group consisted of persons who had been forced to withdraw from Simpson's Christian Missionary Alliance between 1907 and 1911... These four bodies were drawn together partly by necessity and partly by theological affinity' ('Pentecostalism', pp. 939-40).

51. For the three major doctrinal challenges (trinitarian, sanctification, and evidential tongues speech) and resulting definitions see Blumhofer, *Assemblies*, I, pp. 217-43. While the earliest general councils avoided written doctrinal or creedal declaration, in the wake of the trinitarian challenge, the 1916 council passed a document named the Statement of Fundamental Truths. These 16 basic tenets addressed the Trinitarian question asserting the fledgling denomination's orthodox position. The Statement also defined a Pentecostal distinctive, Spirit baptism, advocated a baptistic or reformed type of progressive sanctification, supported premillennialism, recognized two ordinances—water baptism and the Lord's Supper—and endorsed a more Arminian than Calvinistic theology. Because the Statement did not intend doctrinal comprehensiveness, it omitted such doctrines as the virgin birth. Later, as the A/G moved toward evangelicalism, it added formal statements concerning the virgin birth and verbal inspiration of Scripture. However, A/G pastors and evangelists most often preached the so-called four cardinal doctrines of the church: Salvation, Baptism in the Spirit, Divine Healing and the Second Coming. See below for the Foursquare or Fourfold Gospel.

Missouri, systematized a burgeoning foreign missions program, founded training centers for ministerial candidates, coordinated weekly denominational publications, and initiated support systems for Christian educational programs.

The depression years of the 1930s caused economic hardships for the working-class Pentecostals, but the A/G enjoyed a tranquil period of relative isolation and rapid growth. During this era historian William Menzies explains that

> the denomination was relatively untroubled by internal conflict, and, isolated from the larger church world, forged ahead quite apart from the struggles afflicting the more traditional American churches. For example, the tremendous upheaval occasioned by the Fundamentalist-Modernist debate which rent the unity of several of the great denominations held but little concern for the Pentecostals. Few important changes were made in policy or structure. It was a period of 'undifferentiated growth'.[52]

The sect-like A/G, sequestered from most of the church world during this period, interacted with the outside world through evangelism. Their rosters proved their growth. For example, membership and the number of churches more than doubled during the 1930s. In the first 15 years the American A/G had grown to 91,981 with 1612 churches, but by 1939 the membership was 184,022 with 3494 churches.[53]

There were subtle changes among adherents amid these early decades of growth. While 'separation from the world' characterized the continuing attitude of A/G people, inconspicuously participants began to 'embrace some of the new things their culture offered'.[54] For example, A/G people, albeit with some reluctance,

> admitted that movies could be used for their own ends; that radio offered a medium for evangelization (Aimee McPherson began broadcasting over the nation's first church owned radio station, KFSG, in Los Angeles in 1924); in short, that the world's new technology had much for them to appropriate in accomplishing their task.[55]

As the second generation of A/G adherents moved into prominence

---

52. Menzies, *Anointed to Serve*, p. 145.

53. Kendrick, *Promise*, p. 95. Growth continued at this rate through the 1940s and 1950s, so that in 1959 the denomination reported 505,552 members attending 8094 assemblies.

54. Blumhofer, *Assemblies*, I, p. 260.

55. Blumhofer, *Assemblies*, I, p. 260.

other changes were on the horizon. The early Pentecostals forged their movement with their own intense and immediate experiences, but, as children grew within the movement, the challenges of institutionalization and transfer of the tradition to the next generation demanded attention. As the denomination attempted to address these dynamics, they implicitly modified some of their cherished sensitivities. For example, they de-emphasized somewhat their millenarianism even as they revised the original restorationist idealism. Both of these shifts were apparent as leaders produced plans to train the next generation of leaders through Christian education.[56] With these changes the A/G began to emerge from its isolation.

In the 1940s the A/G commenced a five-decade pilgrimage from religious and cultural isolation toward engagement with and leadership among other Christians. Before the 1940s the A/G remained relatively segregated from all other forms of Christianity including other Pentecostal groups. The 1940s, however, brought changes. In 1942, A/G leaders Ernest S. Williams, J. Roswell Flower and Noel Perkins were sent by the denomination to participate in an Evangelical gathering in St Louis. The evangelical gathering resulted in the formation of the National Association of Evangelicals (NAE), which wished to represent groups of conservative Protestant churches. Although Fundamentalist and Evangelical Christian leaders continued to oppose Pentecostal teaching, the A/G discovered a new level of acceptance and interaction among the members of the NAE. Later in the decade the A/G would help to found two other interdenominational organizations that would further accelerate their flight from seclusion: the Pentecostal World Conference, formed in Zurich in 1947, and the Pentecostal Fellowship of North America established in 1948. The A/G has provided leadership in both of these groups since their inception.[57]

Some A/G leaders moved even farther into the mainstream of the

---

56. Blumhofer points out that the shifts were accompanied by continued widespread adventist language. Nonetheless, 'Assemblies of God leaders began to face the likelihood of committing their work to another generation'. And the 'challenge of communicating the heritage, then, contributed to the transformation of the movement' (*Assemblies*, I, pp. 260-61).

57. The Pentecostal Fellowship of North America was disbanded in 1995 with the hope of establishing a more inclusive Pentecostal fellowship/organization.

The A/G also joined an organization with strong ties to the NAE, the National Religious Broadcasters' Association.

religious community. Early in the 1950s, David du Plessis, an A/G pastor, discovered a warm welcome from executives of both the World Council of Churches and the National Council of Churches of Christ in America. They were keenly interested in his Pentecostal testimony and requested his frequent participation in the Councils' ecumenical activities. While du Plessis encountered stiff resistance from A/G denominational executives, his leadership in ecumenism and in the Charismatic renewal served as a symbol of latent A/G interest in developing dialogue and fellowship with other Christians.[58]

During the 1960s and 1970s, the A/G role of interactive leadership continued to grow within two streams: Evangelicalism and Charismatic renewal. These two streams remained quite distinct during the sixties and seventies, and the A/G actions with the two remained dissimilar and separate. Officially, from the denomination's headquarters, the A/G persuaded interaction with conservative Evangelicals primarily through its participation in the NAE. In fact, Thomas F. Zimmerman, general superintendent of the A/G (1959–85) served the NAE as its president.[59] But some have argued that Evangelicalism through the NAE has impacted the A/G more than it has influenced Evangelicalism.[60] Clearly, a certain 'evangelicalization' of the A/G occurred during these decades, in part due to the denominational leadership.

During the same decades, the 1960s and 1970s, the Charismatic renewal claimed the attention of the religious world. The official A/G

---

58. By 1962 the A/G imposed restrictions on du Plessis that he could not abide. Thus, under pressure he resigned from the A/G. In spite of his resignation as an A/G minister, du Plessis continued to view himself as a part of the denomination. His ecumenical activities only grew as did his interaction with Pentecostals and Charismatics. In 1980 du Plessis became an A/G-credentialed minister again.

For examples of the ecumenical involvement of other A/G leaders, see Cecil M. Robeck, Jr, 'The Assembles of God and Ecumenical Cooperation: 1920–1965', in Wonsuk Ma and Robert P. Menzies (eds.), *Pentecostalism in Context: Essays in Honor of William W. Menzies* (JPTSup, 11; Sheffield: Sheffield Academic Press, 1997), pp. 115-50. Also, Daniel E. Albrecht's 'Pentecostal Spirituality: Ecumenical Potential and Challenge', *Cyberjournal for Pentecostal/Charismatic Research* 2 (1997) (http://www.pctii.org/cybertab.html), and his 'Variations on Themes in Worship: Pentecostal Rites and Improvisations' (Geneva: World Council of Churches, forthcoming).

59. In addition to participation in the NAE, Zimmerman, during his tenure as General Superintendent, served on numerous boards of evangelical agencies.

60. See Blumhofer, 'Assemblies of God', in *DCA*, p. 87.

position toward the renewal remained uneasy and ambiguous. Never-theless, an extensive grass roots interaction emerged between many A/G ministers, laity and churches and people of various mainline denominations who were interested in Charismatic renewal. This inter-action occurred in local A/G churches and in other Charismatic forums but rarely within sanctioned denominational (A/G) channels. In spite of the lack of official authorization, many local assemblies found a new reason for being, and they discovered Christian fellowship in a broader context than they had dared to dream. Many A/G pastors became con-sultants, teachers and speakers to grass roots ecumenical groups of the renewal, even as Charismatics from mainline churches were invited to pray with, speak to and participate in worship with A/G congregants. So, two different dynamics during the 1960s and 1970s drew the A/G out of its isolation into the broader streams of Evangelicalism and ecu-menical Charismatic renewal.

The participation in Evangelical and renewal streams, together with other factors (e.g. socio-economic and education factors) produced a progressive acculturation among A/G adherents. Members of the A/G moved increasingly into a middle-American mentality and way of life. A denomination of people that once bore the stigma of rejection by other churches and 'the world' as a badge of holiness, by the 1980s delighted in their new-found popularity. The price for and product of their acculturation proved an uneasy identity.[61] The A/G epitomizes the American success story. It emerged from humble, isolated circum-stances to a high-profile interaction and leadership within global enter-prises. Before we turn to consider our second Pentecostal denomination, we must first note some of the characteristics that distinguish the A/G.

Some Distinguishing Characteristics
Several times since the 1970s church growth agencies have cited the A/G as the fastest-growing American denomination. By 1997 2.5 mil-lion adherents attended nearly 12,000 assemblies in 56 districts, cover-ing all of the United States, and were served by more than 32,000 ministers. The denomination's tradition continues to encourage entre-preneurial-type ministers whose innovative ideas produce ministries sensitive and relevant to the populace. However, due to abuses of such

61. See Paul B. Tinlin and Edith L. Blumhofer, 'Decade of Decline or Harvest? Dilemmas of the Assemblies of God', *The Christian Century* (10–17 July 1991), pp. 684-87, for a critique of the denomination's identity struggle.

entrepreneurial approaches and a continued centralization tendency, the A/G's church bureaucracy exerts more denominational control than in the past. The traditional primacy of the local congregation stands in tension with this increasingly hierarchical form of leadership and structure.[62]

The strength and vitality of the A/G continues at the grass roots level. The pace that Springfield sets does not characterize the denomination as much as the vital congregational interaction within local communities. Local pastors and their people to a large extent continue to shape the A/G tradition.[63]

The print medium helped create the A/G (e.g. E.N. Bell's *Word and Witness*), and the A/G has continued its dependency upon publications and other media. For example, circulation of the denomination's *Pentecostal Evangel* has climbed to more than 280,000 making it the nation's most widely circulated weekly Protestant magazine. However, the *Evangel* accounts for only a fraction of the total publications of the A/G's publishing center, the Gospel Publishing House. The denomination's division of communications coordinates a radio–television department, a media center, an office of information and various publications.

Perhaps the most notable characteristic of the A/G exists outside the borders of the United States. From the founding of the denomination the A/G supported an aggressive foreign missions approach. In 1996, for example, members gave some 235 million dollars to world ministries, a sum which approaches 70 per cent of the denomination's total expenditures. American missionaries (1775 professional missionaries) work together with indigenous A/G churches in 148 countries. Each of these countries has its own A/G denominational structure. Together

62. The formal polity of the A/G represents a mixture of Congregational and Presbyterian elements. From the beginning the A/G members believed that the local church should relate to the central organization, the General Council, on a purely voluntary basis. At the local level the government remains strictly congregational. However, the A/G blended elements of Presbyterian polity into their congregational foundation. For example, a central administrative organization functions to facilitate missionary, educational and publishing efforts as well as supervising clergy. The primitive central administration envisioned by the early General Councils has evolved into a complex, increasingly centralized government.

63. Sociologist Margaret M. Poloma confirms this. See her *The Assemblies of God at the Crossroads: Charisma and Institutional Dilemmas* (Knoxville: University of Tennessee Press, 1989), esp. pp. 66-87.

these organizations serve more than 25 million adherents in 146,000 churches. A high percentage of the American missionaries help by teaching in more than 1000 Bible training institutes, extension programs and colleges around the world.[64]

The A/G first appeared on America's religious map as a reluctant denomination seeking to restore the New Testament charisms to the church and to preserve the positive results of the Pentecostal revival. Its story progressed, incorporating themes of restorationism, evangelicalism, ecumenism and popular cultural adaptation. In part, the story reveals the process of acculturation from sect isolation toward mainstream interaction and influence. The process prompted one observer to note that 'the A/G perceives itself as an evangelical denomination with a difference. But the difference is increasingly obscured by religious and cultural change.'[65]

International Church of the Foursquare Gospel

Not many Americans have heard of the International Church of the Foursquare Gospel (Foursquare or ICFG). Dwarfed by larger Pentecostal denominations, such as the A/G, the Foursquare name and reputation remain relatively obscure on the American religious terrain. While the denomination may suffer from low name recognition, its colorful and controversial founder imprinted her name on the minds of her contemporaries. Aimee Semple McPherson (1890–1944), the gifted and often flamboyant evangelist, founded her Foursquare Church the day she opened the spectacular Angelus Temple on 1 January 1923.[66] For all the doctrinal similarities, the Foursquare story unfolds in a different fashion from that of the A/G. While the A/G resulted from an amalgamation of several groups and theological streams, the Foursquare emerged under the ministry of one charismatic leader. Sister Aimee, as her followers called her, established a heritage upon which

64. See *Biennial Report of The Assemblies of God* (Springfield, MO: Executive Presbytery for the 47th General Council, 1997) and 'The Assemblies of God: Current Facts…' (1997), published by the Office of Public Relations of The Assemblies of God, Springfield, MO.

65. Blumhofer, 'Assemblies of God', p. 88.

66. The official incorporation of the ICFG transpired 30 December 1927, in California.

the Foursquare denomination continues to draw today more than 50 years after her death.

Sister Aimee's Life and Early Ministry

Born Aimee Elizabeth Kennedy on 9 October 1890, near Ingersoll, Ontario, Canada, to hard-working and pious parents, Aimee received religious and musical training in her rural home.[67] Her religious background consisted of a mixture of Methodism and Salvation Army. Her father, James Morgan Kennedy, a farmer and bridge builder, played the organ and led the choir at the nearby Methodist Church. Aimee learned her music from him. Mildred (Pearce) Kennedy, Aimee's mother, exerted a great religious influence upon her daughter. Mother Kennedy's religious training had been undertaken by the Salvationists, when she was orphaned at the age of 12. Later Mildred Kennedy joined the ministerial ranks of the Salvation Army. Although her active service ceased when she became a wife and mother, her commitment did not. In fact, she vowed to dedicate her child to the ministry, a dedication that later culminated in the life of her famous daughter.

Aimee made first contact with Pentecostalism through a young evangelist, Robert James Semple, who came to Ingersoll with the Pentecostal message in the winter of 1907, one year after the Azusa Street revival had begun. Aimee not only accepted the Pentecostal doctrine and experience, she married the evangelist the following year (12 August 1908). The couple demonstrated a deep commitment to spreading the gospel. And Aimee with her husband entered extensive evangelistic efforts immediately following their wedding. This was the beginning of what would emerge as an international Pentecostal ministry.

From the days of their courtship, Aimee and Robert Semple envisioned themselves as missionaries to China, but began the ministry

---

67. Aimee Semple McPherson, *This Is That: Personal Experiences, Sermons and Writings* (Los Angeles: Echo Park Evangelistic Association, 1923); *idem, The Story of my Life* (Hollywood, CA: International Correspondents, 1951); Lately Thomas, *Storming Heaven: The Lives and Turmoils of Minnie Kennedy and Aimee Semple McPherson* (New York: William Morrow, 1970); Cecil M. Robeck, Jr, 'McPherson, Aimee Semple', in *DPCM*, pp. 568-71; Kendrick, *Promise*, pp. 153-63. Two recent biographies of McPherson have helped to illumine her fascinating and provocative life: Edith Blumhofer, *Aimee Semple McPherson: Everybody's Sister* (Grand Rapids: Eerdmans, 1993), and Daniel Mark Epstein, *Sister Aimee: The Life of Aimee Semple McPherson* (New York: Harcourt Brace Jovanovich, 1993).

together in revival campaigns both in Canada and the United States. In 1909 they began an important association with William H. Durham of Chicago. Durham, the earliest chief proponent of the baptistic concept of sanctification in modern Pentecostalism and influential Pentecostal leader, ordained Robert and Aimee to the Pentecostal ministry. The couple accompanied Durham as a part of his evangelistic team. The Semples ministered along with Durham throughout the northern states and Canada for several months before embarking on a missionary term to China.

After only a few months in China, their mission was cut short due to Robert Semple's untimely death (19 August 1910) resulting from malaria. Aimee, not yet 20 years old, remained in China only long enough to give birth to her daughter, Roberta, one month later (17 September 1910). Upon her return to the United States, Aimee engaged in Salvation Army work in New York City for a short time before relocating to Chicago in 1911.

In Chicago Aimee Semple became Aimee Semple McPherson, when she met and married Harold Stewart McPherson (1890–1968).[68] Though Aimee again enthusiastically re-entered church work her husband showed less inclination toward religious work. Harold did act as advance man for some of Aimee's meetings, but eventually the couple separated and subsequently divorced.[69] During the ten years of their marriage (1911–21), however, Aimee's ministry did grow substantially. Her appealing message and ministry took her from small churches to tents and eventually to the main halls and auditoriums across the United States.[70]

While she received ordination from the A/G in 1919 as an 'evangelist', McPherson's ministry sought to be ecumenical.[71] In fact, she

68. The couple married on 24 October 1911.

69. Born to the McPhersons was Rolf Potter Kennedy McPherson on 23 March 1913. The couple divorced in August 1921.

70. In 1917 McPherson launched her first major publication, *The Bridal Call*, a monthly magazine. This periodical allowed her to test her writing skills. By it she was able to disseminate the core of her message and solidify a group of followers, especially along the East coast.

71. McPherson held ministerial papers with the A/G until 1922, when she voluntarily returned her credentials to the A/G headquaters. The issue of ownership of church properties probably helped induce her resignation.

appealed broadly to Christians across denominational lines, a rarity among early Pentecostals.

> Her meetings were always interdenominational or ecumenical. They were supported by many people and pastors within historic mainline churches. Her vision was interdenominational from the start, and the cornerstone of Angelus Temple was inscribed to read that the Temple was dedicated to 'the cause of interdenominational and world-wide evangelism.'[72]

Sister Aimee took her ecumenical world-wide evangelism on the road. By 1918 her transcontinental evangelistic tours through the nation's major cities brought her broad-based interdenominational support and a level of national notoriety that few preachers enjoyed.

In 1921, encouraged by Los Angeles followers, she decided to build a church in the LA area. She purchased property near Echo Park and proceeded to design and build Angelus Temple. In order to raise funds for the construction (it was a 'pay-as-you-go' project) McPherson crisscrossed the United States, preaching and taking offerings for the new flagship church. Less than two years later she dedicated the 5300 seat temple.[73] It certainly was a contrast to most Pentecostal-storefront type churches and missions of the day. 'The impressive sanctuary with its striking dome, stained glass windows depicting the entire life of Christ, great proscenium arch, choir lofts...balconies...and red carpeted aisles...became the heart of Foursquaredom.'[74]

With the completion of Angelus Temple itinerant evangelist McPherson became Pastor McPherson.[75] Sister Aimee settled down to care for her burgeoning flock and to lay the foundation for a new denomination.

---

72. Robeck, Jr, 'McPherson, Aimee', p. 569.

73. With its completion this sanctuary became the largest church in the United States, valued at 1.5 million (1921) dollars. See Vinson Synan, 'Fulfilling Sister Aimee's Dream: The Foursquare Church Is Alive Today', *Charism* (July 1987), pp. 53-54.

74. Kendrick, *Promise*, p. 156.

75. McPherson actively involved herself as pastor. For example, in addition to all administrative roles she presided over 21 services at the Temple per week and preached to 20,000 persons per Sunday. In addition, 'she often wrote dramas, pageants and oratorios that were presented by the Temple's huge staff. Her dramatic services captured the imagination and curiosity of the public' (Synan, 'Fulfilling Sister Aimee's Dream', p. 54).

The Emergence and Development of the Foursquare Denomination
Aimee McPherson brought a plethora of skills and talents to her
pastoral role. She wrote numerous books, broadcast her message via the
new medium of radio, developed social ministries for the Los Angeles
poor, initiated ministerial training, composed and published hymns and
choral pieces, wrote and produced full-length sacred operas, preached
sometimes more than 20 times per week, continued to travel periodically as an evangelist, all the while overseeing a vast and ever-increas-
ing set of ministries emanating from Angelus Temple. Clearly, McPherson's talents as a religious innovator were combined with her gifts of
organizing and administrating.[76]

The growth of the ministries of Angelus Temple under McPherson's
leadership during the 1920s proceeded as follows:

> To the temple were added the Prayer Tower (February 1923); the radio
> station KFSG (Kall Four Square Gospel, February 1924); a five-story
> building housing the Lighthouse of International Foursquare Evangelism
> (L.I.F.E.) Bible College (January 1926), founded in March 1923 to train
> pastors, evangelists, and missionaries; a denominational bookstore, 'Ye
> Foursquare Book Shoppe' (1927); and the Angelus Temple Commissary
> (September 1927).[77]

Though McPherson persisted in her ecumenical endeavors, the
transition from a single church, Angelus Temple, to a denomination
occurred quite naturally and at first unintentionally.[78] As a part of the
growing Temple organization, in 1923 Sister Aimee established an
Evangelistic and Missionary Training Institute.[79]

> Many of the students after receiving training in the school launched at
> once into mission and church work. Branch churches began springing
> up, especially in areas adjacent to Los Angeles... Within two years after

76. See Robeck, Jr, 'McPherson, Aimee', p. 570.

77. Cecil M. Robeck, Jr, 'International Church of the Foursquare Gospel', in
DPCM, pp. 461-63 (462).

78. According to McPherson, the emerging denomination, with its multiplication of churches, was 'not premeditated by us. We did not first draw the blueprints
and then build a work to fit them but the work sprang up everywhere and we had to
hasten to put the needful amount of scaffolding under it to hold it together' (Aimee
S. McPherson, 'The Church of the Foursquare Gospel', *Foursquare Magazine* 27
[May 1954], p. 17, as cited by Kendrick, *Promise*, p. 158).

79. This association would later emerge as the Lighthouse of International
Foursquare Evangelism (LIFE) Bible College (January 1926).

the opening of the Angelus Temple, thirty-two churches had been established in southern California alone, and some fifty other places were appealing to the mother church for services.[80]

The emergence of these new branch churches called 'Foursquare Gospel Lighthouses', together with the other extended ministries of the Temple, made clear to McPherson the need for a new corporation, a denominational design. In 1927 the Church of the Foursquare Gospel was formally incorporated.

During the 1920s and 1930s, the ministries of the Temple and the burgeoning Foursquare denomination took shape. Not only were the educational, missionary and publishing programs cultivated during these decades, but church polity and doctrine developed under the guidance of Sister Aimee. The polity of the new Foursquare denomination emerged within an essentially episcopal framework reflecting McPherson's Methodist and Salvation Army background more than her A/G connection. Mrs McPherson acted as the president, a position with broad powers. As president she presided over all conventions, boards, cabinets, councils and committees. Six other administrative officers assisted her with the division of denominational responsibility, while regional and district supervisors functioned to oversee the churches and pastors. The power of the central legislation of the Foursquare resided in the Annual Convention, which consists of denominational officers, all ordained and licensed ministers, and one lay delegate per one hundred members of every Foursquare church.[81]

The Foursquare name and doctrinal understanding derived, in part, from a visionary insight of Mrs McPherson. While preaching from the Ezekiel 1 text in an Oakland crusade in 1922, McPherson reported a 'divine inspiration', wherein she understood the four faces of the four cherubim to represent the four ministries of Christ. She subsequently proclaimed 'The Foursquare Gospel' and identified Jesus Christ as Savior, Baptizer with the Holy Spirit, Healer and Coming King.[82] Consciously or not, McPherson drew upon theological streams that ran deep

---

80. From the 'History of Foursquaredom' (unpublished mimeographed manuscript prepared by LIFE Bible College, n.d.), p. 1; and McPherson, 'The Church of the Foursquare Gospel', p. 17, as cited by Kendrick, *Promise*, pp. 157-58.

81. Kendrick, *Promise*, pp. 159-60, and Robeck, Jr, 'Church of the Foursquare Gospel', p. 462.

82. See Aimee Semple McPherson, *The Foursquare Gospel* (n.p.: Echo Park Evangelistic Association, 1946).

within the nineteenth-century Holiness movement and into the twentieth-century Pentecostal movement. The emphases of her Four-square gospel reflect the Fourfold gospel of A.B. Simpson's 1890 work *The Four-fold Gospel*. Early Pentecostals reappropriate the four symbols of Christ's ministry as their central teaching with a particular Pentecostal slant.[83] But perhaps McPherson expressed them more clearly and succinctly than any other pioneer Pentecostal. She certainly popularized these cardinal doctrines. Through her Echo Park Evangelistic Association she solicited hundreds of preachers from a variety of denominations who promised to proclaim these four doctrines.[84]

In 1944 Aimee Semple McPherson's sudden death traumatized the congregation of Angelus Temple and the Foursquare denomination.[85] But Rolf McPherson (1913–), who succeeded his mother as president of the Foursquare churches, stabilized the congregations with able administrative and pastoral care. The Church of the Foursquare Gospel flourished for more than four decades under the leadership of Doctor McPherson.[86] When 'Doctor' assumed the presidency, the denomination numbered some 400 churches in North America with 200 foreign mission stations and 22,000 church members, but, before he retired in 1988, the denomination included 1250 churches in the United States, more than 15,000 world-wide with an international membership of more than one million.[87] In addition to the numerical growth, Rolf McPherson

83. Donald W. Dayton demonstrates the intricate movements from Holiness sources into Pentecostal churches of theological concepts. He locates the four main doctrines that later represent the core Pentecostal beliefs within the Holiness groups of the nineteenth century, particularly in A.B. Simpson's Christian Missionary Alliance construct. See Dayton, *Theological Roots of Pentecostalism*.

84. Later in the development of the denomination McPherson penned a Declaration of Faith, a doctrinal position containing 22 articles of faith. These articles represent, according to Kendrick, 'the basic tenets of the several baptistic Pentecostal bodies'. The Foursquare articles reflect the same concerns as outlined in the A/G fundamental truths. 'Little separates the doctrinal position of the ICFG from that of the Assemblies of God', according to Robeck, Jr. See Aimee Semple McPherson, *Declaration of Faith* (Los Angeles: International Church of the Foursquare Gospel, n.d.); Kendrick, *Promise*, pp. 160-61; Robeck, Jr, 'Church of the Foursquare Gospel', p. 462.

85. See Thomas, *Storming Heaven*, pp. 339-46.

86. Cecil M. Robeck, Jr, 'McPherson, Rolf Kennedy', in *DPCM*, pp. 571-72.

87. The membership in the USA was about 200,000. See Robeck, Jr, 'Church of the Foursquare Gospel', p. 462.

guided his church into ecumenical relationships. In the 1940s the Four-square joined the Pentecostal Fellowship of North America and the Pentecostal World Conference. Subsequently, in the 1950s the denomination entered the National Association of Evangelicals and the National Religious Broadcasters. When the Charismatic renewal emerged in the 1960s, the Foursquare churches 'embraced the Charismatic movement as being a legitimate move of the Spirit'.[88] As a result of their ecumenical openness, the Foursquare churches not only grew but changed.[89]

Foursquare: A Changing Denomination
The spectacular originality and explosive growth of the 1920s Four-square could not be duplicated.[90] However, changes during the past two decades reshaped the denomination, so that the Foursquare Church of today again reflects an original burst of innovative creativity and accompanying growth. The profound changes came in the wake of the Charismatic renewal. New attitudes toward worship emerged. Such traits as flexibility and diversity surfaced and were nurtured until they became dominant characteristics among the churches and their leadership. A commitment to social responsibility reappeared, while the number of American churches skyrocketed from some nine hundred in 1980 to more than *nineteen* hundred in 1998.

Charismatic reappropriation. The Charismatic renewal served as a catalysis for the reappropriation of Pentecostal symbols. Many Four-square congregations, for example, transformed their routinized worship styles under the impact of the renewal. As a result Foursquare

88. Jack Hayford, quoted in Steve Lawson, 'The Foursquare Church Faces the Twenty-first Century: A Pentecostal Denomination Reshapes its Message and its Methods so It Can Reach Contemporary Society', *Charisma* 18 (March 1993), pp. 16-26 (25-26).

89. Vinson Synan asserts that the 'Foursquare church has been the most affected by the Charismatic renewal. To many outsiders, the worship services of the church are such that Charismatics from mainline denominations feel immediately at home' ('Fulfilling Sister Aimee's Dream', p. 54).

90. Even Sister Aimee could not match her achievements of the first decade of the Foursquare. The dramatic growth of programs, ministries and adherents of the 1920s slowed somewhat during the mid-century decades, but the 1970s brought new growth. See Wayne E. Warner, 'International Church of the Foursquare Gospel', in *DCA*, p. 578.

churches retained the Pentecostal symbol of (charismatic) praise/worship but reappropriated it, giving it centrality and adjusting its meaning. Church on the Way, a Van Nuys Foursquare congregation typifies the denomination's charismatic reappropriation.[91] Pastor Jack Hayford attributes the changes in his own church to the congregation's commitment to worship and to the Word of God. Hayford led a faltering congregation into a reorientation toward charismatic worship. 'We emphasize the spirit of worship as distinct from hip or hype worship.'[92] Hayford believes in God's sovereign commitment to 'visit [the congregation] with His Glory', and therefore the authentic congregational response should reflect 'an open and expressive attitude'.[93] Attitudinal change characterizes the Foursquare in general.

Renewed flexibility. The denomination in recent years nurtured the attitude of flexibility. Foursquare leaders cite the New Testament metaphor of new wine requiring new wineskins as symbolizing their desired flexible approach to contemporary society's needs. The denominational hierarchy has freed local pastors to employ innovative methods within their community's context. Foursquare leaders now play the role of facilitators, adhering to a decentralized approach. While there remains a pastoral accountability, 'pastors have great liberty to express themselves in ministry', says Pentecostal historian and Foursquare observer, Vinson Synan. Insider John Amstutz, concurs, citing flexibility as a major strength of the present Foursquare denomination. Professor Amstutz points to the contemporary training and ordination programs as evidence of the Foursquare's renewed flexibility.[94]

Growing diversity. A growing diversity within the denomination represents yet another characteristic and consequence of the reshaping process at work. Former Foursquare president John Holland explains one

---

91. During the 1970s and 1980s, Church on the Way emerged as the largest Foursquare congregation, with a membership of close to 8000. In 1969 only a handful of faithful Foursquare adherents attended the dying church. But today the church appears as the 'modern day counterpart to Angelus Temple' (Synan, 'Fulfilling Sister Aimee's Dream', p. 53).

92. Hayford, quoted in Lawson, 'The Foursquare Church', p. 19.

93. Hayford, quoted in Lawson, 'The Foursquare Church', p. 19.

94. Both Synan and Amstutz quoted in Lawson, 'The Foursquare Church', p. 20.

way the denomination encourages diversity, 'We encourage pastors to use their giftings and individual strengths to reach those in the community around them.' Thus, he claims, 'You will not find a "typical" Foursquare congregation.'[95] The diverse 'giftings' produce a variety of methods and together they produce diverse congregations. For example, the range of Foursquare churches spans from one congregation in Hawaii that meets under a palm tree to a Traditional church in Fresno, to a baby boomer-oriented megachurch in Seattle, to a racially mixed congregation in the Chicago area. The growing diversity makes a place for people of color and women both in congregational participation and in pastoral leadership.[96] Diversity is fast becoming a hallmark of the Foursquare people.[97]

Social conversion. While the roots of social concern run deep in the Foursquare soil, the denomination's leadership recognizes that in recent decades the churches have often ignored social issues.[98] Something of a socio-political conversion occurred in 1992. In the annual meeting of the Foursquare church, leaders repented of racism and a suburban orientation that avoids the social problems of the cities.[99] Denominational executives admitted publicly that by not 'energetically ministering to minorities', they were guilty of racial bias. Then President Holland

95. Lawson, 'The Foursquare Church', p. 20.

96. Though figures concerning people of color within leadership of the Foursquare are not available, the denomination reports that 40 per cent of its ministers are women. See Robeck, Jr, 'Church of the Foursquare Gospel', p. 463; and Carol A. Chapman, 'Women Leading the Church into the Twenty-first Century', *Charisma* 18 (March 1993), p. 24.

97. See W. Terry Whalin, 'Breaking the Rules to Build a Twenty-first Century Church', *Charisma* 18 (March 1993), p. 22; Chapman, 'Women Leading', p. 24. Lawson, 'The Foursquare Church', p. 20.

98. For example, the commissary that Sister Aimee opened in 1927 helped to feed and cloth 1.5 million people during the Depression. McPherson's commitment to the work of the commissary was in part responsible for a severe financial crisis that the church faced in the 1930s. The work of the Aimee commissary still goes on today. See Robeck, Jr, 'Church of the Foursquare Gospel', p. 462.

99. I do not mean to suggest that the Foursquare denomination in recent years ignored all social issues and persisted in no social programs. On the contrary, many Foursquare churches, for example, continued in the founder's vision of helping the poor. The issue emerges as an insight from the leadership that they needed to take a greater responsibility to engage actively in social issues, particularly those touching race and the inner city.

asserted that if they have avoided particular people groups, even unintentionally, it counted as sin. In acts of recognition and repentance the annual meeting did not conclude until the leaders and pastors committed themselves to an active social outreach. The repentance seemed real, it remains now to live out the social responsibility of the denominational conversion.[100] The Foursquare church represents a vibrant class of Pentecostalism. Secure in its history, it reaches toward the future as it creatively adapts in order to address its world. I turn now to consider the newcomer to the arena of Pent/Char denominations.

Vineyard Christian Fellowship

The Vineyard Christian Fellowship appeared on the American religious scene in the 1980s. By the end of that decade a shrewd religious observer noted:

> One of the most remarkable developments in American evangelicalism over the last decade has been the appearance of a new phenomenon known as the 'Signs and Wonders movement.' The movement is a blending of evangelical commitments and charismatic practices. Those associated with this recent trend affirm the continuation of all the miraculous gifts mentioned in the New Testament and yet refuse to be labeled Pentecostals or Charismatics.[101]

If the Signs and Wonders movement claims a founder, John Wimber, pop musician turned preacher, deserves the appellation. From 1977 until 1994 Wimber pastored the thousands who attended Anaheim Vineyard Christian Fellowship Church, a Signs and Wonders church. And, until his death in 1997, he led both the 450 church, burgeoning US denomination called the Association of Vineyard Churches (USA) and

---

100. Presently, emerging signs of social responsibility and active outreach are apparent. For examples, see Steve Lawson, 'Preparing to Solve Twenty-First Century Urban Problems', *Charisma* 18 (March 1993), p. 26; and *idem*, 'The Foursquare Church', p. 24.

101. Ken L. Sarles, 'An Appraisal of the Signs and Wonders Movement', *BSac* 145 (January–March 1988), pp. 57-82 (57). Vineyard Churches can be thought of as a subset of the 'Signs and Wonders movement'. Some authors employ the terms synonymously. Related phenomena, the so-called 'Toronto Blessing', emerged in the early 1990s in a Vineyard Church in Toronto, which has since disassociated itself from the Vineyard Churches. Nonetheless, the Toronto Blessing involves signs and wonders similar to the rest of the movement, albeit with its own particular strain of religious experiences.

the 250 Vineyard congregations abroad.[102] In order to give a context to the local Vineyard Fellowship that I will describe in Chapter 2, I must consider John Wimber's life, ministry and positions as they relate to the Vineyard association of churches, and the chief emphases of the Vineyard spirituality.

John Wimber and the Vineyard Story
John Wimber admitted that he knew very little about God or religion when he converted to Christianity in 1962.[103] From that time, however, Wimber's life was increasingly focused on religious issues. Beginning with his conversion, age 29, John Wimber engaged in evangelism. He testified to anyone who would listen that while his career as a rock/jazz musician, composer and record producer soared, his life spiraled into despair. Both John and Carol, John's wife who also converted, enthusiastically told friends of their new found 'freedom from guilt and fear of death,...purpose for living'.[104] Wimber wanted to train for some kind of religious vocation so he enrolled in a Bible college associated with the Evangelical Friends and studied sociology and theology. In 1970 John accepted the pastorate of a Quaker church in Yorba Linda, California. Despite Wimber's apparent success as a pastor (the church grew) he left in 1975 disillusioned.[105] 'I began to lose the kind of joy and peace that I thought would accompany such success. I was dissatisfied with my life and did not understand why. It was a disquieting and confusing time.'[106]

102. Lee Grandy, 'Wimber Plots New Course for Vineyard', *Charisma* (22 February 1993), p. 64; 1997 statistics from Association of Vineyard Churches, see their website, www.avc.vineyard.org.

103. See John Wimber with Kevin Springer, *Power Evangelism* (San Francisco: Harper & Row, 1986), p. xv. See also James R. Coggins and Paul G. Hiebert, 'The Man, the Message, and the Movement', in their edited work, *Wonders and the Word: An Examination of Issues Raised by John Wimber and the Vineyard Movement* (Winnipeg, MB: Kindred Press, 1989), pp. 15-22; C. Peter Wagner, 'Wimber, John', in *DPCM*, p. 889, and *idem*, in 'Vineyard Christian Fellowship', in *DPCM*, pp. 871-72, for Wimber's biographical information.

104. Wimber with Springer, *Power Evangelism*, p. xv. Between 1964 and 1970, Wimber says that he and Carol converted hundreds to Christianity and taught numerous Bible studies. See John Wimber's *Power Healing* (San Francisco: Harper & Row, 1987), cited in Sarles, 'An Appraisal', pp. 59-60.

105. Coggins and Hiebert (eds.), *Wonders and the Word*, p. 15.

106. Wimber, *Power Healing*, p. 23, cited in Sarles, 'An Appraisal', pp. 59-60.

As the former pastor of a fast-growing church, Wimber found a niche as a consultant for the southern California Fuller Evangelistic Association. For the next three years he flew all over the United States advising hundreds of churches seeking a growth formula. But the young Quaker consultant continued deeper into disillusionment. The churches seemed to Wimber bent on programs and efforts characterized by 'a lot of action' but void of authentic 'work of the Holy Spirit'.[107]

Until this period Wimber recalls,

> I had always avoided Pentecostal and Charismatic Christians, in part because it seemed that often controversy and division surrounded their ministries. Also, my judgment of their ministries was colored by a pre-supposition that charismatic gifts like tongues, prophecy, and healing were not for today. (As a dispensationalist, I believed the charismatic gifts ceased at the end of the first century.)[108]

Personal contact with Fuller Seminary's church growth expert C. Peter Wagner and with Wagner's writings softened Wimber's opposition to Pent/Char practices. Wagner, a non-Charismatic Evangelical had studied the evangelistic methods and spirituality of Latin American Pentecostals and had concluded that the Latin Charismatics offered a rich resource to other evangelicals. John Wimber saw Professor Wagner as a 'credible witness'. Wagner's documented cases of 'healing and deliverance from evil spirits...in South America' forced Wimber 'to reconsider [his] position on the charismatic gifts'.[109] Though he remained skeptical of the validity of the charismata in contemporary Christianity, Wimber sought out books concerning Pent/Char phenomena. He also pursued 'Third World students at Fuller Theological Seminary's School of World Mission' who gave him 'first-person testimonies of the miraculous'.[110] A rereading of the New Testament combined with the Pentecostal witnesses he had encountered initiated a process of re-evaluation of the place of spiritual gifts in the contemporary church, and particularly in its evangelism.

The pivotal event in Wimber's exploration occurred in 1977, when Carol Wimber experienced a dramatic healing of what she tagged 'personality meltdown'. While asleep, Carol dreamed that she was

---

107. Tim Stafford, 'Testing the Wine from John Wimber's Vineyard', *CT* 30.11 (8 August 1986), pp. 17-22 (19).

108. Wimber with Springer, *Power Evangelism*, p. xix.

109. Wimber with Springer, *Power Evangelism*, p. xix.

110. Wimber with Springer, *Power Evangelism*, p. xix.

filled with the Holy Spirit. When she awoke, Carol was speaking in tongues.[111] John's skepticism melted away in the light of his wife's healing and glossolalic experience.[112]

Carol, a woman of faith and intellect, had since her Christian conversion pursued a reasonable and biblical foundation for her faith. As she came to insight she sought to give 'a clear and logical presentation of the gospel'.[113] While John traveled as a consultant, Carol began a Bible study/prayer group that grew to 50 members.

> In 1977, at what he believed was very direct guidance from God, [John] began to pastor [the group]. He soon resigned his position as a church-growth consultant. The church met in a high school gymnasium. Wimber began to preach from the Gospel of Luke, and was struck by the many healings and exorcisms Jesus did. Wimber offered repeated altar calls for healing, but the church prayed for months without seeing a single healing occur. It was a humiliating, gut-wrenching time when many people left the church in disgust. Yet Wimber would not give up. He believed that God would not let him. He was determined to see God heal people, and eventually—after ten months—he did. One young woman was healed in her home of a fever, and Wimber's exultation knew no bounds. 'We got one!' he yelled at the top of his lungs on the way to his car.[114]

The church exploded and multiplied into a movement of signs and wonders.[115] Soon after their first healing the congregation experienced more healings and charismatic manifestations. A stream of non-Christians were attracted and converted to Christianity and the emerging Vineyard spirituality. The church first called itself Calvary Chapel— Yorba Linda, but in May 1982 it changed its name to Vineyard to identify with Kenn Gulliksen and his seven Vineyards. By that time the church numbered 700, mostly young people. Three years later, after relocating to Anaheim, Wimber's Vineyard had reached 5000 members and some 120 other Vineyards had emerged.[116] John Wimber again was

---

111. See description of Carol Wimber's process from opponent of the charismata to advocate in her 'A Hunger for God: A Reflective Look at the Vineyard's Beginnings', *The Vineyard Newsletter* 2 (Autumn 1987), pp. 1-3, 7 (1-2).

112. See Wimber, *Power Healing*, pp. 31, 43.

113. Wimber with Springer, *Power Evangelism*, pp. xv-xvi.

114. Stafford, 'Testing the Wine', p. 19.

115. In the first ten years of the church it grew to 6000 (Wimber with Springer, *Power Evangelism*, p. x). For a description of the emerging Vineyard movement see Wimber, 'A Hunger for God', pp. 1-3, 7, and Wimber, *Power Healing*, pp. 44-45.

116. Many of these new Vineyard congregations existed as independent churches

invited to consult and speak to churches, but now as one who proclaimed the work of the Spirit and the Spirit's charisms in church life and growth.

Vineyard's Emphases

Vineyard emerged in the 1980s. As a part of the broader Pent/Char movement of the twentieth century, it draws upon the symbols and spirituality of the movement. In that way it reflects similarities with the Foursquare, A/G, and other Pentecostal churches. But it also seeks to relate to the hesitancies that Protestant evangelicals have felt and voiced concerning Pentecostalism. Thus, Wimber preached a Pent/Char type spirituality but tended to avoid some of the traditional Pentecostal terms. Wimber and the Vineyard churches are forging a new vocabulary, adjusting theological concepts (categories) and developing their own style.

Vineyard worship. The typical Vineyard worship service bears the marks of Pent/Char worship. Many phenomena such as expressive and sometimes ecstatic praise, glossolalia, prophecy, words of knowledge, prayer for healing and lengthy sermons represent similar components. On the other hand, Vineyard worship seeks its own style. They often spend 30–50 minutes worshiping through songs, worship music that members of the Vineyard ministries have composed. The music and the worship period reflects the mode of Charismatic renewal worship and praise but with a definite Vineyard flavor. While excitement and high expectancy characterize the Vineyard services, the meetings also tend to be more relaxed, 'hip', even 'laid back'. No doubt such traits reveal the targeted group. The Vineyard style seeks and attracts the young.[117] John Wimber, the model for all Vineyard pastors,

> speaks in an offhand, unrehearsed manner... He is also a thoughtful, original Bible expositor. He communicates to educated evangelicals. His

prior to affiliating with Wimber. Other churches dropped out of a denomination to join the Vineyard Fellowship. See Coggins and Hiebert (eds.), *Wonders and the Word*, p. 19.

117. Wimber's first explosive growth occurred in 1981 and 1982; when the Vineyard Anaheim numbered 700 the average age was 19 and 21 respectively.

Vineyard's propensity for attracting the young seems to have continued throughout the 1990s. Vineyard continued to attract not only the baby boomers but their children, the so-called 'busters' or 'x-generation'.

style—cool, humorous, fatherly—is exactly pitched to baby boomers. It is a style redolent of Ronald Reagan: an awfully nice neighbor leaning over the back fence, presenting what used to be considered extreme without sounding mean or pushy.[118]

Vineyard preachers emulate Wimber's style, because it helps to create the Vineyard 'feel' for the worship service. The typical Vineyard service reflects the traditional Pent/Char service 'made over' for the 1990s and beyond. The reshaping of Pentecostalism via Vineyard utilizes familiar Pent/Char themes but configures them differently.

Power in the Vineyard. The concept of power claims a central place in Vineyard's vocabulary, theology and experience. Pentecostals speak of power, God's power and the endowment of power. Historically, they link Spirit baptism with spiritual power. In the Vineyard, however, the linkage appears looser. The view of Spirit baptism varies within the Signs and Wonders churches, but Vineyard teaching often suggests that baptism in the Spirit is part of an evangelical conversion.[119] In some Vineyards the category of Spirit baptism receives little attention at all.[120] Though the view of Spirit baptism seems ambiguous among the Vineyards, the emphasis on power towers above other teachings.[121] The Vineyard vocabulary demonstrates the point. Such terms as 'power evangelism', 'power healing', 'power encounters' permeate sermons, seminars and Vineyard's vernacular.

118. Stafford, 'Testing the Wine', p. 18.
119. C. Peter Wagner, 'Third Wave', in *DPCM*, pp. 843-44.
120. In Chapter 2 I will discuss the 'Valley Vineyard Christian Fellowship' (VVCF), one of the selected churches. The VVCF rarely deals with Spirit baptism as a category.
121. The different views of Spirit baptism among Third Wavers is illustrated by the following: 'In February of 1987 Kevin Springer conducted a poll of 2,041 people who attended a healing conference at the Anaheim Vineyard... One of the questions Kevin asked concerned the participants' understanding of "the baptism of (or in) the Holy Spirit." Of those who identified themselves as evangelicals...forty-five percent thought it was "an experience distinct from and subsequent to the Holy Spirit's work of regeneration in which the Christian is empowered for service and witness"... Forty-nine percent "thought it was "the initial action of the Holy Spirit, which happens at the time of conversion, that incorporates an individual into the body of Christ. Any later experiences with the Holy Spirit are better called 'fillings' ".' Only a very small minority (less than 3%) asserted a classical Pentecostal definition. Kevin Springer (ed.), *Power Encounters among Christians in the Western World* (San Francisco: HarperSanFrancisco, 1988), p. 214.

The Vineyard understanding of power is rooted in Wimber's concept of kingdom of God.[122] Wimber described the process by which he developed his notion of and practice of power:

> While my understanding and practice of evangelism, the Holy Spirit, and church growth were undergoing a revolution, [following charismatic experiences] I still lacked a biblical theology that integrated the three, a grid for understanding how they are supposed to work together and fulfill God's purpose on earth. This last element—a solid, evangelical theology—is the foundation on which all practice must stand.[123]

Wimber's search for a theology to support and integrate his experience culminated in his reading of evangelical theologian George Eldon Ladd. Wimber admits, 'It was not until I read his [Ladd's] book *Jesus and the Kingdom* that I realized how his work on the kingdom of God formed a theological basis for power evangelism'.[124] Wimber was convinced, as he alternated between readings in the New Testament and in Ladd, that the kingdom of God manifests itself as an invasive force. The thrust of the kingdom appeared in Jesus' preaching as well as his actions, Wimber recognized. Thus, Wimber reasoned the kingdom of God must not only be presented in the church's preaching of the good news but in its demonstrative deeds. The deeds of Jesus that interjected the kingdom as an invasive force, according to Wimber, were very often works of healing and exorcism. These actions demonstrated the power of the kingdom over Satan's kingdom. Wimber read the commission of Jesus to his followers as a charge to do what Jesus did, proclaim the gospel and demonstrate its power.[125]

In association with C. Peter Wagner, Fuller Seminary's professor of Missions and Church Growth, Wimber began to think in terms of the

---

122. Wimber with Springer, *Power Evangelism*, pp. 1-14.

123. Wimber with Springer, *Power Evangelism*, p. xx.

124. Wimber with Springer, *Power Evangelism*, p. xx. For Ladd on the Kingdom, see *Crucial Questions about the Kingdom of God* (Grand Rapids: Eerdmans, 1952), *The Gospel of the Kingdom* (Grand Rapids: Eerdmans, 1959), *The Presence of the Future* (Grand Rapids: Eerdmans, 1974), *A Theology of the New Testament* (Grand Rapids: Eerdmans, 1974).

125. Those that follow John Wimber 'believe that a purely cognitive approach falsely separates Jesus' word from his work. Jesus' work, as they read it, is a work of supernatural power against demons and sickness' (Stafford, 'Testing the Wine', p. 18).

'power encounter'.[126] Missions history, according to Wagner, portrays numerous examples of missionaries who converted animistic peoples through power encounters—a confrontation between gods. John Wimber extends the concept of power encounter to include where the kingdom of God confronts the kingdom of evil. Signs and wonders mark the battle Wimber preaches. Healings and exorcisms particularly demonstrate the power of God today, as they did in Jesus' ministry.

Divine healing, knowledge and appointments. Divine healing traditionally characterized the Pentecostal churches. Vineyard carries on the tradition, though adjusted.[127] Prayers for healing in the Vineyard bear high levels of expectancy. They represent to the Vineyard people an opportunity for the manifestation of supernatural power. While Vineyard teachings appreciate the role of modern medicine and counseling, members of the Vineyard focus on divine healing as God's intervention, a sign of God's compassion and power. Also, some healings (and exorcisms) require a power encounter. Vineyard adherents believe that modern medicine and psychology cannot fully address these needs, because such needs embody a spiritual dimension requiring spiritual attention or deliverance. The healing rites in these cases epitomize the power encounter.

Often the charismatic gift, the word of knowledge, operates as insight that facilitates the healing prayer of the Vineyard faithful. The process of prayer for healing typically includes discernment and insight, which help to direct the prayer session. Word of Knowledge, perceived as supernatural in its source, can be shared with the one in need. Wimber teaches that such knowledge comes during particular moments, moments he calls 'divine appointments'. Wimber wrote,

> A divine appointment is an appointed time in which God reveals himself
> to an individual or group through spiritual gifts or other supernatural

126. Wagner's study of Pentecostal missions changed his negative assessment of the Pentecostals. His understanding of the 'power encounter' proceeded from the work of anthropologist Alan Tippett. See Wimber with Springer, *Power Evangelism*, pp. 15-31.

127. A sympathetic behavioral scientist, John White, addressed the question of efficacious power and authentic healing. White has interviewed thousands prayed for at the Vineyard and, while he 'carefully points out that his evidence is strictly anecdotal, he believes there is plenty to convince a skeptic'. See Stafford, 'Testing the Wine', p. 20.

phenomena. God arranges these encounters—they are meetings he has ordained to demonstrate his kingdom (Eph. 2.10).[128]

These appointments with attending charisms benefit not only healings but evangelism as well. They provide the key to effective evangelism. Wimber explains that God gives a believer a word of knowledge as a message to be shared with a particular person, 'the astonishing, supernatural nature of the message often penetrates that person's defenses', opening them to the gospel.[129]

Vineyard's impact and challenge. No one can yet predict the impact of the Vineyard or Signs and Wonders movement. It may in time simply blend into the evangelical landscape or it may emerge as a dominant trend that supersedes even the influence of the preceding Pentecostal movement. To this point, the Vineyard, like the broader Pent/Char movement, 'carries a surge of evangelism, of praise, of expectation of the Spirit's power...reopen[ing] forgotten modes of ministry'.[130] Consequently, Vineyard centers have proven very attractive to American baby boomers and more recently to the so called 'x-generation'. Leaders of the Vineyard show a predilection for popular culture, and their churches effectively combine cultural elements with Pentecostal symbols to form their ethos. The young come seeking and they seem to find in the Vineyard a spirituality for today, complete with contemporary worship, relevant teaching and supernatural manifestations.

While some Evangelical, mainline Protestants and Pentecostals have questioned some of the emphases of the Vineyard,[131] they often recog-

128. Wimber with Springer, *Power Evangelism*, p. 51, and see also pp. 51-65 for Wimber's conception of 'divine appointment'.

129. Stafford, 'Testing the Wine', p. 21. Stafford also quotes other Evangelicals and Pentecostals who differ from Wimber's understanding and emphasis on supernatural power and the use of the word of knowledge and other charisms. Traditional Pentecostals (e.g. A/G and Foursquare) have used the word of knowledge but have typically been wary of the kind of application Wimber suggests. They note the danger in 'personal prophecy', charismatic words given to individuals. Wimber's practice and understanding apparently claims no uniqueness among Pentecostals, but his emphasis does. His doctrine that 'divine appointments', with attending personal words of knowledge, hold a normative place in healing rites and evangelism contrasts with the mainstream Pentecostal teachings.

130. Stafford, 'Testing the Wine', p. 22.

131. For examples of critiques of the Vineyard emphasis see Ben Patterson, 'Cause for Concern', *CT* 30 (8 August 1986), p. 20; Coggins and Hiebert (eds.),

nize in the Vineyard an authentic spiritual impulse as well as an implicit challenge.[132] The challenge comes not only from its dramatic growth and appeal, but from its spirituality. One religious writer suggests that the Vineyard spirituality challenges 'a view of the church that has no expectation of God's power above and beyond our techniques'. The 'Signs and Wonders movement', he continues, 'would ask us to take risks in order to experience an outpouring of the Spirit.'[133] The Vineyard offers much of what the broader Pent/Char movement offers, namely, a spirituality that consciously opens to the presence and actions of the Spirit, one that seeks to experience God fully while following Jesus' directives and commissionings. Vineyard's place in history awaits history's analysis, but currently it presents a new form of Pent/ Char spirituality with an implicit challenge.

I began this chapter by pointing out the variety within and the global spread of the modern Pentecostal movement. I proceeded to trace the origins and development of the movement's two primary phases and then considered three representative denominations as contexts within which to evaluate Pent/Char spirituality. Now I can turn to examine three selected congregations, one each from the above denominations. These three churches provide concrete examples of Pentecostal spirituality embedded in congregational life and ritual. In subsequent chapters

Wonder and the Word; John P. Schmidt, 'New Wine from the Vineyard', *Direction* 17 (Fall 1988), pp. 42-56; Sarles, 'An Appraisal'; Thomas D. Pratt, 'The Need to Dialogue: A Review of the Debate on the Controversy of Signs, Wonders, Miracles and Spiritual Warfare Raised in the Literature of the Third Wave Movement', *Pneuma* 13 (Spring 1991), pp. 7-32; and Stafford, 'Testing the Wine', quotes the critiques of some church leaders.

132. The Signs and Wonders movement has penetrated particularly some of the conservative evangelical churches. These are groups that, to date, neither the Pentecostals nor Charismatics have greatly influenced. See Wagner, 'Third Wave', pp. 843-44. Some works that suggest and support this charismatic influence among Evangelicals are Tony Campolo, *How to Be Pentecostal without Speaking in Tongues* (Dallas: Word Books, 1991); Charles H. Kraft, *Christianity with Power: Discovering the Truth about Signs and Wonders* (Ann Arbor, MI: Servant Publications, 1989); Springer (ed.), *Power Encounters*; Wagner, 'Third Wave'; John White, *When the Spirit Comes with Power: Signs and Wonders among God's People* (Downers Grove, IL: InterVarsity Press, 1988); Don Williams, *Signs, Wonders, and the Kingdom of God: A Biblical Guide for the Reluctant Skeptic* (Ann Arbor, MI: Servant Publications, 1989).

133. Stafford, 'Testing the Wine', p. 22.

I will specifically discuss the rituals and spiritualities inherent in these communities of faith, but first I must look at the congregational settings to further contextualize this study.

Chapter 2

THREE CHURCHES: CONGREGATIONAL CONTEXTS
FOR PENTECOSTAL/CHARISMATIC RITUAL

In Chapter 1 I traced the broad outlines of the origins and development of the twentieth-century Pentecostal movement. I gave special attention to three particular denominations: the Assemblies of God, the Foursquare and the Vineyard. These three denominations, each in its own way, reflect the larger movement's development and ethos. They also represent the parent organizations of the three churches selected for the field research. In the present chapter I will consider three specific congregations with one particular socio-historical setting.[1] Pentecostal spirituality, like all spiritualities, is experienced, lived out, in the midst of a particular culture during a certain time (era). While at times in this work I will speak in general of Pent/Char spirituality, I will in most cases be drawing on the three specific faith communities portrayed below.

The selection of the three faith communities involved a three-month process. A preliminary research team visited 17 Pent/Char churches mostly within two Northern California counties, seeking congregations that would provide appropriate contexts for the field studies.[2] The

<hr>

1.   The following chapters bear the influence of cultural anthropological studies, ethnographic approaches, and ritual studies. In this chapter I have drawn, particularly, from the approach and useful categories of the congregational studies of David A. Roozen, William McKinney and Jackson W. Carroll, *Varieties of Religious Presence: Mission in Public Life* (New York: Pilgrim Press, 1984).

2.   The preliminary research team included three women and three men from a upper division Sociology and Religion class at Bethany College. Each had experience in Pentecostal churches and had received training in techniques in participant observation. The author coordinated and supervised the team, which followed the James P. Spradley outline of 'Development Research Sequence' in his *Participant Observation* (San Francisco: Holt, Rinehart & Winston, 1980). After weekly church

fundamental criterion for selection focused on the Sunday morning worship service of each church. I looked for churches whose congregants appeared to be thoroughly engaged in highly participatory forms of liturgy. I sought for congregations whose liturgies displayed a variety and wide range of Pent/Char-type rites and practices.[3] I pursued such churches through the church advertisements in the local papers and phone books by talking with local congregants and pastors, and ultimately by visiting churches that seemed like good candidates.

During the selection process, the team narrowed the groups of churches by locale and denominational affiliation. We decided to choose three churches from one locale, the Sea City area,[4] but from three different denominations.[5] After attending services and making

visits the team met to discuss their field notes and impressions. The team functioned from February 1991 to May 1991. They not only helped in the original visits to the churches and the selection process but they help to gather some of the initial data on the three selected churches.

A second research team from a similar class, including two women and two men, also participated in the fieldwork in the three selected churches. Their work was concentrated mostly during the months of June 1992 through October 1992 and focused on particular questions generated during the course of the ongoing study. The author began his fieldwork in December 1990 and continued it on a weekly basis through March 1993. During 1997 and 1998 follow-up field research was conducted, primarily within the three congregations that were the original focus of this study. During the course of this research more than 250 services in the three churches were attended (mostly Sunday services but others also) more than one hundred congregants were interviewed, both formally and informally.

Members of the research teams included Yvonne Albrecht, James Carlen, Craig Fisher, Paige Glass, Mari Prieto, Wes Sanders, Lisa Schmidt, Douglas Shelton, Eve Snow and Bernard Wagner.

3.   The level of participation in and the range and variety of the rites not only suggested a vital ritual community, but these factors would make the spirituality more accessible to this form of study. The more expressive the ritual forms the more data one would have to work with. Also, the highly expressive forms reflect the tradition of the Pentecostal service.

4.   See below for a description of Sea City.

5.   I chose not to include churches whose own denominations consider them as 'ethnic' 'non-English speaking' or 'African-American' congregations. While many of these local congregations draw on a rich Pentecostal heritage and reflect vibrant and authentic Pentecostal ritual, we felt that a cross-cultural analysis among three churches was too ambitious for this study. Also, I chose churches that reflect the more baptistic or reformed type of Pentecostalism, as opposed to the Wesleyan-

preliminary field notes on seven churches in the Sea City (three A/G, two Foursquare and two Charismatic) area, we chose three: one A/G, one Foursquare, and one Charismatic—Vineyard.[6] Of these three, the Foursquare church and the Charismatic church best fit the primary criterion, namely, a liturgy that reveals a variety and range of Pent/Char rites. However, because both of these congregations have been founded since the Charismatic renewal and reflect much of the contemporary styles of Pent/Char worship, we chose as the third church one with a long history in Sea City, an A/G church. This A/G congregation represents a worshiping community with a continuous Pentecostal tradition of some 75 years. I believe that these three churches reflect some of the range of three different denominational histories and ethos as well as a variety of their own congregational expressions. Yet each of these three faith communities reveals aspects of the general Pent/Char movement and its tradition of ritual and spirituality. Since one geographic locale provides the setting for all three of the churches, I will introduce the churches by way of the context of their civic community, Sea City.[7]

From San Francisco, Sea City is a pleasant drive south along the Pacific coast. Bordered by the crests of redwood-covered coastal mountains to the north and east, Sea City wraps around the mouth of a small bay. The area's natural beauty and pleasant climate have made it a popular seaside resort. The modern history of the area began with the natives, the Costanoan (Indians) who first met Europeans, the explorers, in the late eighteenth century. The Spanish established a pueblo and a mission which by the mid-nineteenth century, developed into a port and industrial hamlet, 'Sea City'. In those days, Sea City's port provided access to the lumber industry centered in the neighboring forests and to the tanneries and surrounding ranchos. During the twentieth century, the Sea City area was known for its specialized agriculture, food-proces-

holiness type and churches that maintain a trinitarian theology in contrast to the 'Oneness' or Unitarian version of Pentecostalism. Clearly, with the multitudinous types of Pentecostalism, we needed restrictions. I do not claim that the three churches represent a cross-section of Pentecostalism. However, I do assert that they reflect authentic strands of the movement and its fundamental spirituality.

6.   Prior to the final selection we discussed with the pastors of three churches our desire to study their congregations. In each case the pastor approved.

7.   The names of the cities, churches and individuals have been altered. This chapter refers, for example, to three particular congregations (though it draws from many others), but their names and minor historical details have been altered to protect the anonymity of their constituents.

sing industries, tourism, parks, beaches and more recently its high-tech firms and a major university.[8]

At the dawn of the twenty-first century, Sea City endures no longer as the sleepy little town for the tourists and the retired, as it was until the 1960s. With a population of nearly 50,000 in the city limits, and more than 200,000 within a 20-minute driving radius, today Sea City sees itself as a burgeoning city. Its university has affected not only the size of the population, but has changed the cultural climate. Today, students, along with the business community, artists, retired people and tourists have been mixed together to form a new Sea City, one known for its progressive politics and casual but varied lifestyles, lifestyles not untouched by religion.

Sea City has always had a strong religious presence. Of course religion played a significant role in the culture of the native Costanoans. 'Our religion and daily life are and were inseparable,' insists a descendant of the original inhabitants.[9] The brown-robed Spanish friars introduced another spirituality to the region, when, at the end of the eighteenth century, they brought in Christianity along with other European effects. But in recent years Christianity no longer dominates the religious realm. Instead, Sea City has become a 'spiritual smorgasbord'. The sphere of East Indian influence that now plays 'noticeably on the consciousness of the populace illustrates the range of religions'.[10]

It is difficult to account for the variety of spiritualities in so small an area. There is, however, a sense that the people of Sea City who in recent days have come from many different origins have a more open and accepting attitude toward religious diversity. One local writer

8.   *A...Compendium: People's Yellow Pages* (Santa Cruz, CA: Bootstrap Press, 4th edn, 1980); *Encyclopedia of California* (St Clair Shores, MI: Somerset Publications, 1980); James D. Hart, *A Companion to California* (New York: Oxford University Press, 1978); Edward V. Salitore, *California: Past, Present, Future* (Lakewood, CA: Edward Salitore, 1973); U.S. Bureau of the Census, *State and Metropolitan Area Data Book* (Washington, DC: US Government Printing Office, 1986).

9.   Daniel Lopez, *Carnalisimo Publications*, November/March 1977–78, quoted in *A...Compendium: People's Yellow Pages*.

10.   Donald Haslam, 'Spiritual and Religious Introduction', in *A...Compendium: People's Yellow Pages*, pp. 54-55. Haslam notes the influence on the Sea City culture in 'the lifestyles of hippies and housewives alike'. He recognizes that Indian spiritualities 'are reflected in the city's stores, restaurants and colleges as well as in its art, music and dress'.

reflected on the religious motivation of many Sea City residents, 'People are tired of TV, drugs, money, insecurity, tension and the dog-eat-dog attitude that prevails'. As a result, many 'are engaged in a more profound search for Truth, God or their Self'.[11]

The same climate that has produced a turn toward Eastern spiritualities has also produced a rise of new Evangelical churches, particularly Charismatic and Pentecostal congregations.[12] Other Pentecostal congregations, well-established, have experienced significant growth and revitalization during the past two decades, the period of Sea City's emerging spiritual diversity.

In this Chapter I will consider three Pentecostal/Charismatic congregations in the Sea City area in order to understand better the congregational context that sustains these particular manifestations of Pentecostal ritual and spirituality. The local congregation that 'traditionally has a certain priority' serves as a community of faith and worship that includes the strands of spirituality contained in the larger church tradition and denomination.[13] Toward an understanding of Pentecostal spirituality then, I will in this chapter consider briefly three local churches. The following three 'portraits' will help to provide background in which to consider the worship rituals of these three communities as a reflection of spiritualities in subsequent chapters.

Coastal Christian Center: Pentecostal Tradition in Transition

On Easter weekend one sees them at and around the Sea City Civic Center, across from city hall in the heart of the community. They stand on the steps of the civic auditorium welcoming friends and neighbors to their locally produced passion play that will attract capacity crowds all weekend. They are the members of the Coastal Christian Center (CCC). Their Easter production at 'the Civic' is explicitly a 'gift to the Community' of Sea City. But implied in the 'gift' are the orientations and purposes of a congregational tradition that reveal its dynamic in a series of transitions.[14]

---

11. Haslam, *A...Compendium: People's Yellow Pages.*

12. For example, more than a dozen, mostly Charismatic/Pentecostal congregations, began in the decade of the 1980s in and around Sea City.

13. R.N. Bellah *et al.*, *Habits of the Heart: Individualism and Commitment in American Life* (Berkeley: University of California Press, 1985), p. 227.

14. Edith Blumhofer has characterized the Pentecostal orientation toward the

Coastal Christian can be characterized as a traditional ('classical')
Pentecostal church, an Assembly of God that has been transitioning
from sect-like mentality, with strong restorationist symbols, to a church
that more fully participates in the larger religious community, civic
community and the global community, as the church understands them.

Only a few blocks from the civic center stand the church buildings
that belong to the CCC congregation. The California white stucco style
trimmed in traditional mission brown appears as an early 1950s version
of the classic style. The main building occupies a corner lot and faces
Church Street, one of the main thoroughfares of Sea City. The well-
trimmed shrubberies and modest gardens that outline the Sanctuary and
Christian Education building, reflect the care given the buildings, which
have undergone numerous remolding projects over the past four decades. The upkeep of the church is consistent with the surrounding neighborhood. Nearby side streets, between the civic center and the church,
are filled with Victorian homes in which their residents and the Sea City
community take great pride. Church Street, too, boasts its share of Vic-

---

religious and secular cultures in four successive, overlapping stages (see 'Introduction', in her *Restoring the Faith*). Each of these orientations continues to some
extent in the contemporary congregational life of the CCC and can in part be seen
in a major event of their church calendar, the Easter Weekend at the Civic Auditorium. The 4 main streams of identity (orientations) at work in the CCC and
'played out' in the Easter production are: (1) a restorationist-emphasis portrayed not
only in the passion story but in its view of the 'primitive church' which is central to
the production; (2) an evangelical orientation, is recognizable in the motivation
which is, in part, to make an evangelistic thrust complete with an altar call for
unbelievers and trained 'altar workers', to assist in sharing the evangelical message;
(3) a Third Force (and Charismatic renewal) orientation: charismatic overtones
were toned down somewhat but are distinguishable. The CCC views the presentation as an opportunity for other churches to come together in mutual support of the
Christian message. Several churches have participated, if only with their presence;
(4) engagement in Popular and/or Civic culture: the entire presentation is billed as a
gift to the community (an expensive gift—employing professional musicians and
technical workers to complement and facilitate the massive lay involvement) presented free to all, in the Civic center, 'a neutral' venue. CCC sees this presentation
in the most public auditorium in the city, as an attempt 'to get out into the community.' It is meant to make a 'statement' to the larger community of Sea City, 'we
are interested in you, we are a part of the community'. The presentation is an
attempt to engage in the 'conversation' that makes up the culture of the civic community. Also see Bellah *et al.*, *Habits*, for the metaphor of 'conversation' applied to
a cultural entity (i.e. a society).

torian houses, though most now house small businesses and offices. Newer buildings represent stores and other businesses that string along for about half a mile on each side of the CCC. Half a mile east on Church Street are the two historic churches that gave the street its name. First Church is a mainline Protestant church that has a history of nearly a century and a half. One block farther east is the actual first church of Sea City, a Roman Catholic church with a history of more than two centuries in Sea City.

When compared to these two churches, the CCC is the 'newcomer'. It was in 1922, six years after the original General Council of the A/G, that a group of mission workers from the south San Francisco Bay area crossed the coastal mountains to share their Pentecostal faith with interested folks in Sea City. After four years of Bible studies, prayer meetings and church services, the mission work formally became a church. The 'Good News Tabernacle' incorporated as an Assembly of God in 1926 and called its first pastor. This began what would later become the 'Coastal Christian Center'.[15]

A History of Transitions
The 75-year history of the CCC may be summarized in four main phases: (1) the founding of a sect-like (restorationist) church (mission work began in 1922–World War II), (2) a broadening influence and interaction with the Protestant–Evangelical wing of the church, (3) an emerging self-perception as a Third Force church stimulated by the reception of and interaction with the Charismatic renewal and with increased civic engagement, and (4) the search for a new identity in light of the rapidly changing cultural (and Charismatic) influences. Each of these phases implies a separate though overlapping congregational identity, which in turn implies a stance toward the larger society and groups of Christians within the society.

A sect becoming evangelical. Both the workers from the South Bay mission that planted the church in 1922 and the fledgling Assembly of God 'denomination', only a few years old in California when the congregation of Good News Tabernacle voted to join it, indicate the restorationist and sect-like qualities of the early history of the CCC.[16]

15. The church name was changed to 'First Assembly of God' before it was changed to 'Coastal Christian Center'.
16. For the general restorationist and sect-like qualities of the early Assemblies

By World War II however, the sect mentality of the CCC broadened somewhat. Members of the CCC increasingly recognized an affinity with the other conservative Christians, particularly, the so-called Fundamentalists and later the Evangelicals. The Pastor of the CCC developed an interactive relationship with other ministers in town, and the Assembly cooperated with joint efforts of evangelism and service. Even the internal programs of the church began to reflect borrowing from churches of evangelical denominations more experienced in programming. The CCC progressed from a narrow, very basic program, mostly church services, to a set of diversified ministries and programs offered to meet the needs of its members. I characterize the CCC's self-understanding during this era, mid-1940s until 1970, as 'fundamentalists (evangelicals) with a difference'.[17] The 'difference', of course, emerged from their Pentecostal understanding/experiencing of the role of the Holy Spirit. While its particular understanding of the Spirit's role remained a barrier to wide acceptance by Fundamentalist churches in the area, CCC's three successive pastors of this period each moved the congregation into wider currents of Evangelicalism.[18]

A Third Force church.[19] By the early 1970s other themes began to emerge within the CCC congregation. With the arrival of a new pastor,

of God see Blumhofer, *Assemblies*, Menzies, *Anointed to Serve*, and Grant Wacker, 'The Function of Faith in Primitive Pentecostalism', *HTR* 77.3-4 (1984), pp. 353-75. Also for the early history of the A/G in Northern California see Everett A. Wilson and Darlene Little (compilers), *Seventy-Five Years of Dreams, of Destiny... A Narrative and Pictorial History* (n.p., 1994).

17. See Blumhofer, 'Introduction', in her *Restoring the Faith*.

18. In part, the move toward Evangelicalism can be seen in a group of dissatisfied parishioners that left the CCC, complaining of its lack of growth and evangelical fervor. Upon leaving the CCC, the group rooted itself within a non-Pentecostal, evangelical church in the city. Their affinity for the conservative evangelical ethos apparently was developed within the broadening Pentecostal self-perception of the CCC.

19. In a now famous article in *Life* magazine ('The Third Force in Christendom', *Life* 44 [June 1958], pp. 113-24 [124]), Henry Pitney van Dusen, the then president of Union Theological Seminary in New York, applied the term 'Third Force' to groups of Christians outside the mainstreams of Protestantism and Catholicism. The notion of Pentecostalism as a Third Force within Christianity resonated with ecumenists and with those participating in the emerging Charismatic renewal of the subsequent period. Many Pentecostals began to view their role in the Church as a

Pat Ralston, and a name change[20] came a new openness, an openness that embraced the Charismatic renewal. Concurrently, the CCC began to see itself as a force for church renewal in Coast County.[21] Throughout the 1970s and into the 1980s the CCC and its pastor provided leadership in the Charismatic renewal. During this period the congregation characterized itself as 'a church on the cutting edge'. They saw themselves as 'out in front' in the religious community, providing needed services and leadership. As a result, some even called them the 'in Church'. This seems particularly true among Pentecostals and Charismatics in the area.

This leadership role also gave expression to newly emerging civic concerns. With a higher profile in the community, the 1970s and 1980s marked a time of expansion and growth for the CCC. The church attracted young professionals and business men and women and their families who soon became the backbone of the church. They helped to engage the congregation more fully in civic service and affairs. Pastor Ralston himself took the lead. He guided the church's growth in community involvement. His own heavy involvement in local non-church service groups set the pace for the congregation.[22] Ralston successfully

Third Force for renewal within the Church. See Blumhofer, *Assemblies*, II, pp. 97-106.

Note that 'Third Force' should not be confused with the term 'third wave', which some have suggested as a descriptive term for a 'wave' of revival since the early 1980s. The term third wave refers back to classical Pentecostalism and Charismatic renewal as the first and second waves respectively. In this view, all three waves are a part of the twentieth-century Pent/Char movement.

20. The name of the church was changed in the early 1970s to Coastal Christian Center. The figure of 'Pastor Ralston' includes several of the pastoral staff members of the church.

21. The CCC became active in Charismatic renewal. There were strong ties, particularly, between Roman Catholic Charismatics and the CCC. Joint prayer between members of the two congregations occurred and the lay leader of an active, large and growing Roman Catholic Charismatic group in town often participate in CCC services, at times filling the pulpit. In addition the CCC sponsored an annual Charismatic conference that was held at the CCC, brought in nationally known charismatic speakers and attracted Charismatics from around the Sea City area. Of course, the CCC congregation fully participated in these conferences. Much of the Charismatic renewal activity was fostered by pastor Ralston making him an unofficial leader in the Charismatic renewal in the county. This leadership was extended into the network of Pentecostal churches throughout the city as well.

22. Examples of social/civic impulse within the CCC during this period included

linked service in the community with Christian service in the minds of
his parishioners. Christian service for the CCC focused not only within
Sea City but extended beyond the local area. In fact, during this period
service teams provided building assistance to churches and educational
facilities in developing countries. Teams sponsored by the church completed more than 20 international projects during these years.

The congregation consciously linked this new extended social involvement to their Pentecostal heritage and charismatic ethos which
continued as foundational to the spiritual life of the CCC. However,
because much of the impetus for the congregation's expansion came
from the force of the Charismatic renewal, when those forces began to
subside, so did the growth of the CCC. With the slowing of growth and
expansion, came the need to reconsider the (congregational) self-identity.

As the decade of the 1980s drew to an end, two events coincided to
challenge the principal self-image symbol (i.e. 'Third Force') of the
church. First, the main wave of the Charismatic renewal seemed to have
passed. The waning of the primary stage of Charismatic renewal meant
that the CCC's role of Third Force church seemed less critical. The second event, new forms of Charismatic Christianity began to appear in
and around Sea City, had a similar effect.

During the 1980s the landscape of Charismatic Christianity in and
around Sea City changed. There appeared several new Pent/Char-type
churches. Other churches, perhaps best characterized as neo-Evangelical, were revitalized in part by the adoption of selected Charismatic
characteristics.[23] Both of these types of churches borrowed heavily from

its popular businessmen's breakfasts (pastor Ralston also met regularly with top
business people and interacted with political officials), active involvement and
cooperative projects with service organizations (e.g. Rotary club), sponsoring medical mercy missions, funding of local youth organizations, providing relief to street
people through feeding programs, disaster and crisis assistance (e.g. earthquake
relief), free counseling to the community, support for the pregnancy center and special meetings in the civic center.

23. Some have characterized such churches as the so-called 'third wave' of the
renewal of the Holy Spirit. See above. Also, there was significant borrowing from
Pentecostal forms of worship and spirituality among many evangelical churches
and neo-evangelical churches. See David S. Luecke, 'Introduction, the Changing
Face of Worship', *Theology, News and Notes* 37 (March 1991), pp. 3-4; and James
F. White, *Protestant Worship: Traditions in Transition* (Louisville, KY: Westmin-
ster/John Knox Press, 1989), especially ch. 11, for the claim, in general, of the

the Pentecostal tradition, but were perhaps more in touch with some of the popular evangelical currents and the popular culture of the emerging 1980s and 1990s, than was the CCC. The CCC had in some ways routinized its rituals and activities as its core of young adults moved toward middle age. This routinization made it less likely that it would follow the trends as rapidly as some of the newer developing congregations.[24] The changing terrain of Charismatic Christianity in the area seemed to dilute the need for CCCs primary Third Force role.

Currently, the CCC is regrouping.[25] A newly arrived pastoral staff has developed programs aimed at encouraging a new self-understanding.[26] It is too early to know precisely what new congregational self-identity

influence of the Pentecostal worship on other Christian forms in the recent past. Also, see John Fenwick and Bryan Spinks, *Worship in Transition: The Liturgical Movement in the Twentieth Century* (New York: Continuum, 1995), pp. 105-14, for the influence of Charismatic renewal on the Liturgical movement and the interaction between the Liturgical movement and Charismatic renewal.

24. Another event that produced confusion and congregational self-questioning was a series of failed relocation attempts. Because the church's physical facilities had been restricting the congregations activities and programs for some time, the congregation sought to move to larger quarters. However, political conditions and neighborhood zoning codes stalled several relocation proposals. In the midst of these setbacks, the congregation went through difficult pastoral staff changes, resulting in shifts in pastoral styles. A number of families moved their membership to other churches in Sea City. Many chose to affiliate with the newly emerging 'neo-Charismatic' congregations, others transferred membership to other Assemblies of God, still others to neo-Evangelical churches.

25. By the end of the 1980s and into the early 1990s, the CCC had entered a period of self-questioning. This self-questioning was voiced by one long time member and congregational lay leader: 'I've even wondered what is wrong with us...are we not mature or stable Christians? Maybe we haven't been trained in the scriptures enough.'

These doubts revealed a congregational self-identity that became blurred. The image of Third Force for renewal had lost much of its potency as a dominate theme for self-understanding. Other newly established Charismatic and Evangelical churches in the county became attuned to the contemporary popular culture of the 1980s and 1990s in ways the CCC could not. These emerging churches provided a new backdrop. The CCC was no longer alone in the leadership of the Pentecostal/ Charismatic force in Sea City. Attempts to re-understand its identity in a changing world proved challenging.

26. Part of the regrouping and new programming can be seen in the pastors' approach to lay ministries. The CCC has a tradition of encouraging its members to minister as lay people, however, the new pastoral staff has developed a training

will emerge. But as the church is now again attracting new parishioners, the new members and the old core, together with the leadership, will surely develop a relevant though somewhat altered self-image. Presently, the emerging identity represents a (re)synthesizing of the CCC's historic symbols into a new order that will symbolize Pentecostal spirituality for this congregation. This transition is not the first, it is only the most recent, in the life of this traditional (classical) Pentecostal church.

Membership: Belonging and Participating
The CCC's constitution states clearly its reason for being: 'To establish and maintain a place of worship' and to promote 'close Christian fellowship and edification', while conducting 'the work of evangelizing both home and foreign fields'. All 'departments and institutions...necessary for the propagation of the gospel, and for the work of the assembly' receive support and encouragement. Members of this assembly commit to this purpose. Generally, to be a member means to belong to and participate in this particular faith community. Being a member of the CCC community implies particular things, such as common qualifications, expectations and types of involvement.

In recent years the official membership of the CCC has averaged nearly five hundred.[27] However, barely half of the congregation is

program to cultivate lay ministries. They not only encourage the 'priesthood of believers', they have taken steps to train the congregation.

27. The median age of adults in the congregation is about 45. Among five adult age categories: twenties, thirties, forties, fifties, and sixties and above there is a relatively even distribution of the congregation, roughly 20% in each. Approximately 30% of these are children and teenagers, thus about 70% are over 20 years old. Recent shifts in the congregation suggest that the average age is rising. A number of younger professionals and their families have recently left the church, and the church has recently attracted more blue-collar workers and young people just entering the work force. This, according to a pastor and the treasurer, had an overall effect of lowering slightly the socio-economic level of the church. The CCC has for the past decade or so been mostly a blue-collar congregation, with a sizable minority of professionals, including college professors, school teachers, middle-management executives, entrepreneurs and presidents of small companies. While some of the church's advertisements claim that the CCC is 'where background doesn't make a difference', the socio-economic differences and the presence of people with an assortment of Christian traditions seems greater than the church's ethnic and racial diversity. However, the preponderance of whites, nearly 90%, with minority representation primarily from Mexican-Americans (and fewer African-

officially on the membership roll.[28] A few times each year membership classes present an opportunity to formalize a commitment to the congregation and submit to the common expectations of the community. Congregational leaders encourage participants to consider membership. A short series of classes provides answers to questions from inquirers, gives information about church doctrine and about the programs of the CCC, stipulates the requirements for membership and allows a pastor (and possibly a board member) to interact personally with the 'candidates' for membership. Those who choose to pursue membership comply with the standards of membership as outlined in the church's constitution, including 'a born-again experience (regeneration)', 'water baptism', 'a consistent Christian life', 'subscription to the tenets of faith' of the church [see below], and a willingness to contribute regularly to the support of the assembly according to his or her ability'.

The basic standard for membership however reflects only part of what members expect from one another and from their church in general. CCC members above all expect a worship service relevant to their form of spirituality. Members become most disgruntled over services that do not function according to their sensibilities. They want relevant and biblical preaching and uplifting, heart-warming, high-quality music. Overall they want to feel like they 'have met God' in their worship experience. The worship services as much as any other single activity fosters the sense of belonging to a community.

Americans and Asian/Pacific Islander-Americans) approximates the ethnic/racial composition of the Sea City community. Yet race, ethnicity and gender do not seem to restrict congregational participation. Persons of color and females (who are 50% of the congregation) not only participate fully in congregational life, they are disproportionately found in positions of leadership including that of the official board and the pastoral staff. The church in the past two decades has sought diversity, although it has often resulted in an assortment of theological backgrounds more than in a diversity of color and ethnicity.

28. There is little distinction made between 'members' and others that participate in the congregational life of the CCC. Non-members may not vote in the business meetings of the church, nor are they eligible to be elected to the board of deacons. Few other restrictions are placed on non-members. They may sing in the choir, provide special music in the worship services and even teach Sunday school at times. Non-members are welcome to participate in the outreaches of the church and may receive all the services of the church and its pastoral staff. In fact, generally even the members seldom think in terms of 'who is an official member and who is not'.

Other than the worship services, members expect a Christian education program for their children and youth that nurtures, trains and challenges them toward a Christian commitment. They expect pastoral care and leadership and they have thus employed five staff ministers. Finally, as the constitution states, members want to feel that their church is actively involved in 'evangelism'. To this end, the church employs various programs of outreach. Members support these program with their finances and participation.

Participation in the life of the church, not official membership, is the chief concern of the 'insiders'. Loyalty is judged more on involvement than on the membership card. It is hoped that members and non-members together can be a 'church family'. This hope seems to a great extent, to be realized.

Financial participation is one indication of the congregational involvement. The entire budget is raised through offerings and tithes. The CCC's members apparently give generously, their budget is approximately $1 million annually, an average of more than $2000 per member per year. Such a high level of giving is even more remarkable considering there are very few sizeable gifts, nearly all income comes from weekly offerings from middle-income families. The members of the CCC give particularly heavily to foreign missions, about 20 percent of their annual budget, showing their commitment to 'the spread of the gospel'.

The involvement level of the members is also revealed in a high participation in the CCC's numerous ministries and programs (projects). A program that well illustrates the congregation's involvement is the annual Easter Presentation. Each year some 250 congregants become actively involved in producing a major passion play in the Sea City Civic Auditorium. People band together to function in the multitudinous roles required in such a production. Other activities and programs reveal the same kind of enthusiasm and participation.

To summarize, to be a member of the CCC is to commit to the fundamental purposes of the assembly. That commitment is signified not merely in the signing of a membership card but in truly belonging to the community is demonstrated by certain required qualifications, by fulfilling general expectations of the congregation and by an active level of participation in the life of the community.

Offerings: Integral Components of a Community's Spirituality
Belonging to and participating in the faith community of the CCC are
fundamental to their notion of membership and therefore are essential
to the congregational spirituality. To explore further the integral components of the CCC's spirituality, I move from the question of commitment, participation and giving to the inverse question. What does the
CCC community *offer* its members? Seeking to answer this question, I
will consider four categories of offerings. The CCC provides its members with (1) a theological self-understanding, (2) an orientation toward
the religious and secular worlds, (3) a organized structure for its programs, rites and spirituality and (4) a way of being Pentecostal.

Theological self-understanding. The Statement of Fundamental Truths
outlines the CCC's theology. The Statement represents a creedal presentation from the General Council of the Assemblies of God.[29] These
Truths proceed from a conservative understanding of the Bible.[30] While
16 categories outline the tenets of faith, popularly the Assemblies of
God, the CCC included, have emphasized the 'four main doctrines of
the church' salvation, divine healing, Spirit baptism, and the second
coming of Christ. There is a consensus on the broad framework of these
core beliefs among the congregants of the CCC.

Pastor Pat Ralston voices an attitude of many classical Pentecostals
toward dogmatic theology when he asserts that 'doctrine is important,
but it never saved anybody'.[31] If the focal point of the church is not
doctrine, what is it? Ralston characterizes the church as a body of
believers, the body of Christ, empowered by the Holy Spirit to serve
God in worship (to know him intimately) while serving its neighbors in
the local community and around the world. Pastor Ralston believes that

29. To be a member church of the Assemblies of God is to participate 'voluntarily' in 'full cooperative fellowship with the… District Council…and with the
General Council of the Assemblies of God…while recognizing…[the] right to sovereignty [of the local congregation] in the conduct of its own affairs'. So states the
constitution of the CCC. This congregational form of 'cooperative fellowship' is
standard among the Assemblies of God.

30. The 'Holy Scriptures' are accepted as 'the revealed will of God, the all-
sufficient rule of faith and practice', according to the constitution of the CCC.

31. Traditionally, among Pentecostals, there has been and is 'a certain detach-
ment from some dogmatic concerns that have divided Evangelicals and Fundamentalists' during the twentieth century. See Burgess, McGee and Alexander, 'Introduction', p. 5.

the teachings of the church are clarified as they are worked out through
'ministry to God and ministry to the world'. To grasp the theological
(self-)understanding of the people of the CCC one must comprehend
their practical emphases that mark their orientation toward the broader
religious and secular culture.

An orientation toward the broader religious and secular cultures. A
second provision the CCC community gives to its members is an orientation toward the religious and secular cultures. I have noted some of
the CCC's historical progression from sect-type toward a more church-
type orientation.[32] Pastor Pat Ralston, who has pastored the CCC from
the early 1970s, has moved the congregation away from its sect-bound
sensibilities and self-understanding as much as any other leader in the
tradition of the local assembly. His pastoral spirituality for the past two
decades has moved between two poles of orientation that he calls 'a
getting out there' and a 'centering'.

Virginia Lee, a parishioner since the mid-1940s, and church leader,
characterized Pat Ralston's leadership and orientation as she recalled
his coming to the church: 'Pastor Ralston pushed us out into the mainstream of life...[Before the 1970s] we had been somewhat isolated.'
But isolation gave way to involvement once Ralston arrived. Now we
are 'getting out there into the community', she says with a sense of
satisfaction.

'Getting out there' means at least three things. First, getting out into
both local and overseas Christian service outreaches, secondly, getting
out into the broader religious world, and, thirdly, getting out into local
civic affairs. Ralston seems most pleased with the church's progress in
'getting out' into these three areas. 'We've done our best to put the
church out into the community', he says, as he cites numerous examples of their recent involvement. His examples range from the political
arena to the business community, from the established religious leader-

---

32. Ernst Troeltsch suggested three types—sect, church, and mystical. The CCC
has also been a combination of the three. But its movement has been generally from
sect to church while continuing its dominant mystical orientation. See Ernst
Troeltsch, *The Social Teachings of the Christian Church* (trans. Olive Wyon;
London: George Allen, 1931); see also Bellah *et al.*, *Habits*, pp. 243-48. Bellah and
associates consider Troeltsch's three types as 'dimensions' of 'Christian (and often
non-Christian) religious community'.

ship to social services. In all of his examples Ralston envisions the church 'on the cutting edge of the society'.

Pat Ralston's theme of 'getting [the church] out there' into the community complements his theme of 'centering'. Shortly after he became pastor, he led the congregation to change the name of their church from Assembly of God to Coastal Christian Center. The name change symbolized the emerging self-understanding of the church building as a center not only for themselves but for others. 'The Church,' he often reminded his parishioners, 'is the people, the building is the center'. Ralston wanted a more neutral name, one not packed with sectarian perceptions. He hoped to make the Center an open place where people from the community would feel comfortable to visit and participate in the activities of the congregation. He wanted the church to become more of a center for the community.

Ralston dreamed of having an open church and a church that would become a 'centering' agent within the larger civic community. For Pastor Ralston the church could realize its potential as a centering agent as it made a place for peoples of diverse ideologies, theologies and backgrounds. He believed that the diversity he sought could discover a complementary unity in the gathering together and centering, focusing, on essential Christian experiences. For Ralston these experiences are symbolized in a variety of ritual expressions that he encourages. While Ralston's envisioned goal seems somewhat naive and idealistic, the congregant has, apparently, to some extent achieved the goal.[33]

A structure for programs, rites and spirituality. A third category of what members receive as they participate in the congregational life of the CCC is an organized structure for the programs, rites and spirituality of the faith community. The CCC has a wide variety of programs,

33. The partial realization of Ralston's vision was recognized as during the 1970s and early 1980s, and the church became a center for ecumenical (Charismatic) renewal. People from very diverse backgrounds, including Roman Catholic, Eastern Orthodox and Mainline Protestant, came to the CCC for special meetings and services and together had 'essential Christian experiences'. The other movement toward Ralston's goal was the general broadening of the congregation, that is, the backgrounds of those the church attracted from the time of Ralston's coming were far more varied than prior to the mid-1970s. Ralston characterizes the congregation after his nearly two decades of leadership as 'really multiple congregations'. He insists that they are one in spirit, but their differences of background and ideas persist.

as one expects from an evangelical church of its size. Both a professional pastoral staff and an able group of volunteers provide leadership for the main programs. The five associate pastors head up programs in pastoral care, Adult ministries, Youth ministries, Christian
Education and Music. Within these areas of ministry there are numerous activities and programs that seek to educate, nurture, evangelize
and provide for expressions of congregational life as members of all
ages relate to one another and to the broader community of Sea City.
Unlike some of the younger churches (particularly those I will consider
below), the CCC does not have one dominant program or ministry
emphasis. It emphasizes, as do other churches, home fellowship groups,
Bible studies, mission trips, feeding the poor and healing teams, to
name a few, but these are seen more as a variety of options from which
members choose to participate. The CCC attempts to provide a wide
assortment of ministries in order to service the community and allow
members to serve one another.

If no one program or ministry dominates the church's identity, what
then functions as the common core of the congregation? What helps to
provide cohesiveness amid the diversity? The Sunday service, 'the
celebration', as Pastor Ralston refers to it, is central to the life of the
CCC. The Sunday service is the one time when the whole church
gathers to celebrate their life together as Christians. Describing this
main ritual of the congregation the pastor says,

> We worship the Lord Jesus Christ seriously, joyfully and enthusiasti-
> cally...[Our] worship takes many forms...sometimes it is structured...
> [with] quiet reverence. Other times it is [a] spontaneous...explosive cele-
> bration of praise. [It] involves music, the Word, praise, and both physical
> and vocal response. We all carry the responsibility of seeking God, for
> our worship is highly participatory and open to the possibility that God
> will speak through any of us.

Pat Ralston maintains that the celebration and its forms of worship
are biblical. 'Scripture is our source [our] pattern and principal...[and]
decency and order are our constant watchwords.'[34] While the scriptural

34. 'Decency and order' are relative concepts. But clearly they are observed at
the CCC according to the traditions of the congregation. To help explain characteristic practices of the worship service that may be unusual to visitors, the church
places within the visitor's packet information that explains 'why we...clap our
hands...lift our hands...have audible praise unto God...manifest the gifts of tongues

foundations for the Sunday rites are important, the key to the ritual's effectiveness as a core congregational activity is its participatory nature. The CCC's service of celebration is no place for passive worshipers. While neither visitors nor members are coerced into a particular worship form, the goal of active participation in the rites is implicit. 'Exalting God and edify[ing] all participants are our goals', says the pastor. This is accomplished as each one worships together fully engaged in the ritual of celebration. These rites provide a communal heart-felt, self-expression that which helps to transform the individuals into a community of faith.[35]

A way of being Pentecostal. Finally, the CCC offers its members a *way of being* that understands and employs religious symbols in a particular fashion. It is a way of being Christian that is infused with the classical Pentecostal tradition yet susceptible to new elements (symbols), to creative ritualizing and developing new mixes of the symbols, and to new configurations during key transitions.

Hinting at the importance of the continuity of the Pentecostal tradition within the CCC, Elaine, a public school teacher who has been a member of the CCC for more than a decade, says 'longevity!' is the church's strength. When asked what she meant by 'longevity', this wife and mother of two, who was born into the A/G denomination, explained:

> It seems our church [CCC] can withstand anything...church problems, differing styles of pastors, and worship leaders, people [parishioners] with differences, opposition from neighbors, resistance from the city council and it's still there, still going...sometimes not as big or as strong but still going.

Elaine's remarks are revealing. They point to the tension in the CCC's recent history, a tradition grappling with another transition. But most of all her remarks convey the understanding that her church community is rooted in a tradition that is strong, resilient and persistent.

Elaine implies a basic impulse, need, of the CCC congregants, that of being a part of a 'community of memory'.[36] While the people of the

---

and interpretation...prophecy'. These worship practices, along with others, are justified with proof texts and explanations.

35. In the following chapters I will discuss in depth the Sunday rites and ritual.

36. Drawing upon Josiah Royce, Bellah and his associates speak of a 'community of memory' as a fundamental category of society; it can be primarily religious, civic, or political. See *Habits*, pp. 152-62.

CCC seldom use the term 'tradition' to describe themselves, they none-theless depend upon and feel secure within the tradition of their specific congregation and its denomination.[37] Other Pent/Char churches have emerged in Coastal County in the last decade. Many of these have attracted many new members and seem quite vital, but they cannot yet offer the tradition, rooted in a community of memory, of this Assembly. They are not grounded as securely in the classical Pentecostal her-itage.[38]

But while the CCC is a community rooted in a classical Pentecostal tradition, it is not a static tradition; its rituals and other symbols are not unchanging. For example, new congregational self-identities have emerged during transitional moments in the (religious and secular) culture(s). Such was the case in the early 1970s when the CCC responded to Charismatic renewal by recognizing its new role of lead-ership, a force for church renewal and ecumenism.

Another example of the dynamic in the tradition is how worship practices change and evolve, while yet continuing within the Pente-costal ethos. The forms of congregational singing illustrate the evolu-tion. Traditionally, the CCC sang predominately gospel songs (enthusi-astic hymns of a testimony genre); in recent years the gospel songs have been sung less frequently. The CCC's congregation now predominantly sings worship choruses (short repetitious hymns explicitly directed to God). This shift signals a change in the form of worship and the config-uration of the symbols of the worship service. It reflects a dynamic rather than a static tradition.

In summary, the CCC offers its members a community, with a partic-ular theological self-understanding, an orientation to both the religious and secular cultures, a structure for the faith community's life and tradi-tion rooted in a classical Pentecostal heritage that is dynamic in its incorporation of fresh elements. Together these elements of the CCC's spirituality help the congregants define themselves and their devotion to God and neighbor. I turn now to a second congregation, the Light and Life Fellowship.

37. This is somewhat distinct from the two churches to follow, the L&L and VVCF.

38. This grounding in a tradition is in tension with but not antagonistic toward the openness to others, their backgrounds and practices that has marked the ecu-menical dimension of the CCC (see above).

Light and Life Fellowship:
Reappropriating the Pentecostal Symbols

Tucked away within a quaint, hundred-year-old Sea City neighborhood, on a wooded hillside, adjacent to a three-block, village-like business center and surrounded by an attractively landscaped parking lot stands a converted theater now the home of the Light and Life Fellowship (L&L). 'The building', as the congregation refers to it, is modest but well kept both inside and out. Though it does not have the look of a theater anymore, neither does it appear to be a church, at least in the traditional sense. There is a small sign that indicates the name of the church at the entrance to the parking lot by the sidewalk that runs along Main Street which runs through the village. The chief religious indicator is the subtle symbolism contained in the large mural painted on the south side the church building. Northbound motorists and pedestrians face the mural as they drive or walk through the village approaching the hill that leads out of the small business center. The mural is of the sea coast. Prominently perched above the cliffs of the ocean is a lighthouse whose beams of light pour out of the lighthouse tower and metaphorically connect to the name of the church: Light and Life.

Walking into the sanctuary of the L&L is like walking into someone's living room or family room. Warm blue blends with earth colors, the arrangement of the chairs, the gestures of the people, all projecting the feeling of 'family', the sense of a close community. Normally, about 150–175 chairs arranged in large semi-circle fashion are filled with active and attentive worshipers.[39]

There is no doubt that the church service is at the center (core) of the spirituality of the people who call the L&L their 'church home'. The symbol of that core is the sanctuary where they gather. It is their 'family room', the place where they experience most intensely their common life and their uncommon God.

Entering the meeting room has an immediate effect. A sense of warmth, acceptance and safety begins to enfold those who move into the service. It is a place where people can let down their guard and be embraced by a community of caring people.

---

39. The L&L presently has three services on the weekend, and most parishioners attend one of the three. On an average weekend, in the three services combined, about 400 congregants will gather for worship at the church.

The L&L Story

The L&L was founded in 1981 in the home of a young 26-year-old native Californian and his wife who 'felt called to start a church'. William Barrett (his friends call him 'Willie'), a recent graduate of a southern California college and former hippy, had been converted to Christianity as a freshman and subsequently studied for the ministry at a Pentecostal, Foursquare, college. To look at the handsome, six feet two inches plus, conventionally dressed, well-poised pastor today, it is difficult to guess that he was truly a 'hippy'. Willie still characterizes himself as 'naturally casual' and at heart 'a hippy and left wing'. Perhaps his unconventional tendencies had something to do with his choice to move to the culturally progressive and politically liberal coastal community of Sea City.

Acting on their sense of 'calling', Willie and his wife Barbara moved to Sea City. They had no formal support or direction from their denomination, the International Church of the Foursquare Gospel.[40] Rather, in typical Pentecostal-entrepreneurial style Willie set out to start a church 'on faith' with particular ingenuity.[41] Willie and Barbara rented an apartment, found jobs and set out to learn the culture of the city. 'We wanted to discover what they were doing in town,' Willie remembers. During the first nine months they learned the local customs, penetrated some of the 'native' subcultures of Sea City, while they were working at their jobs and visited various local churches. Within their first year they had a 'good feel' for the uniqueness of Sea City and its people groups.

After nine months they were ready. Willie and Barbara invited their new neighbors and fellow workers to a Bible study in their home. The first meeting of what was to become the L&L had eight people in attendance: Willie, Barbara, a married couple the Barretts had known

---

40. See Chapter 1 for a description of the ICFG.

41. Willie did inform his regional superintendent that he intended to start a church, but denominational identity was of little importance to those Willie wanted to reach. His church was not going to be very 'churchy'. As a result, Willie minimized the denominational connection. The involvement of the L&L with the parent denomination has increased in recent years. This has been a gradual connecting process. In fact, many in the congregation today have little if any loyalty to the International Church of the Foursquare Gospel. Their loyalty is primarily on the congregational level.

for years who wanted to assist in starting a church, and four other friends from work and acquaintances from the neighborhood.

The style of this and other initial meetings was 'informal, attempting to engage non-Christians'. Willie was interested in 'evangelizing the unchurched', those that could not relate well to the forms of church life in the Sea City area. In the very first Bible study one young man who worked with Willie at the Freeze Dry plant 'prayed to receive Christ as Savior'. Willie's attempts to make 'the gospel relevant to the lives of the unchurched' apparently were successful. His Bible study grew.

Within months Willie rented a bigger apartment to accommodate the Bible study. This began the growth. In the first four years Barrett rented a series of sites around Sea City to accommodate the emerging congregational life. From 8 people in 1981 the group grew to 40 within the first two years, as the Bible study developed into an untraditional church, one that reflected Willie Barrett's intent to reach out to people the churches of Sea City in general were missing.

Willie intentionally avoided many traditional symbols associated with the organized church, believing they often communicate ineffectively or negatively to his target groups. For instance, the L&L took no offerings, though he would keep an offering box in the rear of the meeting room for those who wished to contribute.[42] He chose terms more culturally generic than those often used in churches, for example, the 'building' instead of sanctuary, the 'meeting' instead of the service or liturgy. Rather than liturgical language, Willie sought to speak plainly, using more 'standard' Sea City English. Even when explaining scriptural texts he viewed them through the lens of the Sea City culture and communicated them in the language of the people. As a result various groups from the coastal communities were attracted. In fact, there were so many surfers that found a 'home' at the L&L that the church was dubbed 'the Surfer Church'.

But the L&L did not become merely a religious enclave for surfers. It continued to reach out to other individuals and groups in non-traditional ways. 'We did not want to put up any barrier to the gospel. We wanted to make it available in a form that people in Sea City could relate to,'

---

42. Regular offerings (collections of money) are still avoided at the L&L. Little or no mention is made of an offering in the services. Members do support the church. They drop in contributions and tithes into the collection box on a small table in the back of the sanctuary as they enter or leave the church, or sometime during the service, as they remember.

recalls Willie. Their strategy attracted university and college students from the nearby institutions. Coeds discovered a message and a style they could relate to, and they with the surfers and others from the Sea City culture forged a new community of faith.

By the fifth year the congregation had grown to nearly three hundred. In need of a site that could accommodate the burgeoning congregation and root it in a more permanent location, the L&L discovered the old theater only a few miles from their rented facility. They had limited funds, but, with the help of the Foursquare denomination and the dedicated support of the families in the congregation, the church obtained a loan and purchased the theater for their own.

Throughout the 1980s the congregation continued to grow in number and mature in faith in their new facility. As the congregation completed its first decade it had gained stability. Many of the young surfers and university students had settled down, married and started families. Other young families discovered the L&L and the base of the congregation shifted somewhat from singles in their early twenties to married couples in their late twenties and thirties. Feeling that the initial phase of 'church planting' had been successfully accomplished, Willie Barrett believed that he had completed his work in Sea City. The time had come for him to start another church.

Early in 1990, with the blessing and financial support of the L&L, Willie and Barbara Barrett made plans to move up the California coast to another city that they believed was in need of a new congregation. A young man from the L&L congregation, just 30 years old, who had recently completed his theological training, was chosen to be the new pastor. David Markowitz became the second pastor of the L&L in the spring of 1990. The pastoral change was surprisingly uncomplicated.

Carolyn Johnson, young working mother, member of a worship team and married to a lay leader in the L&L, reflected on the change of pastors:

> It was a smooth transition. And it was time. Willie was a great pastor, but so is Dave... In many ways they complement each other. Willie preached about shared ministry but he was the founding pastor and it was difficult for him to give up control to people in the congregation. Dave shares leadership and ministry better. Dave brings a strength in organization too.

Others remember the transition as an important time in the church, marking new leadership and a new phase in its life. Some years later, it now appears they were correct, for the L&L is in another stage of development.

The traits of an 'untraditional' church persist at the L&L, though tempered somewhat. Today the music 'is less rowdy, less rockin' out type', according to Carl, a single man in his late twenties who joined the L&L seven years ago while a university student. The aging trend in the congregation also continues and with it a tendency toward the more traditional. The majority of new members are no longer late adolescents and singles in their early twenties. Now young families populate the church. In fact, often the Sunday congregation reflects a 'thirty-something' generation, predominately people in their thirties most often with children in hand.[43]

The ethos and manners of the congregation are still far from 'orthodox' when compared to many mainline or Evangelical Protestant churches. Many of the original non-traditional marks remain, but Pastor Dave and the staff he has put in place emphasize stronger organizational underpinnings for the congregational life. They believe in a more structured approach to ministry than did Willie Barrett. At the same time Dave and his associates have sharpened the focus of pastoral care and expanded the counseling services of the church. Their movement toward structure has not, however, squelched the congregation's creative impulse. In some areas of church life, including the liturgy, Pastor Dave has actually increased the level of experimentation. For instance, though Dave is an excellent preacher, he has explored broadening the homily time to involve dramatic presentations of the gospel. The liturgy in general and the music in particular, continue to be experimented with creatively. Although the non-traditional style of congregational life and creative liturgy are important dimensions of the L&L, they really are part of a more fundamental dynamic, that is, the rediscovery and reappropriation of Pentecostal symbols.

43. Currently, the church is mostly working class, with a minority of professionals. It is approximately 80% white. The non-Anglo, ethnic/racial composition of the congregation is predominately Hispanic, about 12%. There is no significant disparity between the distribution of male and females in the congregation. The congregation, except for the age composition, is quite reflective of the Sea City community.

Rediscovering and Reappropriating Pentecostal Symbols
The L&L offers its members fundamental dimensions of congregational
life, ritual, community and an organized structure within which to nurture a congregational spirituality. In each of these three areas symbols
foundational to Pentecostalism have been rediscovered and reappropriated.[44] In an attempt to be relevant to the unchurched, and to those
'turned off by the church', L&L has avoided many symbols associated
with church, even the Pent/Char church (e.g. choir, hymnals, ministers
on the platform, special vestments or even dress suits for ministers).
They considered these symbols to be non-essential and often inhibitory
to those they wish to reach. However, most of their energies are spent
not avoiding but discovering. The L&L offers it members rediscovered
and reappropriated symbols of ritual, community and structured programming and thus has defined, developed and nurtured a Pent/Char
spirituality that is their own.

Reappropriated Ritual Symbols
One of the most important things that the L&L offers its members is
vital and meaningful ritual.[45] Their form of ritual life I have described
as a rediscovering and reappropriating the Pentecostal ritual symbols.
The L&L is a young congregation that has experimented with forms of
worship that suit them as an emerging community. Naturally, they have
been influenced by the Protestant, Evangelical and Pentecostal traditions, but in their own minds they have set aside many of the prescribed
forms of worship. While they have avoided merely accepting the traditional forms of ritual life, they have not ultimately rejected the underlying Pentecostal symbols (e.g. healing, tongues, the word, prophetic/
charismatic utterances, free expressive worship). Nor have they denied
a basic mystical (Pentecostal) presupposition that God is near and can

---

44. I do not use the term 'rediscover' to suggest that the Pentecostal symbols
were lost. Rather, I use the term to indicate the process by which this relatively new
congregation is coming to find their own way. While they are securely attached to
the classical Pentecostal tradition—which in some cases through the process of routinization has a diminished understanding of its own symbol—they are attempting
to locate, re-understand and then reappropriate historic Pentecostal symbols in their
unique context of the L&L congregation.

45. The ritual process will be the focus of the analysis in the ensuing chapters.
Here, I intended only to sketch the significance of the ritual to the L&L congregation.

be encountered intimately. In fact, they continue to uphold a fundamental Pentecostal value, namely, the value of promoting affective
mystically oriented religious experiences.[46]

The effect of maintaining a traditionally Pentecostal, foundational
(presupposition and) value, is that the L&L has rediscovered many of
the symbols that Pentecostals have long held dear. The L&L has, however, in many cases (re)appropriated the symbols according to the
emerging congregation's own needs, insights and understanding.

Among the traditional Pentecostal symbols that have been rediscovered and reappropriated by the L&L congregation is that of 'free expressive worship'. Classical Pentecostals have long been known for their
propensity toward enthusiastically expressive forms of worship. Over
the decades of the twentieth century, however, stylizations and patterns
of worship have emerged.[47] Routinization has had its effect. These
routinized practices, particularly those within the classical Pentecostal
liturgy, have become for many Pentecostal churches 'the way it is
done', leaving less room for innovation and spontaneity.

The L&L from the beginning avoided many of these routinized

46. For the centrality of experience in the spiritual life see Donald L. Gelpi,
Charism and Sacrament: A Theology of Christian Conversion (New York: Paulist
Press, 1976) esp. chs. 2 and 4; *idem, Committed Worship: A Sacramental Theology
for Converting Christians* (2 vols.; Collegeville, MN: Liturgical Press, 1993); *idem,
Experiencing God: A Theology of Human Emergence* (New York: University Press
of America, 1987), wherein he grounds his entire theology in his understanding of
human experience. For Gelpi experience, as he defines it, serves as a transcendental
category derived from North American philosophy. And he cogently argues that
experience can be an appropriate foundational category for Christian theology.
Gelpi further develops his construct and explicates his notion of the importance of
experience in contemporary theology in his *The Turn to Experience in Contemporary Theology* (New York: Paulist Press, 1994). Also, as examples of the importance of experience to Pentecostal spirituality, see Spittler, 'Spirituality', pp. 800-
809, who claims that experience is 'by far the most pervasive' Pentecostal value
and that 'Pentecostals consider personal experience the arena of true religion'; and
socialist Poloma, *Crossroads*, especially Part 1, where she argues that 'the promo-
tion of religious experience is what distinguishes Pentecostalism from a myriad of
non-Pentecostal evangelical churches'.

47. Examples of areas in which stylizations and patterns occur include the kinds
of music sung, the way charismatic speech acts are presented, the way glossolalia is
practiced in the liturgy, the way an altar call is given (and other forms of response),
the way people raise their hands and the emergence and use of Pentecostal parlance
and language patterns.

Pentecostal patterns. Pastor Willie felt that many of these were simply culturally irrelevant to those he wanted to attract, the unchurched. Yet the Pentecostal symbol of 'free worship' was 'rediscovered' by the emerging L&L congregation. This rediscovery is due, in part, to the common Pentecostal value that prompts religious experience. This value is founded on a belief that an encounter with the (Holy) sacred is possible and should be encouraged in the liturgy as well as in private spirituality.

The rites that the L&L offers its people are symbolically expressive; they show a reappropriation of the Pentecostal symbol of free worship (classical Pentecostals call it 'spontaneous', 'unprogrammed', or 'non-liturgical' worship). An example of this reappropriation is the use of dance at the L&L, which is perhaps central to their understanding of free worship. Classical Pentecostals, in the tradition of the Holiness movement, have rejected all types of social and liturgical dancing. The exception to this ban is the infrequent expression of 'dancing in the Spirit', a form of ecstatic dance-like movement.[48]

The liturgical dancing at the L&L is seldom intensely ecstatic. When ecstacy is connected, the ecstacy is normally a result of the expression of dance rather than dance the result of the ecstacy. Thus, the type of dance at the L&L is certainly less explosive. The dancers move in a natural fluidity, and there is little to suggest a dramatic 'inbreaking' of the supernatural. In fact, dance at the L&L reveals a principle of their reappropriation: the supernatural can be experienced in a 'natural', almost casual manner.[49]

The dance movements at L&L are most often choreographed and

48. 'Dancing in the Spirit' typically erupts explosively, symbolizing a highly ecstatic state. It is believed that one has been moved, almost irresistibly, by the Spirit. For Pentecostal involvement in dancing see Frances Bixler, 'Dancing in the Spirit', in *DPCM*, pp. 236-37; also T.B. Pierce, 'The Dance and Corporate Worship', *The Pentecostal Evangel* (2 November 1986), pp. 8-10. See Chapter 3 for a discussion of kinesthetic dimension of worship and for other references to sacred dance.

49. Even charismatic gifts (e.g. words of prophecy and charismatic speech acts, see Chapter 4 below) are presented in a more 'natural' way than 'in old time Pentecost'. Seldom is there a 'biblical' (King James version) sounding, traditional Pentecostal-type, formulaic style, such as 'thus saith the Lord'. Instead, in a normal-sounding vocal tones and cadence a member may suggest, 'I believe God is saying...' This less explosive, less ecstatic manner is a reappropriation. Yet it still symbolizes the presence of the Spirit to the congregation.

practiced by the dance team in their weekly rehearsals. However, often congregational members spontaneously join in the dance with the team. Planned or spontaneous dance and other physical movement in the liturgy of the L&L is fundamental to the worship. People feel free to move to the music as they worship and praise, and they feel freed as they do. Most people in the congregation do not directly participate with the teams of dancers. They are affected by them, however. Worshipers lose some of their own inhibitions and move kinesthetically with the movement of the dance teams surrounding them.

Dance is only one example of a reappropriation of the symbol of free worship. The L&L have actively encouraged a 'wide range of expressions of worship'. They believe that with a wide range there are more opportunities for varying temperaments and tastes. The L&L seeks to be inclusive. The leaders hope that with a larger group of appropriate expressions each person can feel free to 'enter in' to the worship, participating with others in a unifying variety of expressions.

Elements of Community
Secondly, the L&L offers its members an accepting and supportive community characterized by contemporary relevance with accountability and much of the feel and function of a family. Within their supportive community they have developed a matrix for their 'dramatic conversation' and decision-making.[50] The community's conversation concerns matters of significance. Together they discuss and help each other to define their corporate and individual identities, mission(s) (i.e. purpose in life), and ways of relating within the faith community and in the world. Their community conversation has helped them to rediscover and appropriate symbols of community that come to define them.

The L&L has worked to become an accepting, supportive and caring community. Leon LeMon, a young professional who has been a member for six years, remembers, 'Many of us were beaten up and battered when we came to L&L...we [he and his wife] needed a safe place, a caring community'. Pastor David Markowitz sounds a similar theme: 'Our church is an ark, a refuge and a place of safety.' People who have been abused in various ways, including religious abuse, have discovered at the L&L a supportive community, a healing community.

Tolerance marks the L&L community. Recognizing that sometimes

---

50. Bellah *et al.*, *Habits*, pp. 27-51, speak of cultures as a 'dramatic conversations about things that matter to their participants' (p. 27).

the church is perceived to be intolerant, they have been working toward a community that is tolerant and inclusive. In several interviews parishioners spoke of the 'unchurchy', 'non-traditional' characteristics of the L&L as symbols of tolerance and inclusiveness. 'Just look at the way people are dressed', one 30-year-old carpenter/contractor instructed. 'People can feel comfortable coming to church wearing what they want. You don't have to have a suit and tie or be dressed up or wear expensive clothes. You can be accepted just the way you are.' This young businessman, husband and father of two, spoke for many others. Casual dress for members of the L&L symbolize an attitude of inclusiveness.

Another reason why clothes are an important symbol for the L&L community is that casual dress is seen as culturally more relevant. The L&L community attempts to meet the contemporary needs of the Sea City culture without putting up unnecessary barriers. Since Sea City 'is a laid back sort of place', one congregant told us, 'we want our church to relate'. A casual attitude toward clothing assists them toward cultural relevance. Likewise, they believe that the contemporary music (i.e. the band, the worship team, the style and genre of musical expressions) helps keep the faith community a contemporary and relevant force.[51]

While there is a casual, 'laid back', attitude with apparently little pressure to conform to rigid standards, the community of the L&L often uses the word 'accountability'. Both from the pulpit and in our interviews we heard the language of accountability. Some pointed to the necessity of accountability in connection to spiritual gifts. They spoke of the 'dangers of people [presumably Pentecostal] from outside the community' who 'try to take over' with some kind of charismatic domination or some other misuse of the charismata. Others spoke of the 'balance' brought to the congregation through accountability to one another. One husband and wife, the Garcias, with a Baptist background, told us that they 'learned the hard way the need for accountability'. In another congregation, they experienced a domineering pastor who was able to maintain an unquestioned authority by claiming a charismatic mandate and thus avoided any accountability to the congregation. The Garcias represent many at the L&L who believe that part of the strength of their

51. In conversation with parishioners, I discovered many who saw most churches as neither contemporary or relevant. Churches, according to them, are often too 'churchy'. By that I assume they meant that 'churchy' symbols did not relate to them, that is, they neither understood such symbols nor were such symbols seen as vital.

community originates in the willingness of parishioners and leaders alike to be accountable to one another.

The metaphor used most at the L&L to describe their faith community is 'family'. The image of family fits in several ways. Even visitors are taken in by the 'homey atmosphere', the family room feel to the sanctuary. It is not merely the arrangement of the objects in the sanctuary, it is more the attitude of the congregation. They relate to one another much like a super-family. This does not blur the lines of the actual families within the congregation, it only seems to enhance the nuclear family roles. But family members seem to participate in two family structures, that of the nuclear family and the church family. This is clear in the roles of children at the L&L. Children are very much a part of the L&L community, and they are not simply shuttled off to Sunday school. They are encouraged to be a part of the worship service, at least for the first half hour. The congregation has a tolerance for a certain amount of background sound, a kind of buzzing of numerous children whispering to parents or being corrected. But much as in a family room the interaction emerges naturally and neither parents nor other congregants seem negatively affected by the children's presence. Charismatic worship proceeds, children and all. Pastor Markowitz summarized the primary metaphor for their community when he said concerning the congregation, 'We want to be a family, a functional family…we are *becoming* a family. When you become a family you are responsible for one another, for the children…we are all involved in this project, this family, and together we are all parenting.'

The L&L fellowship is attempting to rediscover what a community is and how members of a contemporary community can effectively relate to one another. Their appropriated discoveries help to make their congregation a community of accepting, supportive, relevant people, a family.

Structure for Spiritual Life

The third primary element that the L&L offers its members is an organized structure within which to nurture a congregational spirituality. Here I will consider briefly the structure for the spiritual life of the congregation in two dimensions, programs and leadership.

What started in the early 1980s as evening Bible studies in a young couple's home has evolved into a church with an organizational structure of church programs that are meant to facilitate the spiritual life and growth of its members. Over the years, many of the more 'standard' church programs have been put in place (e.g. Sunday school, children's programs, youth program with its own pastor, a mid-week Bible study); however, the L&L has discovered ways of programming that seem to fit their needs better. On the surface, some of their programs appear foreign to Pentecostalism, but in most cases they have reappropriated a Pentecostal symbol to express better their congregational experience.

An example of such a reappropriation is the way the L&L has reappropriated the symbol of expressive worship. Pentecostals have long been known for their expressive forms of worship, and music has traditionally played a primary role in the expressive forms. At the L&L music is still integral to their appropriation of expressive worship, but different forms of music have been put in place. For instance, there is rarely 'special music' (i.e. solos or ensembles, vocal or instrumental performances), as had been common in Pentecostal churches, nor is there a choir. There is a worship team that provides accompaniment to the congregational singing, which is emphasized. But the expressive worship is more than the music for the L&L, it is kinesthetic movement as well. Though movement in Pentecostal worship has a tradition, it was always recognized as a spontaneous movement (lifting hands in praise, or dancing in the Spirit). But, as I mentioned above, the L&L has incorporated dance into their form of expressive worship. And they have endeavored to make this form available to all. While many traditional Pentecostal churches have rehearsals for their age level choirs, the L&L has age level classes for their unique form of liturgical dance. Members in the classes not only practice dance but they worship with dance during the classes, and then, if they wish, they are prepared to express their worship in the Sunday service in dance;[52] Although one need not go to the class to participate and worship in dance in the services. The classes are meant to facilitate not restrict the expression. So, while a choreographed dance in Pentecostal liturgy was (and still is) unthinkable, the L&L has reappropriated the common Pent/Char symbol of expressive worship in dance.[53]

52. Some never feel comfortable to dance in the services, but they enjoy the learning and the times of worship in the classes. Also, it should be noted that the dances practiced are a blend of group and individual choreography that is based on particular congregational worship choruses that are sung in the liturgy.

53. This reappropriation can also be seen in the portfolios of ministerial staff at the church. Pentecostal churches the size of the L&L typically have a minister of

New ways to express the symbols of fellowship and community have also been discovered by the congregation at the L&L. A very old Pentecostal idea, nearly extinct, is a 'family camp'. Though 'old timers' remember 'camp meetings' and family camps, most Pentecostals in the Sea City area have long since ceased to practice this ritual. The L&L, though, has resurrected this symbol of fellowship. Once a year the entire congregation takes over a retreat center and has a family camp. It is a time of community building, of 'becoming family together'. Similarly, each quarter the congregation structures a special Sunday service at a park, the beach or a local retreat center. These settings allow not only for a combined liturgy in which the whole congregation can participate, but they present a structure for fellowship in the context of a picnic, potluck, or some other activity that allows them to share with one another. The weekly home group fellowships also reflect a desire to rediscover some of the elements of community that early Pentecostals claimed. The L&L places a particular emphasis on community building by attempting to reappropriate old symbols of fellowship.

The L&L's understanding of outreach also shows signs of reappropriation. The symbol of evangelism as sharing the gospel is being understood more broadly than in the traditional Pentecostal way. Sharing the good news is applied not only to preaching or forms of proclamation (e.g. evangelistic meetings or crusades). The L&L has become interested in sharing in society's social needs. The food pantry is only one example. But it illustrates a grass roots impulse within the congregation that has become a sizeable ministry of sharing and reaching out to those outside of the faith community.[54]

Another sign of an emerging understanding of outreach and reappropriation of sharing the gospel, is the understanding of foreign service and missions work. Pentecostal denominations and churches have been disproportionately involved in overseas service ministries and missions

---

music, and at L&L they have an assistant pastor, Donna Delaney, who is the minister of arts. Among other things, she works with the dance classes and coordinates with the leader of the worship team (who leads the congregational worship in song) the songs and possible dance expressions.

54. The 'food pantry' is feeding or supplementing nearly 1000 persons on a weekly basis, one half of whom are children. With this outreach has emerged other services, including counseling (of various sorts), bilingual ministries and other food distribution ministries.

evangelism.[55] The L&L has not only broadened the understanding of what a missionary does, but, as importantly, they have rethought who can be a missionary. The result has been a shift in their emphasis from a professional and denominationally trained, approved and supported missionary to a lay missionary, one that emerges within the local church and then connects with a para-church missions organization (e.g. Youth with a Mission or Wycliffe Bible Translators). In the L&L's short history there are numerous examples of people from within the congregation who have been encouraged to go overseas for short-term service, three months to two years. In these foreign service outreaches and in the local humanitarian expressions, such as the food pantry, the L&L has been conceiving of gospel outreach as primarily lay involvement. Professional ministers are recognized for their training and expertise, but their expertise functions as a resource to facilitate lay projects rather than to dominate the gospel expressions.

Just as programs and their attending symbols have been reappropriated, often with the impetus of the laity at the L&L, so too has the symbol of leadership. The expressions of authority and charisma and the combination of the two have played a significant role in the twentieth-century Pent/Char movement. The tension between this historically lay movement and its periodic spawning of strongly authoritarian leaders is well known. The L&L has worked to understand and implement forms of leadership that facilitate congregational growth, help to give guidance and provide leadership that has a sense of authority while avoiding domineering authority figures and other oppressive forms of authoritarianism.

The result of their quest for balanced leadership has been a re-emergence of lay leadership and decision-making. They have developed a group of elders, all lay, who, together with the church council, work with the pastors to lead the church. They together work to discern appropriate direction in matters of import. The elders work with the other congregants to understand the 'pulse of the people'. However, their leadership is not only in decision-making. One of the most important roles of the elders is that of teaching and preaching. While the pastoral staff is trained in preaching, and Pastor Markowitz brings most of the pastoral messages, he encourages, trains and allows the elders to bring homilies to the congregation. Thus even the power of the pulpit, a

---

55. Barrett, 'Twentieth-Century Renewal'.

strong force in the Pentecostal tradition, is layicized. Consequently, the L&L can offer its members a leadership structure that has become more widely shared, accountable and service oriented and, conversely, less centralized, authoritarian and controlling than many of the traditional models. With a reworking of the dynamic of leadership and a revised understanding of programming, the L&L provides a structure for nurturing its congregation's spiritual life.

The congregation of the L&L appears as a vital and contemporary expression of Pentecostalism. As a new congregation it has drawn on the symbols of the past, an emerging faith community that has rediscovered and reappropriated traditional Pentecostal spirituality. I turn now to our third congregational sketch, Valley Vineyard Christian Fellowship.

Valley Vineyard Christian Fellowship: Combining Pentecostal, Evangelical and Cultural Influences

Just a short drive inland from the Sea City municipal limits toward the coastal mountains is a small community, adjacent to Sea City, that shares Sea City's mailing address and much of its culture, Valley Town. Valley Town hosts Valley Vineyard Christian Fellowship (VVCF), a church of some 200–225 'members', most of them solidly middle-class whites in their twenties and thirties.[56] This youthful congregation meets together in a newly built pseudo-Spanish-style office building on Valley Drive, the main street in the area. The VVCF rents about two-thirds of the building, which it shares with two small business firms. Several small businesses and high-tech enterprises border the VVCF building. Two international computer firms do business a few blocks away.

---

56. The Valley Vineyard Christian Fellowship (VVCF) of Valley Town is a local expression of a burgeoning contemporary movement. The Vineyard movement often identified as a part of the so-called 'third wave' (movement), or 'signs and wonders movement', is a group of some 450 churches concentrated in the Western States, with a smattering of churches throughout the United States and about 250 churches overseas, that emphasis the miraculous, the supernatural and signs and wonders. See bibliography, the works of John Wimber and C. Peter Wagner and other works on the Vineyard movement.

The VVCF is a young congregation with about 70% of the adults in their twenties and thirties. About 87% are Caucasian, which is close to the general Sea City composition, but reflects a higher percentage of people of color than does the population of in the area of Valley Town. It is about 94% Caucasian.

Nearly all of these companies and their structures have sprung up in the last 15 years.

The office building that the VVCF calls home has a pleasant exterior with two driveway entrances each with an attractive sign that indicates the name of the church and the times of its services. Inside the building, the 'sanctuary', though tastefully arranged and decorated, has the look of a hotel conference room. A small platform midway on the far wall as one enters from one of the two entrances draws the attention. About two hundred chairs tightly surround the three sides of the platform. When the room is between services, few religious symbols can be found. There are, however, signs of contemporary technology that occupy conspicuous spaces in the sanctuary. The platform seems filled with synthesizers, monitors and the latest high-tech musical instruments (it looks like the stage of Saturday Night Live or a platform of a rock concert in miniature). The lights, sound and projection systems are all run from a technical booth in the rear of the room, and it has its own prominence. Just looking at the icons of technology, one might guess the proximity of Silicon Valley.[57]

Historical Aspects of VVCF

Another connection to the Silicon Valley is a winsome, 36-year-old former chef from San Jose, Tom Allen. Pastor Tom's boyish smile and quick wit might suggest a calling of a comedian, but his intensity about life, natural gifts of leadership and motivational skills suit him for the pastorate. Pastor Tom is an entrepreneurial-type pastor. He is not afraid to experiment with new ideas. This is evidenced not only in the programming that he initiates in the church but also in the worship structures and dynamics of the services.

In Tom's (he is often called by his first name) heart of hearts, he knows he is a motivator. His sermons betray this fact. Even when he makes the announcements of church events, he is in a motivational mode. Tom personally engages in a variety of services and ministries in the Valley Town and surrounding community, and he weekly challenges and motivates his congregation to follow him into more active involvement. For example, the extensive food distribution program of the church is spearheaded, organized and implemented by Pastor Tom.

---

57. The VVCF has moved into another rented building in Valley Town. Although there have been necessary changes that come with such a move, the surroundings and the sanctuary are substantially the same.

From making the special 'deals' that purchase the foodstuffs to the recruiting of the volunteers that transport and deliver the food in a pick-up truck caravan, Pastor Tom's personality propels the work.

Listening to his preaching/teaching is somewhat like listening to a TV motivational expert. His tone is upbeat. His mannerisms are casual, lacking ecclesiastical form or stiffness. The language Tom uses is sprinkled with contemporary jargon, attempting a cultural relevance. All the while he is unfolding biblical texts, using personal examples and giving a heavy dose of direct application to daily life.

Tom's style emerges out of his experience as much as personality. He is a convert. In fact, Tom's quite dramatic conversion happened less than a decade ago. The pastor often refers to his 'BC' (before Christ/conversion) days, his heavy cocaine use and the sense of meaninglessness that pervaded his 'life without Christ'. Pastor Tom generally fits the convert type. He is a true zealot. He attacks issues. He does nothing half way. He engages in forceful rhetoric, absent of gentle persuasion. No, those who follow him are captured by his straightforward, no holds barred approach.

Tom Allen brings his approach and his message to Valley Town and to its Vineyard Fellowship. In addition to his basic evangelical challenge to a converting relationship with Christ, Tom's concerns center around the 'power of the Spirit to do signs and wonders' (primarily healing) and a deep interest in 'caring for the poor and needy'. Tom sees both of these components as central to the gospel message.

The 'power of God to work mightily' grounds all of Pastor Tom's messages and his programs. His concern for the disadvantaged and hungry and his interest in 'power healing'[58] have been his foci since his conversion. He tells the story of his immediate post-conversion zeal that sought expression:

> I wanted to do something for Jesus, I wanted to be like Jesus. I read in the Bible Jesus fed the hungry, I could relate, I was a cook. So I took the left over soup from the restaurant and went looking for some poor and hungry people.

Within weeks, Pastor Tom discovered a church in his Silicon Valley city that had an extensive feeding program. He met the lay woman,

58. 'Power Healing' is a term coined and described by John Wimber (former leader of the Vineyard movement) in his *Power Healing*. Both the term and the practice are pervasive at the VVCF. See Chapter 1.

Mary Holden, that ran the program. He offered his help. Mary not only incorporated Tom's zealous attitude and his soup but promptly led him into preaching and praying for the sick. 'To my surprise people were healed when I prayed for them, the power of God was on me, I had the anointing.' So, as a brand-new convert Tom Allen became actively involved in ministering to the poor and needy. Feeding, preaching and praying for healing remain his main preoccupations.

The VVCF is a new church, begun in the late 1980s. Pastor Tom, then a chef living and working in the south San Francisco Bay area, was becoming increasingly involved in lay charismatic ministry. When asked how the church came into being, in his own characteristic way Tom insists that God 'told me to start a church in Valley Town'.

Following the 'divine directive', Tom, his wife Joyce and their two children moved into Valley Town and worked full time at establishing a congregation. Beginning with a small Bible study in Valley Town, Tom Allen launched his church. Ned, a retired businessman and one of the few members over 50 years old, recalls the beginnings of the congregation:

> Tom started with a handful of us, just seven. First, we met in a living
> room of Tom's and Joyce's town house for a Bible study... My wife and
> I took a vacation—when we returned at the end of the summer the group
> had grown to about thirty.

By the next May, one year later, the congregation numbered approximately 75 people and had moved into a portion of a rented office building for its services. Four years later the church boasted a weekly attendance of nearly 250. Though a young congregation, the VVCF has an emerging congregational self-understanding that in part reflects a theological self-understanding.

Theological Self-Understanding
Formal statements. The VVCF summarizes its theology in seven statements, which the congregation calls 'We Believe'. These brief proclamations, creedal in form, are adapted from the Vineyard Ministries International. The VVCF's theological summarization is derived from a conservative reading of the Bible and includes the belief that the Scriptures are 'fully inspired by God and without error. They are our written authority and guide in all matters of faith and practice'. Foundational to the VVCF's beliefs is the understanding of personal conversion, an

individual acceptance of Christ as savior. The result of this 'faith alone' experience is that 'you will be born again'.

Like the Pentecostals and Charismatics, the VVCF emphasizes the gifts and workings of the Holy Spirit. The distinction is the more mainstream Evangelical emphasis on 'the Holy Spirit who [comes] at the moment of conversion...to live in all believers, to empower them to grow into the likeness of Jesus' character and to follow Him in His work'. While Pentecostals in general also believe this statement, they would emphasize another subsequent event of Spirit empowerment, commonly called the 'Baptism in the Holy Spirit'. The VVCF avoids 'Spirit baptism' language, at least in their formal statement. In practice, however, many of the congregation claim Spirit baptism and think of it as having been initiated in an event subsequent to their conversion.

The statement of beliefs also highlights the 'personal, visible return of Christ when he will fully establish the Kingdom of God'. Again, while this formal statement is definite about Christ's second advent, it avoids statements of sequence and chronology and the rhetoric of 'rapture' and 'tribulation' that produce points of controversy among many Evangelicals. The 'We Believe' document remains consciously vague on these matters. Pastor Tom believes that 'it is not important to make ["exact"] statements...unless it can help people better serve the Lord'. Avoiding specificity in theology, especially in controversial areas, has helped the VVCF's purpose of relating broadly to conservative Evangelical emphases while incorporating the traditional Pentecostal emphases, if not the terminology.

The VVCF's formal theological summary reflects the congregation's beliefs, but to comprehend clearly the theological self-understanding of the church one must consider issues they have chosen to emphasize in practical ways. For Pastor Tom, formal theology matters little, relevance emerges in application.

Emphases. One does not have to attend the VVCF for very long before recognizing the main emphases of the local congregation. The worship services themselves point to the important elements of the VVCF community: worship, signs and wonders, social outreaches and motivation and equipping for Christian life and ministry.[59] These emphases reflect core beliefs of the VVCF.

59. The VVCF has 'An Invitation to You', a small tract-like invitation given out by church members that in addition to listing service times and location briefly

When asked why they were initially attracted to the church or what
they appreciate about their church, VVCF members often respond 'the
worship'. 'The worship' means something very specific. It does not
refer to 'worship' in the sense of the entire Sunday service, as the worship service. No, 'the worship' refers only to the first phase of the Sunday ritual, the worship in song, the congregational singing. But 'worship' represents more than just hymn or chorus singing. Their 'worship'
has a high level of individual engagement. It represents a highly participatory rite that involves the congregation in forms of worship that
alternate between the somewhat free-wheeling celebrative mode and a
consciousness that incorporates a deeper more mystical-contemplative
mode. It is hard to believe that anyone who does not appreciate the
VVCF form of 'worship' would integrate well into the congregation. It
is at the core of the identity of the church and it implicitly calls one to
participate fully in its worship forms.[60]

People are also attracted to the VVCF by its language of 'power',
'signs and wonders' and 'divine healings'. As we have indicated, these
symbols are at the center of the Vineyard Ministries International. Vineyard represents a 'signs and wonders' movement, emphasizing 'power
healing' and 'power evangelism'.[61] The VVCF, with its charismatic

describes the congregation: 'We are a Christ centered fellowship emphasizing
balanced worship, Bible teaching, and the workings of the Holy Spirit.' 'Priorities'
listed are 'healing teams', 'feeding the needy' and 'raising up the chosen generation'. This description of the 'fellowship' and its priorities conveys essentially the
same emphases we discovered in field research: worship, social outreaches (particularly 'feeding the needy'), signs and wonders ('the workings of the Holy Spirit' and
'healing teams'), and a motivation for Christian life and ministry ('raising up the
chosen generation').

60. For a more extensive descriptive analysis of modes of worship, e.g., the
celebrative or contemplative modes of sensibility, see Chapter 5 below.

61. 'Power Evangelism' and 'Power Healing' represent terms used widely in
the Vineyard movement; they are also titles of two books written by John Wimber.
Other books dealing with power and signs and wonders by or about Wimber include
Power Points: Seven Steps to Christian Growth (San Francisco: HarperCollins,
1991); Springer, *Power Encounters*.

These books argue for the place of healing and signs and wonders in the contemporary times. Wimber (and Pastor Tom) believes that the 'miraculous' is an
ordinary part of the normal Christian life. These 'power' books encourage their
readers to become personally involved in the power of the Holy Spirit and the ministries of the Church (e.g. evangelism, healing) in that power. Even the book con-

pastor Tom, emphasizes this same cluster of symbols both in the Sunday ritual and the outreaches of the church.

Signs and wonders and power evangelism come together in a particular way for Pastor Tom.[62] He sees a primary role of the church as caring for the poor. 'The poor and needy' are nearly always referred to in Tom's pastoral messages.[63] He believes in feeding the poor, but insists that the church needs a deeper level of commitment. The members of the VVCF seek to meet other needs of the poor they feed. They have discovered an openness among the socially disadvantaged. 'We ask them if they have a need we can pray with them about... Often they say "yes",' indicates a young college student who has helped in the food ministry for more than a year. Here is where Pastor Tom focuses on what he calls the 'supernatural'. The pastor, through a charismatic awareness, discerns the need and prays. Often the request is for healing. Pastor Tom, and others in the congregation who he has trained, report 'miracles', healings and other answers to these prayer requests.

Pastor Tom's synthesis of social ministries and charismatic prayer forms the basis of his pastoral teaching/training. Tom has mobilized a high percentage of his people to work with the poor and to believe for signs and wonders. Tom Allen is a motivator and 'equipper' (i.e. trainer). His messages sizzle. He packs them with pop jargon, seasoned with excited expectation, and always linked to biblical texts. The purpose of his messages is often to encourage, stimulate congregational members to believe in their potential to be successful in ministries. Other than evangelism, the ministry most often encouraged is that of service to 'the poor, the hungry, and the needy'. The form of this service is primarily to work among them; feeding and charismatic praying. Pastor Tom's motivational and training skills are evidenced by the high level of involvement and general congregational emphasis on social outreaches oriented by charismatic ('power') expectations.[64]

cerning the 'basics of spiritual growth' is linked to the 'power' terminology, that is, *Power Points*.

62. Although Tom Allen has a particular application of these concepts, when asked how he conceives of healing and signs and wonders (power ministry in general), he indicated that he was in complete agreement with John Wimber.

63. In the early stages of our field research we noted often more than six references by Pastor Tom to the 'poor' or 'needy' during the scope of individual Sunday services.

64. More than 50 people have regularly involved themselves in the feeding

Programs and Activities

Pastor Tom's propensity for motivation and equipping undergirds the 'philosophy' of programming at the VVCF. The four general emphases of the VVCF are reflected in the programs and activities established by the church. Of course, the Sunday worship services, their corresponding children's programs and Wednesday night prayer meeting are integral to the church's life.[65] Beyond the liturgies, however, the programs most significant to the character of the church are those born out of the Pastor's 'vision'. Speaking of his original impulse, Pastor Tom recalls, 'Our vision was to plant a church that would feed the poor, heal the sick, restore families and equip believers for the work of the ministry'. These aims are today central to the programs and activities of the VVCF.

As we noted above, the church channels much of the energy into 'feeding the poor'. An elaborate food acquisition and distribution program involves scores of church members. The food distribution ministry has two primary destinations. Locally, in perhaps the poorest section of Sea City, food is distributed biweekly to approximately 200 families in need. The second destination is Mexico. Helping a missionary feeding program in an extremely poor village 30 miles south of the Mexican border is also a part of the outreach of the VVCF. Members transport food along with building materials to a village in Mexico at

program and some 60 people often participate in the quarterly Mexico trips. Though numbers, as well as the individuals, vary from a congregation of 250, the level of involvement is notable.

65. Programs and activities that are 'standard' in many protestant churches (e.g. Sunday school, youth groups, choirs, etc.) are less central to the life of the VVCF. In part this is a function of the church's short history. Its programming is less sophisticated, owing to its newness. Also, there is a certain reaction against some 'church-like' programs. One older woman, who had come from a more mainline church previous to her involvement with the VVCF, voices the feeling of many at the VVCF. She is suspicious of 'traditional things' in the church. Her misgivings were specifically in response to the pastor's announcement of the establishment of an official group of deacons for the congregation. She fears that as 'the church [becomes] more and more organized and traditionalized that it [will] lose some of the power of God'. Rendering it 'more of a social institution' than a church. Vineyard is attempting to distinguish itself as 'not just another church' or merely a 'social institution'. Thus their most dominant programs and activities strive to portray a uniqueness in keeping with their uniquely perceived 'calling'.

least four times a year. These quarterly trips provide an on-going opportunity for congregational members to minister 'by caring for the needy' in the manner of their training. Several congregants pointed to the Mexico missions as extremely important and central to the identity of the VVCF.

Tom has also trained people for other programs essential to the VVCF. The Home group program represents one such core activity. The pastor calls this activity an 'essential and [the] most powerful expression of the church family'. These weekly gatherings meet in members' homes with usually fewer than ten adults. Pastor Tom says that within 'the small group... We learn to love, pray, heal, exercise spiritual gifts, and give and receive affirmation and insight'. In fact, much of the so-called charismatic activity occurs in these settings.[66]

Another program that is characteristic of the VVCF is the prayer or ministry teams. Tom Allen often teaches about divine healing.[67] In most of the services of VVCF there is a 'ministry time' that is often the final phase of the Sunday ritual. This ministry time is primarily a healing rite patterned after the model of John Wimber, leader of the Vineyard Ministries International. In the ministry time, trained healing teams practice 'techniques' of healing prayers and interviews with those who come to be ministered to.[68] These teams function primarily in the Sunday services, however, these trained individuals are encouraged to take their healing prayers outside the church to the needy, friends and neighbors.

Each of these programs, feeding the poor and caring for the needy,

66. For instance, charismatic words (e.g. words of wisdom, knowledge, prophecy, etc.) are encouraged in the home groups at the VVCF. In contrast to the CCC, L&L and many classical Pentecostal churches, charismatic utterances are restricted in the Sunday services at the VVCF. Another contrast is the apparent absence of 'messages in tongues' and accompanying 'interpretations' in the VVCF community. Neither the Sunday ritual nor the home groups practice this 'rite'. Tongues speech is however practiced devotionally as private prayer in both settings during congregational 'concert' prayer.

67. At times he will do a series of, for instance, Sunday night teaching sermons that deal with divine healing. One church member recalls that 'a couple of years ago Tom taught on healing for nearly six months'.

68. The form of healing prayers at the VVCF is taught by Pastor Tom and patterned after John Wimber (see Wimber, *Power Healing*). The practice generally includes prayers, interview (speaking about the perceived need) and charismatic insight and words. See Chapter 4 for a discussion of 'altar/response' and rites of healing.

home groups, and prayer/ministry teams, relates in some (broad) way to the VVCF's concept of Evangelism. 'At the [VVCF], the most effective evangelism results from modeling the life of Jesus Christ through feeding the poor, healing the sick and loving one another'.[69] The church's relationship to 'the world', according to Pastor Tom, is 'to love people...and serve them in humility'. The 'church family' is to 'relate to the world in healing love and power'. Each of these characteristic programs of the VVCF are outward looking. They proceed from the concept of worship and relationship to God that the congregation expresses and experiences in the Sunday ritual.

Organization and Leadership Structure

Implicit in our previous remarks, Pastor Tom Allen is the central figure in leadership structure of the VVCF as well as the overall organization of the church. No doubt his centrality results in part from his position as the *founding* pastor and to his style/type of charismatic leadership. Most of the people involved with Tom in the leadership of the VVCF are lay and volunteer. Only two other staff receive salaries, an associate pastor and a church secretary.

Tom summarized his 'philosophy' of 'structure and leadership' when he wrote,

> Structure and leadership in the church exist to give life and freedom to the [church] family. Our structure here at Vineyard enables us to better communicate, educate, channel resources, and restrain harmful behavior. It is set up to serve...help [people discover] areas...most enjoy[able], serving the Lord. Leaders in this church must be servants of the family.[70]

In keeping with this understanding, the church has structured '*three levels*' of decision-making leadership: elders, trustees and home group leaders. The four elders assist the Pastor Tom in decisions concerning what he calls 'financial and spiritual issues'. The three trustees, on the other hand, are involved solely in the determinations regarding the church finances. While the third level of the lay leadership structure is for the home groups, home group leaders. Though each of the home group leaders has direct leadership in his and her home meeting, the

69. From the booklet 'Vineyard Christian Fellowship', a local publication of the VVCF that explains the church by describing its philosophy of ministry, its programs and it basic doctrines.

70. From a booklet published by VVCF to inform inquirers about the church.

influence of these leaders is felt throughout the church.

But none is as influential as Tom Allen. Even the leaders in the aggregate are not as influential or powerful as Pastor Tom himself. While Tom believes that all of 'these leaders…contribute to the decision making process of the church', he is ultimately in charge.[71] The VVCF shows few marks of democracy in its governance.[72] Pastor Tom is not only the founding pastor, he is typically the charismatic leader. He believes that God called and 'anointed' him to pastor this congregation in Valley Town and the people of the church seem to agree.[73]

Consistent with Pastor Allen's understanding of his own charism he says, 'We seek to recognize leaders, both men and women, who prove to be *anointed* by God to equip the congregation for the work of the ministry' (emphasis mine). Congregants uses the term 'anointing' often in the VVCF. Anointing symbolizes a recognized charismatic enabling, usually for a particular ministry. Though the congregation is involved in discerning anointing among its members, Pastor Tom in the end is the one who validates the 'anointing upon' particular individuals. He does not adhere to 'democratic methods of picking elders or other leaders'. Instead, he says the 'anointing is obvious', and when he recognizes it he asks that person to become involved an area of ministry or leadership.

The VVCF has divided its ministries into five main ministry areas each requiring its own leadership: worship, Christian education, food

71. The three levels of leadership ultimately remain under the control of Pastor Allen. He appoints each of those who fill leadership roles. There apparently is no accessible constitution or written governing policy that defines or limits pastoral control. There is some minimal regulatory supervision of the local church and its pastor from the Vineyard International. It is primarily in the person of the 'overseer', who is a Vineyard pastor in the region.

72. I have noted above the tendency toward authoritarianism in Charismatic congregations.

73. It should be noted that, while the congregation in general seems to comply with Tom's form of leadership, there have been some who have questioned its wisdom. In interviews with former members of the VVCF, a common theme emerges. Tom's strong, controlling leadership is seen by former members as domineering, stifling gifted people who want to emerge into leadership roles. Apparently there is a tension between the stated purpose of sharing leadership and the reality. This is not to say that there is no democratic dimension in the church. An egalitarian freedom to minister healing rites, for example, stands in contrast to the pastoral control in the organizational realm.

distribution, home groups and prayer 'soaking' ministry.[74] 'Worship', the first part of the liturgy, is led by the associate pastor, Ron, who brings his abilities as a professional musician to the leading of the worship team and the band. Ron also ministers in pastoral counseling. The Christian education of the VVCF receives direction from Dee Long, a young woman who works as the church secretary but volunteers her time to lead the children's ministries at the church. The food distribution and social ministries have been coordinated by various lay leaders, but Pastor Tom closely oversees them. Gil Bertson leads what Pastor Tom calls the 'prayer soaking ministry'. 'Prayer soaking' exemplifies a form of intercessory prayer. Teams of prayers seek to assist the church's ministries of healing through intercessory prayer. They provide healing prayer rites by appointment for those who have been prayed for during the ministry time of the Sunday ritual but are still seeking healing.[75] Leadership of these ministries helps to form the overall framework in which the congregation is supported.

Combining Pentecostal, Evangelical and Cultural Symbols
Having considered the VVCF, even in this cursory manner, it becomes clear that this congregation draws upon and adapts the Pentecostal tradition to its own vision. The Vineyard movement in general has been called a 'third wave' movement.[76] This designation suggests both a similarity to the Pentecostal and Charismatic movements of the twentieth century (these being the first two waves of renewal) and a distinction between this third wave and the others. The VVCF fits the classification, third wave, to the extent that there is a strong connection phenomenologically to Pentecostalism and that the VVCF reflects its own variations on the Pentecostal themes.

    While the VVCF has avoided the term 'Pentecostal', its styles of

74. These area ministries could be seen as requiring a fourth level of leadership adding to the three levels explained above. However, the five ministry areas are somewhat overlapping with the three levels of leadership.

75. Of the decision-making processes for the ministry areas, Dee Long says, 'Tom sets the direction for the leaders and leaves them with the freedom of how to get there'. Dee's statement stands in tension with the general congregational organization decisions that are supposedly up to the elders, trustees and home group leaders, but are primarily controlled by the pastor. See above. This may again be a sign of more freedom within what is designated 'ministry' as opposed to organizational control.

76. Wagner, 'Third Wave'.

prayer, its emphasis on the charismata and many of its rites betray a strong dependance on Pentecostal spirituality. Some of the VVCF's traits suggest a return to emphases that were perhaps more salient earlier in the Pentecostal movement. The VVCF's strong emphasis, for example, on divine healing and on signs and wonders seems rather extreme when judged by some contemporary Pentecostal standards. On the other hand, the VVCF de-emphasizes some of the traditional Pentecostal symbols. For example, they seldom explicitly speak of the 'baptism in the Holy Spirit'.

The VVCF has attempted not to be 'pigeonholed' as Pentecostal. Along with their impulse to avoid categorization, they have consciously included and adapted many of the Pentecostal phenomena while incorporating conservative Evangelical and contemporary cultural symbols.[77] In some ways the third wave designation seeks to attempt to bridge the traditional gap between conservative Evangelicals and traditional Pentecostals. Pastor Tom attempts to reach out to Evangelicals, as did John Wimber at the national level of the Vineyard movement.[78] Tom avoids tight doctrinal statements that might separate him from other Evangelicals, even statements concerning the charismata that are very important to him.

But even more important to an understanding of the VVCF than the Evangelical adaptations, is the inclusion of elements and symbols of the contemporary popular culture. I have mentioned the great reliance on high technology and the forms of contemporary music as only two elements that symbolize the inclusion of many of the elements of the pop culture into their spirituality. These inclusions are justified, as they have attracted 'baby boomers' and more recently the so-called 'busters' or 'x-generation'. In fact, many of the distinctions made between the VVCF, as a so-called third wave church, and traditional Pentecostalism, are distinctions due to cultural adjustments.[79] So, while the VVCF might

77. On the Pentecostal propensity toward popular culture, see Blumhofer, *Restoring the Faith*; Wacker, 'America's Pentecostals'; and *idem*, 'Pentecostalism'.

78. Apparently, John Wimber hoped to convince the conservative Evangelicals of the legitimacy of the charismata, divine healing and signs and wonders in the contemporary church. See his *Power Evangelism* (with Springer) and *Power Healing*.

79. This seems clear when it is noted that many similar popular cultural influences (e.g. casual attire for services, rock 'n' roll forms of music, no choir, no special music, contemporary musical instrumentation, no organ, a casualness toward

be called a third wave church that shows signs of combining Pentecostal, Evangelical and cultural symbols, I would argue that the church
is very much a part of what I have called the twentieth-century Pente-
costal/Charismatic movement with the attending spirituality.[80]

Summary

The three selected congregations all participate in the Pent/Char movement of the twentieth century. They demonstrate their Pentecostalism in
both similar and differing ways. In similar fashion, members of each of
the three congregations manifests a typical Pentecostal propensity for
mystical experiences of the Spirit both in the liturgy and in personal
life. They claim to experience God as supernatural and to receive supernatural helps, gifts and empowerment. All three emphasize the sense of
divine commissioning that facilitates their understanding of purpose
and meaning in life. But the three churches also differ within the Pentecostal movement. In part, their differences reflect the point at which
each one entered the movement's evolutionary process.

   The CCC, for example, emerged within a few years of their denomination's founding and only a decade and a half after the Azusa Street
revival. As a result, today's CCC congregation reflects the heritage and
the imprint of successive transitional phases of the movement and their
denomination. Compared to the other two congregations, the CCC
appears less trendy and perhaps less able quickly to adapt to the swift
movements of the contemporary culture. The CCC's relatively longer
history, its chronologically more mature congregation, and its more
mainstream Evangelical tendencies, account for its resistance to some
popular cultural influences.

   On the other hand, both the L&L and VVCF were born into the
Pent/Char movement at a later stage in the movement's life. As a result,
they reflect a different phase of the movement's evolution. Though they
both reflect the influence of the Charismatic renewal and to some extent
are products of the neo-Pentecostal stage of the movement, they do not

---

the sanctuary that avoids use of religious symbols, has no pews but chairs, does not
seat ministers on the platform, uses only a small pulpit) displayed at the VVCF are
reflected also in the worship of the L&L, which is a part of a traditional Pentecostal
denomination.
   80. For the designation Pentecostal/Charismatic movement, see Barrett, 'Twentieth-Century Renewal'.

make the same ecumenical connections, as the CCC. They show less of a Third Force tendency. Instead, they both seek to be a new form of Pentecostal Christianity with an emphasis on relevantly relating to the contemporary culture. The VVCF envisions itself as a part of a so-called 'third wave' within the twentieth-century movement. It seeks its own unique place in the movement by attempting to combine Pent/Char practices and beliefs with those of the Evangelicals and the pop culture. While the L&L appears more comfortable with the Pentecostal designation than does the VVCF, it actively pursues cultural relevance while reappropriating the traditional Pentecostal symbols.

The three churches also offer the same essential elements to their members, though their emphases differ. Each of the three churches creates a Pent/Char faith community rooted in ritual, a community that assists its constituents with an orientation toward society and life in general. They each help their congregants to realize meaning in their lives, meaning refined through a Pent/Char filter, while providing a structure for community life. In other words, the three congregations exhibit similarities in the components of their rites, beliefs and structures.

The emphases and configurations among these Pent/Char components however vary from congregation to congregation. For example, while all Pentecostals proclaim divine healing, the VVCF, following its parent organization, stresses divine healing as a part of its emphasis on signs and wonders. They speak more about and seek more ardently demonstrations of 'supernatural' power than do the leaders and members of either the L&L or CCC. Another example, each of the three congregations refer to its faith community as a 'family', but the L&L clearly emphasizes human growth within a nurturing environment as the priority of their congregation. They seek to heal and help those in need and return them to the larger society better able to contribute. They display many of the traits of a traditional American extended family.

Empowerment remains a common Pentecostal theme, but the theme varies among these three churches. Perhaps the contrast is greatest between the L&L and VVCF. Both churches emphasize empowerment, though they view it quite differently. For the L&L community power comes fundamentally through a nurturing environment permeated with the Pent/Char practices, while the VVCF congregants regard empowerment as solely a dramatic inbreaking and supernatural event.

Approaches to the life beyond the boarders of the faith community also differ. The L&L and VVCF give little guidance to their congregants regarding the orientation to the society except concerning personal evagelism and individual moral direction. The CCC, in contrast, chooses to emphasize its place as a congregation in the civic community. Its rites and programs reflect this civic-mindedness. The congregation, aware of their Pentecostal reputation as 'holy rollers', seeks to perform its rites in a non-offensive manner, palatable to the outsiders (this contrasts with the other two churches). Similarly, the CCC incorporates programs that reach out to the community (e.g. Alcoholics Anonymous, Easter at the civic center) and, while maintaining a classical Pentecostal perspective, the pastors and leaders of the CCC encourage engagement in the civic affairs of Sea City. These contrasts represent congregational distinctions within the Pent/Char tradition, yet all three faith communities reveal the core of the Pent/Char spirituality, a core that will become more apparent as I now proceed to consider the rituals of these three churches.

Chapter 3

SELECTED ELEMENTS AND DOMAINS
OF THE RITUAL FIELD

In the previous chapters I have sought to lay a foundation for the study of our ritual with descriptive discussions of two contextual spheres of Pent/Char ritual. In Chapter 1 I began with the broad context of the twentieth-century Pent/Char movement. The scope narrowed to consider ritual in the context of three specific congregations. In this chapter, I will begin to consider selected elements within the ritual fields of these three congregations to gain a better understanding of Pentecostal ritual dynamics and Pent/Char spirituality in general. Here, I focus upon six components of the ritual field. First, I will look at three fundamental components: time, space and identity as they serve to 'frame' and define the ritual and the people. Second, I will appraise three other elements: sight, sounds, and movement as these assist the 'dynamic' of Pent/Char experience. In subsequent chapters I will consider other primary elements of the Pentecostal ritual field, the rites themselves (Chapter 4), the modes of sensibility that pervade the ritual (Chapter 5), and the consequences of the ritual (Chapter 6).

The abstraction 'ritual field' encompasses a conceptualization that includes the contexts, elements and dynamics of a ritual.[1] To help explain the concept of 'ritual field', Ronald Grimes, a leading ritologist (one who studies ritual) suggests two images, a playing field and a swirling pattern of metal filings in the midst of a magnetic force. The

---

1. The ritual field is the broadest context in which the ritual process emerges and interacts. One might think of this process of interaction as a dramatic ritual 'conversation'. This conversation is not limited merely to verbalization, it may include the kinesthetic, the visual, the felt and the auditory dimensions of communication. A conversation filled with drama. See Bellah *et al.*, *Habits*. 'Conversation' is the 'stuff' of which communities are made. In Chapter 6 I will consider community building as potential consequence of the Pentecostal ritual.

ritual field, Grimes explains to would-be ritologists, 'is a physical-social place where one goes to do a study, as well as a pattern of interconnecting forces'. He further describes the ritual field as 'both the locus of ritual practice and the totality of a ritual's structures and processes'.[2] The ritual field comprises what James Spradley has called 'cultural domains' or categories of cultural meaning.[3] I have considered several interacting and overlapping cultural domains of Pent/Char ritual during the field research, they include ritual time, ritual space (and the objects in the space), ritual identities and roles, ritual sight, ritual sounds and language, ritual actions and behaviors and gestures.[4]

Together these components of the Pent/Char ritual culture help to make up the ritual field, with which the Pentecostal ritual process emerges.[5] The Pentecostal ritual drama, like a text, constructs a 'world'.[6]

2.   Grimes, *Beginnings*, p. 10. See also Victor Turner, *The Forest of Symbols: Aspects of Ndembu Ritual* (Ithaca, NY: Cornell University Press, 1967), pp. 260-78. Turner first describes his own journey toward developing the concept of 'ritual field', then describes the potential components of the field and finally applies the concept to his description and analysis of the Ndembu rites.

3.   Spradley, *Participant Observation*, pp. 87-91.

4.   See Spradley, *Participant Observation*, pp. 73-84; and Grimes, *Beginnings*, pp. 19-33. Both of these have suggestive categories (domains) for thinking about the ritual field from which we have drawn.

5.   The congregations of the three churches each creates its own specific ritual field so that its 'species' of the dramatic conversation (e.g. ritual performance) might have a conducive context in which to emerge. They craft their particular context in order to worship as they wish. Each church ritually shapes the field into a 'world' of its own creation. This world then sustains the interchange, the conversation, the dramatic ritual of the congregation. The dynamic plane of this interaction consists of a conversation among the faithful and between the faithful ritualists and their God.

6.   As I have suggested, each of the three Sea City churches creates a 'world', a ritual context in which to express and experience its forms of worship. The ritual actions, utterances, affections and experiences together construct a ritual world, a matrix, that affects its participants. Once constructed this world helps to provide intensification and formation of experience for those who have created it and for those who are adopted into it (e.g. Pentecostal veterans, neophytes and converts). Pentecostal ritualists within their created ritual world come to share in a common ethos and world view (see Clifford Geertz, *The Interpretation of Cultures: Selected Essays* [New York: Basic Books, 1973], p. 113, where he claims that 'any religious ritual, no matter how apparently automatic or conventional involves [a] symbolic fusion of ethos and world view'). The ritual world, then, impacts its ritualists as it affects their world view and ethos. The better we understand the contextual ritual

According to Grimes, 'a [ritual] performance creates a microcosm in gestural and concrete form. The temporary cosmos generated by a rite...is a way of condensing the plural realities of a people.'[7] In this chapter, I am interested in how the three congregations arrange, manipulate and negotiate selected domains of meaning and how these domains 'frame' or define the contours of their ritual, thereby expressing their world view and their spirituality.[8] To understand a Pent/Char world view and spirituality better I now approach three 'key components of any framing that is on the worldview, or cosmological, scale':[9] time, space and identity. In the second section of the present chapter, I will consider how these other selected domains of the ritual field give meaning to Pentecostal ritualists.

world, that Pentecostals create and experience, the better we will understand the spirituality of the Pentecostals. See Ricoeur, *Hermeneutics*, esp. ch. 8, 'The model of the text: meaningful action considered as a text', where Ricoeur deals with meaningful actions (e.g. ritual drama) as a text with reference to a 'world'.

7. Grimes, *Ritual Criticism*, p. 90. For the development of a concept analogous to Grimes's 'microcosm' or 'temporary cosmos' created by the ritual, see James W. Boyd and Ron G. Williams, 'Ritual Spaces: An Application of Aesthetic Theory to Zoroastrian Ritual', *Journal of Ritual Studies* 3 (Winter 1989), pp. 1-43, where they present a model dependent on aesthetic theory that uses the category of 'ritual spaces' to speak of the created world of the ritual field.

8. Grimes, *Ritual Criticism*, p. 91. Grimes follows Erving Goffman's conceptualization of 'frame analysis', the 'examination of the ways people define social situations'. Understanding how people frame their world is important, because perceptions of reality are produced and worlds are constructed from their frames. To analyze a frame (or cultural domain) one must study its boundaries and how they are maintained and crossed with a goal of understanding the definitions or borders that organize the experience of the group. See Erving Goffman, *Frame Analysis: An Essay on Face-to-Face Behavior* (Garden City, NY: Doubleday, 1974).

9. Grimes, *Ritual Criticism*, p. 92. Grimes supports his claims for the primacy of these three components, time, space and identity, for understanding a people's world view by following Michael Kearney, *World View* (Novato, CA: Chandler & Sharp, 1984) esp. chs. 3 and 5. Symbols of space, time and identity can be thought of as 'frames' or cultural domains that provide a context within which a people organize and define their social situations. The most comprehensive frame is the world view. Smaller frames or domains, also, help to order perceptions of reality and produce 'worlds'.

Three Primary Ritual Field Elements: Ritual Time,
Ritual Space and Ritual Identity

Pentecostal Ritual Time

A central fact of Christianity in general is its temporality;[10] Christians believe revelation takes place in time. Likewise, Christian worship occurs in time. In a Pent/Char liturgy, in spite of the flexible time spans 'the when' affects the worshiper.

Pentecostals both shape time and are shaped by sacred and ritual time (in their own way).[11] In Pent/Char ritual, time sanctifies and is sanctified, or, one could say, time frames the Pent/Char ritual experience and the Pentecostal ritual experience frames time. The three main frames of Pent/Char ritual time operate in three cycles, the cycle of weekly and annual services and events, the lifetime cycle (that involves rites of passage and an eschatological sense of time) and time as experienced in the cycle of worship service itself.

Weekly and annual cycle. The traditional church year is not observed, except for Christmas and Easter, in any of the three Sea City Pentecostal churches. More attention is given to annual congregational events, such as family camp, special evangelistic meetings, seminars and retreats than to the ecclesiastical calendar.[12]

For each of the Sea City Pent/Char congregations, the weekly organization of time is very important. The main Sunday morning service and evening service, and a Wednesday night prayer/Bible study service

10. See White, *Protestant Worship*, pp. 18-19, 192, 201, for discussion of temporality in Christianity with some application to Pentecostal Christianity. For the importance of an understanding of time in the Christian liturgy see *idem*, *Introduction to Christian Worship* (Nashville: Abingdon Press, rev. edn, 1990), pp. 52-87.

11. For a discussion of the dynamics of the temporal system and ritual, see Catherine Bell, *Ritual Theory, Ritual Practice* (New York: Oxford University Press, 1992), pp. 124-30.

12. Except for special observances of Christmas and Easter, the holidays more noted in the three Pentecostal congregations are secular/civil holidays (e.g. July Fourth, Labor Sunday, Thanksgiving Day, New Year's Eve, Mother's Day and Father's Day). These observances help mark Pentecostal expressions as those of 'popular religion' or even 'civil religion'. For a discussion of civil religion see Robert N. Bellah, 'Civil Religion in America', *Daedalus* 96.1 (Winter 1967), pp. 1-20; for popular religion see Williams, *Popular Religion in America*.

or a midweek family night divides the ritual time.[13] The services, together with vital home group meetings and weekly ministry involvement, provide the central pattern of sacred time for Sea City Pentecostals.

Lifetime cycle and passages. If services and events function as main rituals that give rhythm to the weekly and annual cycles, Pentecostal rites of passage provide the key moments in a lifetime cycle. Conversion, often referred to as 'salvation', emerges as the most important lifetime event for the members of the three congregations. Pre-conversion and post-conversion divides time into distinct categories. Conversion radically reshapes life, one is truly a Christian when one is 'saved'. Seen as distinct from conversion, baptism follows the salvific event, but in none of the three churches does baptism rise to the same level of importance as the event of conversion.

Spirit Baptism reigns as the second most significant rite of passage. If conversion represents the doorway into life as an Evangelical Christian, then, the baptism in the Spirit marks the entrance into life and spirituality as a Pentecostal Christian.[14] The 'Pentecostal life' marked by an openness to the presence and power of the Spirit characterizes the Pentecostal experience.

The events of 'healings' also shape the Pentecostal life cycle. Divine healing is among the most significant key events for most of the members of the three congregations. A majority of members claim to have been healed by God at some time in their lives. These healings make up a part of the overall life cycle of the Pentecostal congregation and the individual congregant. Pentecostal sacred time, and with it the Pentecostal reality, is shaped by divine healing as a part of the cycle.[15]

13. The L&L, because of the size of the congregation and limited space in their sanctuary, has a Saturday night and two Sunday morning services in lieu of one Sunday morning service. All three services however are essentially the same.

14. Spirit baptism is less emphasized at the VVCF. While there is a significant emphasis on 'signs and wonders', even more so than at the CCC or L&L, and encouragement toward an openness to the spiritual gifts and their operations, the event of baptism in the Spirit is seldom discussed in pastoral messages. Many members of the VVCF do however claim Spirit baptism.

15. For two examples of sociological analysis on Pent/Char healing as a set of 'alternative healing' beliefs and practices to the dominant medical system (and thus expressions of an alternate world view), see Meredith B. McGuire, *Ritual Healing in Suburban America* (New Brunswick, NJ: Rutgers University Press, 1988); and

Together with conversion, Spirit baptism, and divine healing, the time in the life cycle is framed in light of an eschatological event. While the rhetoric and expectation of the second advent of Christ may have cooled somewhat from the earliest Pentecostals, the congregants of the Sea City churches still define their lives to a great extent by 'the Second Coming'. For them the eschatalogical event symbolizes God's reign and divine presence[16] and thus shapes their whole sense of time, sacred or secular.

Time in the worship setting. The sense of divine presence keys the understanding of the framing of time in the third cycle, time as experienced in the service, the liturgy, itself. Ritual time in the Sunday services in all three of the churches separates into three main phases or foundational rites, the worship, the pastoral message, and the altar/response. This tri-part structure will be discussed in the next chapter. Here, I wish only to note it as the frame in which God's presence is perceived and experienced in ritual time. These three phases have a progression, but the existential dimension of the ritual holds the progressive dimension in tension. Pentecostal ritualists not only move through the expected procession of the liturgy, but they make room for momentary encounters with the divine. These encounters seemingly suspend the ongoing nature of the ritual time, often as events of ecstacy, short moments 'suspended' in the overall momentum of the ritual. Such events can have a long or short 'duration' in real time.[17]

Poloma, *Crossroads*, pp. 51-62. For a more comparative religions-type approach, see Cox, *Fire from Heaven*, where he develops the idea of Pentecostal healing as an expression of 'primal piety'. Referring to religion in general and Pentecostal spirituality in particular, Cox claims that 'whenever primal piety re-emerges, the link between health and spirituality emerges with it' (p. 108). See esp. ch. 5.

16. See Land, *Pentecostal Spirituality* and his 'Pentecostal Spirituality: Living in the Spirit', in Louis Dupre and Don Saliers(eds.), *Christian Spirituality*. III. *Post-Reformation and Modern* (World Spirituality Series; New York: Crossroads, 1989), pp. 479-99 (490-93). Land has well noted that the spirituality of Pentecostals is shaped by an understanding of 'God as eschatological presence'. This presence is experienced in time and helps direct believers toward the divine workings in history, which will ultimately move toward a divine goal, the *telos*.

17. For a discussion of how Pentecostal ritual can shape the experience of time, see Salvatore Cucchiari, 'The Lords of the Culto: Transcending Time through Place in Sicilian Pentecostal Ritual', *Journal of Ritual Studies* 4 (Winter 1990), pp. 1-14.

Pentecostal Ritual Places/Spaces

If time frames the Pent/Char field of ritual then space provides physical boundary.[18] Christianity in general is territorial. Its central doctrine of the incarnation, locates it both in time and space. Pentecostals have often claimed to transcend narrow spacial limits that traditionally have defined worship settings (e.g. specific church buildings and styles of sanctuaries). Rhetorically, they are apparently indifferent to sacred space. However, the places and spaces of worship play very important roles in the Pentecostal ritual matrix, if for no other reason than that the space in which Pent/Char liturgy occurs helps to shape the ritual as a whole and thereby affects Pentecostal spirituality.[19]

Pentecostals in general adapt; years before they ever constructed sanctuaries, Pentecostals had a tradition of meeting in storefront churches. In this tradition, the L&L congregation met in a series of buildings, including apartments and a vacated bank, before converting a theater into their 'permanent' location. The VVCF today rents office spaces in which to worship. As adaptable as these congregations seem to be regarding a place in which to worship, they seem somewhat unaware of their use of space in ritual. Certainly, they are not preoccupied with the concept of ritual space.

Nonetheless, the space in which they come together to worship has important prominence.[20] In their sanctuaries these congregations 'create a ritual place, a micro-world' in which to experience their God.[21] Each

18. See White, *Protestant Worship*, for discussions on the importance of the dimension of space to Christianity in general and to each of the American Protestant traditions in particular. Also, *idem*, 'The Language of Space', in *idem, Introduction to Christian Worship*, pp. 88-121. For a more general discussion of ritual and the spatial system, see Bell, *Ritual Theory*, pp. 124-30.

19. Cucchiari, 'Lords of the Culto'. Cucchiari notes the 'liminal' dimensions of the space of Italian Pentecostal worship. Later, when I address more directly functions of Pent/Char ritual, I will discuss the concept of 'liminality'.

20. 'Space', at least metaphorically, is significant to Pentecostals. This can be seen in some of their favorite hymns (choruses), such as 'Holy Ground', a devotional song sung often at the CCC: 'Holy ground / We're standing on holy ground. / For the Lord is present / And where He is it's Holy.' Or, a preferred chorus at the L&L, 'I believe in Jesus', which proclaims, '...I believe that He's *here* now / Standing in our midst / Here with the power to heal now / And the grace to forgive'. Space is seen as being 'sanctified' and thereby shaped, altered, set apart by the presence of God.

21. Cucchiari, 'Lords of the Culto', p. 2. The space, shaped and created by the

of the three congregations carefully shapes its own micro-world. This 'world' is a culturally sculpted space molded from the elements of physical space and other elements of the ritual field. In order to understand better the ritual space as an important dimension of the Pentecostal ritual field, I will consider some of the places and spaces that the congregants occupy and move within during their ritual experiences.

Buildings (spaces) reveal an attitude. The fact that two of the congregations worship in buildings not originally constructed as church buildings points to their understanding of space. These buildings make a statement. The buildings of the L&L and VVCF lack the particular barriers, emotional and physical, that church buildings often represent. They are more familiar. VVCF's office building is similar to the ones many in Valley Town and Sea City frequent daily. Additionally the financial advantage appeals to VVCF, as they feel a heavy mortgage could potentially affect their ministry priorities. They value feeding the poor more than a church edifice.

The sanctuary and ritual spaces. Inside their buildings, rented or owned, office building, converted theater or traditional church structure, these three congregations have shaped their worship space. Pentecostals have championed two complementary ideas, that 'God can be worshipped anywhere' and that 'the Christian life should not be confined to the walls of a church sanctuary'. Nevertheless, each of the congregations understands the importance of some fixed place to gather and to worship in an 'auditorium', a 'meeting room', or sometimes called a 'sanctuary'.[22] The physical layout of the three sanctuaries differs. The use of

congregation, in turn affects the ritualists. It is a circular dynamic. Pentecostals 'sanctify' their ritual space through their worship, their ritual. They are then defined in part by their space, the world that they have created. Following Yi-Fu Tuan, social geographer, Cucchiari effectively argues that because culture and human life occur in spaces structured and created for the emergence of human culture, 'one of the most important ways of establishing, renewing, and, perhaps overthrowing cultural worlds is through the ritual manipulation of the temporal and spatial boundaries of human places' (Cucchiari, 'Lords of the Culto', p. 2). This concept seems consistent with Victor Turner's notion of 'liminal space' (see below). Also see Boyd and Williams, 'Ritual Spaces', for a discussion of the creation and function of ritual space as a kind of 'virtual reality' that produces a 'meaning space'.

22. Both the VVCF and L&L have avoided the use of the term 'sanctuary' and have chosen more neutral and less ecclesiastical terms.

space also varies among the three congregations, yet several foundational patterns emerge when one considers the shape and use of the
sanctuary space among the three churches. Here, I will highlight only
three main worship spaces, along with their attending centers. The three
basic ritual spaces within which the three congregations worship are:
the congregational space(s), the leadership space (the platform) and the
altar space ('the front').

Congregational spaces. At some time during the service the congregation moves through, or in some way uses, the majority of the sanctuary space. They gather and greet each other not only in a narthex (if
they have one) but within the confines of the sanctuary as well.[23] As the
members arrive and enter the sanctuary they most commonly congre-
gate first in the back of the sanctuary in the space behind the last row of
chairs or pews. In this 'greeting space', small groups often congeal as
fellow members pause to embrace and speak for a few moments with
one another. At the L&L and VVCF members often continue greeting
one another as they move to their seats. These greetings may continue
for several minutes.[24]

In each case the congregation occupies the majority of the space in
the sanctuary. The sanctuary, outlined by the rows of chairs or the
pews, takes up between 70 and 80 percent of the physical floor space in
the sanctuary. The congregation is not confined to this percentage, nor
hemmed in by the rows of seats. For instance, at various moments in
the service and during certain rites, the congregation fills the isles to
pray for one another or they stream down the aisles and gather in the
front of the platform for a healing service. In these and other ways the
congregation make even the aisles and the front truly congregational
space(s). They seemingly fill the spaces with worship rather than leave

23. The VVCF and L&L have no narthex or foyer. The congregation enter into
the sanctuary from the outdoors.

24. Little emphasis is placed on quiet reflection or meditation in the minutes
that precede the beginning of the service. Greeting and conversing seems to be preferred. The VVCF and L&L have no organ or other instrumental prelude. The only
sounds that fill the space are the happy sounds of friends greeting one another. At
the CCC the emphasis on greeting is nearly as predominant, however, there is normally an informal organ prelude. This seems to draw people a bit more quickly to
their pews and to potential reflection prior to the beginning of the service. But in all
three churches the use of space in the pre-service is mainly for gathering and greeting.

them empty and hollow.[25] The entirety of the sanctuary becomes congregational space at some time during the service.

Platform: Leadership space. If one thinks of the primary congregational space, the outline of the pews, as one pole in a dialectical dynamic, then the other spacial pole in the dialectic would be the platform, the leadership space.[26] The 'platform' is a space with its own divisions and ritual centers that most represents liturgical leadership.

The platform arrangement differs among the three churches, but each is configured in the manner of a concert stage. The CCC has a more traditional concert stage–choir/orchestra approach with the choir and orchestra on the platform behind the chairs for the ministers are behind the central pulpit. The L&L and VVCF have eliminated the choir's and the minister's chairs from the platform and replaced them with a contemporary-looking and sounding band with all the attending equipment.[27] The band, part of the worship team, also replaces the organ and the song leader found typically in Evangelical and traditional Pentecostal churches. The worship team and band fill the platform with musical instruments and high-tech sound equipment. In both cases, the platform resembles a concert stage, but one (the CCC's) looks like a choir and orchestral concert, while the others (VVCF and L&L) mirror a rock concert. Though very different in appearance the function is quite similar. The people on the platform use the space to lead the congregation in worship.

Although the pastor does not sit on the platform at the VVCF and L&L, he moves to the platform from the congregational space when he functions as a liturgical leader.[28] This contrasts with the CCC, where the minister's chairs and the pulpit together act as linked centers and symbolically dominate the leadership space. The established liturgical

25. Even the platform space becomes used often by members of the congregation other than the clergy. For example, individuals or groups of congregants come to the platform for prayer time normally at the end of the service.

26. The word 'chancel' is never heard in any of our three churches. Platform or even stage is preferred. The L&L, as a converted theater, has both a stage and a platform. The platform is directly in front of and lower than the stage.

27. Both of these churches have not only eliminated the choir loft but the actual choir as well.

28. Symbolically, the pastor remaining in the congregational space except when actually functioning in leadership signals a solidarity with the congregation and blurs the distinctions in certain portions of the worship service between the clergy and the congregation. This is intentional.

leaders at the CCC are all visible and present during the entire ritual. When 'designated' time comes actually to lead, they move to the single centered pulpit. Such use makes the pulpit a symbol for liturgical leadership in general rather than a symbol for preaching exclusively.[29]

There is one other center within the leadership space in all three of churches, it is a newer addition, an innovation, the projection screen. With the emerging genre of the newer worship choruses, the use of hymnals has diminished.[30] Concurrently, the practice of projecting the words of the worship chorus onto a screen has become widespread in Pent/Char churches. The projected words and the screens themselves perform a type of electronic leadership as the congregation looks to the screen(s) for the prompting of words with which to worship.[31] Each of the centers on the platform comprise the leadership space, whether a technological device (the video screen), or centers represented by furniture (i.e. the minister's chairs and the pulpit), or centers symbolized by persons (i.e. the ministers and the worship team).

Altar space. The dialectic between the leadership space on the platform and the congregational space yields a kind of synthesis in the altar space. The altar space, frequently called 'the front' is in each of our three churches the area between the platform and the first row of chairs or pew. The altar space is a meeting place. Where the established ritual leaders and the congregants meet, there the congregation symbolically meets their God. The communion table and the altar rail are two furniture symbols where this dual axis of meeting happen. Traditionally,

29. At the VVCF and L&L the pulpit is used only by the preacher and is nearly invisible until it is time for the pastoral message. Symbolically, the pulpit is then only dominant during preaching and is more directly connected to the pastor and the preaching event.

30. Neither the L&L nor VVCF own hymnals. The CCC does still make use of hymnals, but their singing is also dominated by the worship chorus and its projected image onto a screen.

31. While to the uninitiated projections screens can look like a bizarre use of space with an overbearing visual effect, the Pent/Char have in recent years become so accustomed to them that many insist that their worship is enhanced by them. They assert that they are freer to worship without holding a hymnal. They claim that they can physically move as well as focus on God more easily. Evidently, the projected screen is only a prompter. It is not consciously focused upon, especially once the words are known. The words of this genre are normally uncomplicated and repetitive allowing congregants to learn them quickly. Many close their eyes or focus on something else as they sing.

in Pent/Char churches, both of these have helped to define the altar space, though most of the physical area is open space.[32] How the congregants use their altar space helps symbolically to define the space, a place of meeting. Coming to the 'front' normally means to come metaphorically to a ritual center for sacrifice. The sacrifice is made in prayer and in acts of spiritual commitment 'around the altars'. At the CCC and L&L rites of ministry and healing also often transpire in the altar space. At the L&L the space is often used in celebrative actions, such as dance, but in each of these cases the ritualists look to the altar space as a meeting place with the divine.

This meeting with the divine is also symbolized in the fusion of the dialectical elements mentioned above. The liturgical leaders also often meet members of the congregation in the altar space. Leaders come from their leadership space on the platform as congregants come from

32. The communion table, traditionally centered below the pulpit on the main floor below the platform in Pent/Char churches, is no longer a permanent fixture in the ritual altar space at the CCC (it never was in the two newer churches, L&L and VVCF). Eucharistic communion is still received, as always, once per month. On that Sunday the communion table appears. But it is absent the rest of the month. This is a further minimization of the table as a ritual center within the altar space. Pentecostals, the CCC included, have not traditionally focused on the sacrament of communion. Though, as we suggest below, they certainly focus on the divine encounter, a meeting with God, within the general altar space. Their divine–human axis, however, is not located in the center of the communion table, it is not the true altar for Pentecostals. The locus of the encounter is in the altar space itself.

This points to another minimized center, the baptismal font. While all three of our churches practice adult/believer baptism, neither the VVCF nor L&L have baptistries. This is in part the result of using buildings not constructed for ecclesiastical purposes. It may, however, also point to a relative de-emphasis on baptism as a Christian community boundary. We say 'relative de-emphasis' because all three congregations encourage and practice baptism (and eucharistic communion), but relative to other practices these two sacraments are less emphasized. This is not to suggest that these Pent/Char churches are not interested in the sacramental dimensions of worship. Though they seldom use the sacramental language, they certainly believe and experience their God's gracious acts. It seems, in fact, that they recognize God's gracious acts in abundance throughout their liturgy. See White, *Protestant Worship*, p. 200, for a sense of the sacramental quality of Pentecostal worship. Also, see Gelpi's *Charism and Sacrament*, and *idem*, *Committed Worship*, for both a definition of sacrament that is consistent with Pentecostal experience and for an understanding of how charism and sacrament converge in liturgical practice.

their primary space in the pews, and together they meet at the altars.[33] Here they will meet together in order to stand, kneel or bow before their God. In these actions and rites, they use the altar space to symbolize both the leader–congregant axis and the divine–human axis, including leaders, congregants, and the divine.[34]

Thus, the altar space reveals something important in Pentecostal liturgy and spirituality: 'meeting with God' is a primary purpose of the entire ritual.[35] The altar space functions symbolically as an *axis mundi* in Pentecostal spirituality, a sacred space, a place for meeting God, a place for humans to make self-offerings in prayers, actions and ministry rites. And while 'meeting God' occurs throughout the sanctuary space, and throughout the outside world, the altar space most clearly symbolizes and helps to focus the human–divine convergence.[36]

Understanding space. One might say, then, that space to Pent/Char ritual becomes a temporary 'container' of sorts for the sacred, for the human to engage in the sacred. There is a liminal dimension to the Pent/

33. As I will discuss below, liturgical leaders are not confined to the established leaders (those who function from the platform). They may be nearly anyone in the ranks of the Pentecostal congregation.

34. Sometimes, especially at the CCC, the pastor will use the altar space symbolically to meet with the congregation. In fact, he is the only one who moves. He comes down from the platform to speak in another mode with the congregation as a whole. He uses this space to have a sort of 'family talk'. The effect seems to work. It is less formal, he is neither speaking from the pulpit, which symbolizes preaching or leadership in general, nor is he speaking from the raised platform, the place of leadership. Instead, he has come to the space of meeting, the altar. The divine axis is not explicit in these talks. Nor is the leadership role of the pastor dominant. As he speaks from the altar space, the place of meeting, one sense a symbolic conversation within the congregation. Though most of the talking is done by the minister, symbolically he is meeting with other congregants and they together are conversing about 'family business', congregational matters.

35. In the second section of this chapter I will consider the idea of encounter with the divine in Pentecostal spirituality in more depth.

36. The human–divine meeting can be seen more clearly when considering the rites and activities that occur in the altar space. Often congregants testify to a meeting with God or a 'touch from God' located at the altar, as, for instance, (a) altar calls for conversion, where often people experience God in a converting experience, (b) rites of intensification around the altar space, wherein people make commitments in prayer and by acts of dedication to God, and (c) rites of healing and other ministry prayers where congregants and ministers pray with one another.

Char sanctuary.[37] It sets a boundary between ritual life and daily life.[38] During the liturgy, the sanctuary and its ritual spaces become a locus, a center for reality.[39] This is not to say that our congregations view their respective church meeting rooms as sacred in and of themselves; in fact, they avoid such notions. However, during the ritual process clearly the sanctuaries take on a sense of sacred space. The ritual experience largely produces this sense. For it seems that wherever and whenever the congregations gather for authentic Pent/Char liturgy, the space-time dimension becomes sacred to them; the whole sanctuary becomes a sacred center.[40] The sanctuary becomes a space marked off as a center, a place to encounter reality.

A meaning space: A focusing lens. This encounter with reality closely connects to the concept of meaning. The Pent/Char ritual field in general, and its ritual space in particular, defines a dimension of meaning for the ritualists. Within the boundaries of the ritual space (the sanctuary) there are 'imaginative constructions' that produce new 'rules', and with the new rules, altered meanings within the ritual boundaries.[41] The ritual process within the boundaries of the ritual space and time acts as a 'lens' to focus the meaning on the reality encountered within the ritual.[42] New significance is revealed within the boundaries, the ordinary

37. See Turner, *Ritual Process*, pp. 94-130, for an understanding of 'liminality'. Also, we will discuss this concept in Chapter 6.

38. Cucchiari, 'Lords of the Culto', pp. 1-14.

39. For Pastor Ralston the place of meeting is a 'center' and not the 'church'. He explained that the church is comprised of the people. People are the church regardless of where they gather. The people are the church scattered when they are apart and they are the church gathered when they meet together.

40. This is obvious at the various meetings held outside of their own sanctuaries. For the CCC the civic auditorium takes on much of the sense of sacred when the congregation meets there periodically. The L&L has outdoor meetings at the beach and in the parks. The 'gathered' congregation and its ritual 'sanctify' the space in each case. Even the three categories of ritual space, congregational, platform/leadership and altar take shape in the outdoor ritual process. Also, home meetings in all three congregations suggest that the ritual process produces a sense of sacred space.

41. Driver, *The Magic of Ritual*, p. 98. Driver follows Victor Turner in insisting that ritual 'realizes itself in the subjunctive mood'. The ritualists behave in an 'as if' manner, one appropriate to their meaning construction within the sacred space and time but not according to the rules of the work a day world.

42. See Jonathan Z. Smith, who speaks of a holy place or temple as a '*focusing*

is fashioned as sacred and the supernatural becomes mirrored in the rites. The marking off of ritual space then assists Pentecostal ritualists in the process of what Robert Bellah and associates call 'attending', that is, paying attention in a special way and thereby recognizing meaning, not easily perceived in the workaday world.[43]

Transcending ritual space. Though certain elements of Pent/Char meaning are perceived better in the ritual space, the rituals of the three churches point beyond themselves back into 'the world'. These Pentecostals encourage re-entering their daily world, accompanied by their altered understanding of reality and with the experience of the ritual, in order to interact with better and affect their world. A kind of 'spill over', a transcending of the ritual space must take place. Pastors and ritual leaders exhort their people to practice the rites, in some modified forms, outside the congregational ritual space. For example, Pastor Tom of the VVCF, exhorts his congregation to pray for people in need. Tom does not advocate just praying in general ways, he teaches his people to seek out neighbors in need of healing. 'Ask if they would like you to pray for them', Pastor Tom advises. Apparently, some parishioners follow Pastor Tom's instructions and pray in the manner of the healing 'rites' of the VVCF. The testimonies suggest such prayers are being enacted with encouraging results.

This is one example of the spillover of Pent/Char rites out of the ritual space and into the mundane world. In fact, Pastor Ralston's view that the ritual space should be a 'center' from which to launch people into the community equipped, in part by the ritual, represents all three of the congregations. It might be said, then, that a goal of the Pentecostals in these congregations is not only to experience their God within the ritual space of the sanctuary, but is to view the whole world as

lens' that marks and reveals significance. 'The ordinary...becomes significant, becomes sacred, simply by *being there*. It becomes sacred by having [ones] attention directed to it in a special way' (*Imagining Religion: From Babylon to Jonestown* [Chicago: University of Chicago Press, 1982], pp. 54-55, cited in Driver, *The Magic of Ritual*, p. 48).

43. See Robert N. Bellah *et al.*, *The Good Society* (New York: Alfred A. Knopf, 1991), pp. 255-61. Bellah and associates recognize the importance of 'attending', paying attention, to matters of significance in the American society. By 'attending', they mean a kind of 'mindfulness', an 'openness to experience, a willingness to widen the lens of apperception' when it is appropriate.

potentially a sacred space sanctified by the people of God and the spirit of God working through them.

Pentecostal Ritual Roles/Identities

A third element of the ritual field, particularly significant to the understanding of the Pentecostal world view, is liturgical roles and identities.[44] Here, I will consider the ritual roles in two main divisions, congregational identity/roles and liturgical leadership identity/roles.

Congregational identity/roles in liturgy. One thing the three Sea City congregations have in common is the high degree of lay participation allowed, even encouraged and expected, in each of the three liturgical settings.[45] Though it may be an ideal never completely realized, each of the churches in some dimension of its liturgy seeks a 'full democratization of participation'.[46] This kind of democratic and active participation can be illustrated by five of the functional roles that a congregant may play during the liturgy: worshiper, prophet, minister, listener/learner, doer/disciple.

Worshipers. In each of our Pent/Char churches ritualists see themselves as active worshipers with little room for passivity. Worship of God, one of the main functions for gathering, must be done actively with full engagement of the ritualist. The 'worship' segment,[47] normally the first part of the service, is particularly structured to encourage full participation. In a sense, the congregants see their worship as a performance, demonstrating their devotion in worship and praise performed for God, as an offering to God. Though the congregation performs together, in concert, individual ritualists are free to 'worship in their own way'[48] as they give praise in word (e.g. corporate/simultaneous

---

44. For probing questions concerning ritual roles and identities see Grimes, *Beginnings*, pp. 29-30; and Hans Mol, *Identity and the Sacred* (New York: Free Press, 1976).

45. Many observers have noted that Pentecostals characteristically encourage a highly participatory form of worship. For example see Quebedeaux, *The New Charismatics II*, pp. 127-73; Robins, 'Pentecostal Movement'; Spittler, 'Spirituality'; White, *Protestant Worship*, pp. 192-208.

46. This term is White's, *Protestant Worship*, p. 207.

47. I will consider this term and this segment or phase of the liturgy in a chapter to follow.

48. This phrase was used with some variation in each of the three churches, and with certain boundaries is intended to give freedom to the individual worshiper and

praise, individual sacred explicative, testimonies), in song (e.g. congregational worship singing, tongues singing usually in concert), and in action (e.g. lifting hands in praise, dance). The role of worshiper in the Pent/Char liturgy is a performance seen as both an offering unto God and a dramatization of the Pent/Char experience of God.

Role of prophet. While the role of worshiper has an intended direction toward the divine, the role of prophet directs itself to the congregation. Though the term 'prophet' is used sparingly in our churches, various persons in the congregations often function as prophets during the services. To speak prophetically in these congregations is to speak the word of God, normally in a charismatic dimension. In the CCC, prophetic speaking happens during appropriate gaps in the service, often following the preaching, while at the L&L opportunity is made for prophetic 'sharing' during the worship and praise segment of the service,[49] and, when recognized as deriving from the divine, is seen as prophetic. However, the L&L ritualists characteristically use conversational vocal tones and inflections. This is in contrast to some ritual 'prophets' at the CCC, who, in classic Pentecostal style, use the announcement formula 'thus saith the Lord' and affect dramatic vocal tones and rhythms. Regardless of the style, each of our congregations recognizes and encourages prophetic participation and thereby fosters active lay ministry within the liturgy.

Role of minister. The role of minister is not reserved for the clergy in the three Sea City churches. This can be clearly seen in their liturgies. The ritual role of 'care giver' dominates the liturgies. The faithful do not gather only to worship, they gather to share with one another and to care for each other. The Pentecostal services are generally very sensitive to human needs and concerns. Nowhere is the idea of priesthood of all believers more practiced in the Pent/Char spirituality than in the 'ministering' to one another in the services. Believers, not clergy only,

his or her own temperament, background and sense of the moment.

49. Here the VVCF contrasts the other two churches. Such prophetic announcements fall outside the bounds during the worship segment and following the preaching. In fact, only the pastor/preacher may give such utterances (and he does) to the congregation as a whole. For other ritualists, charismatically speaking, the word of God to another is reserved for the ministry time, the final phase of the VVCF's liturgy. During this phase charismatic prophetic words of insight are normal when preforming discernment and healing rites. Congregants may also function as 'prophets' in the home group meetings of the VVCF.

are expected to be involved in healing rites of various sorts and to engage actively in prayers for those in need, particularly those present in the service. Ritualists hold hands with fellow believers or they lay hands on each other as they pray. They anoint with oil and they utter prayers of faith. In so doing they see themselves as ministers, care givers, or priests, roles open to each of them in the liturgical ritual.[50]

Role of listener/learner. A fourth role of listener/learner is open to all, and expected of all Pentecostal congregants. Hearing the voice of God, discerning the word of God, and responding rightly are core concepts within the Pent/Char liturgies. The word may come in various ways, charismatically or in prepared teaching/preaching.

Ritual listening is not passive listening, but listening with a purpose.[51] Pentecostal ritualists want to hear from their God so that they may learn to do God's will and become like God, sanctified in their attributes, attitudes and actions. For Pentecostal congregants listening to God's word represents only half of an integral twofold process. Listening comes first, responding to that word follows. The essential qualities of responsiveness and application help define Pentecostal spirituality.

Role of doer/disciple. Finally, the attribute of responsiveness to the word of God suggests one other ritual role, namely disciple. For these Pentecostals a disciple does not just learn or follow, a disciple does, is 'a doer of the word'. This concept fuels the participatory nature of the ritual. Action and doing are valued highly both in the ritual and in a Christian life of service outside of the church and its liturgies. Disciples minister to needs, heal the sick, speak in the name of the Lord and engage in other activities seen as redemptive and responsive to human need and divine directive.

Liturgical leadership roles/identity. The second main division of Pent/ Char liturgical identity is ritual leadership.[52] In principle any Pentecos-

---

50. This role of minister/priest is not restricted to the liturgy. Each congregation teaches that believers minister and should, for example, pray for and perform simple healing rites outside of liturgy.

51. Of course, there is rapt attention given to a charismatic utterance that is discerned to be 'a word from God'. But sermons and prepared Bible teachings, normally 30 minutes to a full hour, are also listened to intently. Congregants listen closely with open Bible and notepad as pastoral messages are given.

52. For a brief discussion and survey of the literature on 'ritual specialists', see Bell, *Ritual Theory*, pp. 130-40.

tal believer may 'lead' during a given moment in the service.[53] In these Pent/Char worship services, the charismata create a fundamental equality among the members. Anyone may prophesy or perform healing rites, regardless of gender, race, ethnicity, socio-economic status or clerical status.[54] They need only to be 'led/moved' by the Spirit and recognized by the congregation as behaving authentically and appropriately.[55] In this way, the members of the congregation move toward an egalitarian form of ritual leadership, a 'body ministry' within the whole body of Christ, each taking responsibility for ministering and leading.[56] I am not suggesting, nor do the members of the Sea City churches, that there is no 'division of labor' in the ritual. There are distinctions, leadership identities; however, the roles of leadership do not reside with the clergy or other ritual specialists alone.

Ritual leadership as facilitator/coordinator. What then are the roles of the liturgical leaders, lay or clergy? My field research has led me to see the ritual roles of Pent/Char leadership as primarily threefold: the

53. This principle is more true in the L&L and at the CCC than at VVCF. As we indicated above regarding prophecy, leadership in general is more restrictive at the VVCF. In this sense the VVCF, as a so-called 'third wave' church, is less affected by the Pentecostal tradition than the conservative Evangelical tradition.

54. The ideal of leadership for any and all is seldom achieved in any of the three churches. Such egalitarian leadership seems to have been most realized within the charismatic gifts, but when dealing with other less charismatic functions of leadership often a more restrictive rule is implicitly applied. For instance, women seemingly are not discriminated against in charismatic functions within the services. No woman, however, has been the senior pastor of any of the three churches, nor has the idea ever been seriously entertained. On the other hand, women have held other leadership and official pastoral roles (e.g. music, education, dance, administration, board of deacons, treasurer).

55. Recognition by the congregation as one being Spirit-led has to do, in part, with appropriateness. Is the behavior (e.g. the 'leadership'), 'decent and in order'? Does it have pastoral approval? The pastor represents the congregation and functions to safeguard it by discerning with the congregation the appropriateness of a charismatic utterance and/or spontaneous charismatic leadership. But the pastor must not dominate or seek to preserve their own position at the expense of appropriate charismatic leadership. For an excellent treatment of 'discernment' as practiced by Pentecostals, see Stephen E. Parker, *Led by the Spirit: Toward a Practical Theology of Pentecostal Discernment and Decision Making* (JPTSup, 7; Sheffield: Sheffield Academic Press, 1997).

56. See Kilian McDonnell, 'The Ideology of Pentecostal Conversion', *JES* (Winter 1968), pp. 114-15, cited in Quebedeaux, *The New Charismatics II*, p. 127.

facilitator/coordinator, the authority and the expert/specialist. In general, liturgical leadership in the three Sea City churches functions in the role of facilitator/coordinator. Pentecostals assert that the true leader of a thoroughly Christian liturgy is the Holy Spirit. They then reason that human leaders must facilitate and coordinate the liturgy and the ritualists; however, since the Spirit's agenda has priority, ritual leaders should manifest a sensitivity to the Spirit's movings. Any Pent/Char liturgical leader, professional or lay, established or spontaneous, must move with the flow of the Spirit's guidance. Facilitating a fuller participation of persons and their gifts is the goal, then, of all the ritual leaders.[57]

Ritual leadership as authority. A second role of ritual leadership in the Pent/Char service is that of an authority. With openness to spontaneity and the charismata there is a special need for the role of an authority. No person is expected to usurp the divine authority, but the congregation has ways of conferring authority on leaders and then, for the most part, following their lead. For example, an authority functions in the liturgy to evaluate spontaneous charismatic demonstrations. While each ritualist evaluates, discerns and analyzes, most look for a signal from an established liturgical leader (e.g. a pastor) to authenticate the charismatic utterance or performance. A recognizable verbal or gestural sign from the pastor as an authority greatly effects the acceptance or rejection of the charismatic expression.[58]

Ritual leader as expert/specialist. Similar to the authority role, the third leadership identity is the expert/specialist. As we have indicated, fundamentally Pentecostals believe that any believer, gifted and empowered by the Holy Spirit can function in nearly any liturgical role. How-

---

57. Full participation of people and their gifts of course is done within boundaries. For example, in the VVCF, as I have indicated, gift ministry participation is mostly limited to the ministry time and to the home groups, whereas the L&L liturgy makes 'spaces' for particular forms of gift participation during the worship time. The boundaries become clear over time to members of the congregations, though not often explicitly expressed.

58. The office of pastor (associate pastor[s] too) gives authority as a liturgical leader. The pastor's role as leader in the faith community blends into the ritual. But a pastor is more qualified as a leader in liturgy because a special charism has been recognized in him or her. That charism is often spoken of as that of 'caring shepherd', or 'a pastor's heart'. To the extent these characteristics or charisms are perceived by the community, the pastor has charismatic authority both in the liturgy and church life in general.

ever, they also believe that through special or particular training (and calling) one among them can be seen as an expert or a specialist. So, while all must be open to uttering the word of God, a pastor/teacher is to be both gifted and trained to function skillfully in preaching/teaching. Or, while all should pray for, care for and even perform healing rites, some specialists have special healing gifts and possibly more extensive training. Similarly, 'worship leaders' are most often musicians, though anyone may lead in worship.[59]

Three Sensory Domains within the Ritual Field:
Pentecostal Icons and Encounter

Having considered three primary cultural domains of the Pentecostal ritual fields, time, space and identities, and how they frame and give definition (i.e. help to organize experience) within the Pent/Char ritual, I turn now to three other elements of the ritual field, elements more connected to the *senses* of the ritualist. 'Any culturally constructed world, especially one enacted by ritual...does so by invoking and reorganizing sensory data.'[60] While the sensorium organization happens, for the most part, unconsciously among the Pentecostal ritualist in these three churches, one can learn much about their spirituality by considering some of the elements and dynamic of how they organize their sensorium within the ritual field.[61]

While in general the elements of the ritual field provide a matrix for the performance of the Pentecostal ritual, here I want to focus on a specific function. For these Pentecostal congregations, the entire ritual

59. The tension between those charismatically gifted as a specialist and those trained as a specialist seems to be maintained well at both the CCC and L&L (though they at times lean toward the charismatic over the trained expert). The tension collapses often at the VVCF. Training is minimized in favor of the 'anointing'. Even the pastor has very little theological training. He claims complete charismatic authority. Expertise comes from the Spirit's anointing. This is taught at the VVCF to lay people. As a result training is minimized, though certainly not ignored.

60. Grimes, *Ritual Criticism*, p. 96.

61. 'Sensorium' is the term of Walter Ong, who uses it to denote the particular manner in which a culture organizes it sensory data. See Walter J. Ong, *The Barbarian within and Other Fugitive Essays and Studies* (New York: Macmillan, 1962), and *idem, Their Presence of the Word: Some Prolegomena for Cultural and Religious History* (New Haven: Yale University Press, 1967), cited in Grimes, *Ritual Criticism*, pp. 54, 96, 225.

field, and the ritual drama that emerges within that field, is aimed toward an *encounter*. For example, at the CCC they speak of 'meeting God'. 'We have gathered to meet together with God', they say, or, 'We *really* met God tonight', they assert, after a service that was, for them, exceptionally satisfying.[62]

When one considers the practices and rites of Pentecostal worship as a part of the ritual field, one discovers a certain *iconic dynamic* (i.e. the dynamic interaction between the human being and an icon). Pentecostal 'icons' differ from holy painted altar pieces or works by pious artists that surround the chancel, though in some ways Pentecostal icons function within the ritual field similarly to icons of other Christians.[63] Their icons could be considered as windows or doorways into prayer. They have been seen as intersections between the human and divine. [64]

In all three of the congregations, such intersections are sought. The prayers of these congregants and their worship have a particular direction, toward the goal of coming to a sense of the presence of the holy. Thus, elements within the Pentecostal ritual field often are judged, to some extent, according to their assisting facility. Do they help move the ritualists toward the valued human–divine encounter? If the elements of the ritual field facilitate the congregation in their movement toward 'coming into the presence of God', they are accepted as positive. If the elements (e.g. music, preaching, charismatic words, rites of healing, etc.) and dynamics of the ritual field do not lead to this goal, they will be questioned.

62. Similar phrases are used at the L&L and VVCF.

63. For a brief but good discussion of the place of the icon in spirituality, see Kallistos Ware, 'The Spirituality of the Icon', in Cheslyn Jones, Geoffrey Wainwright and Edward Y. Arnold (eds.), *The Study of Spirituality* (New York: Oxford University Press, 1986), pp. 195-98; Paul Evdokimov, *The Art of the Icon: A Theology of Beauty* (Torrance, CA: Oakwood Publications, 1990); and Henri J.M. Nouwen, *Behold the Beauty of the Lord: Praying with Icons* (Notre Dame, IN: Ave Maria Press, 1987). Here, I use 'icon' in a restrictive sense (i.e. a window into prayer, a connecting link in the human–divine relationship). I understand that the theology and spirituality of icons, especially in the Orthodox tradition, are far richer and more nuanced than my usage.

64. Duane Christensen has produced a brief but highly suggestive work that considers icons in a very creative context. Following his lead, I seek here to use icons as a metaphor, one that will hopefully help to view the Pentecostal sensorium in a new way. See Duane Christensen, 'Reading the Bible as an Icon', *TSF Bulletin* (January–February 1985), pp. 4-6.

To illustrate, I will consider three examples of Pentecostal 'icons' that function within the Pentecostal ritual fields of each of the Sea City churches. Each of these three components will be viewed according to its iconic function: Does it serve as an intersection for encounter? Does it provide a pathway into the 'holy of holies'? I will consider the *ritual sounds* that surround the Pentecostal worshiper, *ritual sights* that stimulate the Pentecostal ritualist and *kinesthetic* dimensions of the Pentecostal ritual field.

Sounds that Surround

Walking into any one of these three churches for the first time during the Sunday ritual one might well be struck by a *cacophony of sounds*. However, what an outsider may disdain as sonic dissonance is to these Pentecostals a symphony of holy sounds. These symphonic sounds surround, support and give a sense of security to the Pentecostal worshipers. They symbolize an entrance into the felt presence of God. Among the Pentecostal ritual sounds, *music* especially functions as an auditory icon. It embraces the Pentecostal worshipers in an analogous fashion to the manner in which icons visually surround the Eastern Orthodox faithful in their sanctuaries. Our congregations use their sounds, particularly music, to facilitate the creation of their ritual field. Consequently, the manipulation of Pentecostal musical symbols advances the entire ritual process.

The music of the Pentecostal song service (often called 'the worship'), for example, seeks to help usher the congregation into the presence of God.[65] Many Pentecostal ritualists report that during 'the worship' they sense the proximity of the Holy Spirit and the reality of close communion with the divine heightened during the singing, listening and participating in the music and the other sounds of worship. The sounds of Pentecostal worship are not confined to musical sounds.

Verbal sounds occur in abundance within the rituals of all three of the Pent/Char churches. Concert or corporate prayers (where all pray at once), interludes of prayer (between songs), oral sacred expletives or vociferations (such exclamations as 'hallelujah', shouts, even whoops of wordless sounds) interjected throughout the service provide the mix of sounds that to Pentecostal ears symbolize the gathered community in the presence of God. These Pentecostal verbalizations represent, in part,

65. See D.L. Alford, 'Pentecostal and Charismatic Music', in *DPCM*, pp. 688-95.

both speaking to and hearing from God. They are a main element in the great 'ritual conversation' that includes the congregants and their God.[66]

The Pentecostal world of worship, shaped by the sounds, surrounds the worshiper. As part of the ritual field, these ritual sounds are one of the elements that helps to produce the matrix within which Pentecostals encounter their God and each other.

Sights that Stimulate

The iconic sounds of the Pentecostal service complement the ritual objects that serve *visually* as 'icons'. It is true that typically the Pentecostal sanctuary is quite austere, reflecting the Zwinglian tradition. Nonetheless, Pentecostal believers are visually stimulated to worship. The traditional ritual symbols (objects) are displayed as a part of the ritual context: the Bible, the pulpit, the altar rail and the musical and technical instruments, to name the most obvious. The sight and presence of these ritual objects with their symbolic overtones help to create the ritual field in general and to act as sights that stimulate.[67]

The sight of the Bible held high in Pastor Markowitz's (L&L) hand as he preaches, on the lap of a worshiper at the VVCF or held close to the breast of a testifying 'saint' at the CCC, visually demonstrates the importance of the symbol in the three Sea City churches. Bibles dot the 'landscape' everywhere during the liturgies. The physical symbol signifies a particular understanding of the Word of God to these Pentecostals.[68] Of course, this understanding is linked closely with the sight of the pulpit.

The pulpits in these three sanctuaries vary somewhat in their physical characteristics, size, material composition and style, but in each case they have a central niche on the platform. The pulpit at the CCC and VVCF may be used for a variety of purposes (e.g. leading of congregational singing and the performance of special music at the CCC, the

---

66. This stress on verbalization is why, among others, W. Hollenweger, R. Spittler and S. Land have rightly noted the orality of Pentecostal spirituality (Hollenweger, *The Pentecostals*; Spittler, 'Spirituality'; Land, *Pentecostal Spirituality*; *idem*, 'Pentecostal Spirituality'.

67. The 'sights' are affected by the lighting. The lighting is subdued during some phases of the service and brighten during others. This effect is most dramatic at the VVCF and L&L.

68. In a subsequent chapter I will deal with the concept of 'word' and 'Word of God' in these congregations.

making of announcements, pastoral prayers at both the CCC and VVCF) and by persons functioning in liturgical leadership (lay and clergy), yet predominantly the function of the pulpit is tied to the preacher. Together the pulpit, the preacher, and the Bible make a triadic visual statement as to the focus on the Word of God in these Pentecostal liturgies.

This focus is even sharper in the L&L ritual field. During the first 40 minutes or so of the Sunday morning ritual the pulpit is nearly out of view on the far right-hand side of the platform. The focus during this time period in the liturgy is predominately on worship and praise, and the worship team and band lead from the stage directly behind the platform. They visually fill the stage, while the small platform, a 12 feet semi-circle, 1 foot below the stage, is empty. One forgets the platform is even there. When the worship and praise period is completed, the modest wooden pulpit is unobtrusively moved to the center of the platform during a time of congregational greeting. It seems to appear almost from nowhere. The pastor begins his message and the effect is to refocus, to move from the worship and praise to a focus on the 'Word', the pastoral message. At the L&L this ritual object, the pulpit, is visually the most potent, but it is a significant symbol in each of the three Sea City churches.

Another important ritual object is the altar (rail). Unlike Roman Catholic and some mainline Protestant churches, the 'altar' is not synonymous with the 'communion table'. The altar (space), as we noted above, is represented by and derives its name from the altar rail, a place of prayer.

In the CCC sanctuary, for example, the altar rail is in the front of the church on the level of the congregation below the platform, between the pulpit and the front row of chairs or pews.[69] It is in two parts, cor-

69. Recently, the altar rail was removed from the CCC. It was determined that the rail itself was not functionally important. The church seldom uses it for communion, the congregation most frequently receives communion while seated in the pews. Also, for general 'altar calls', when all or many of the congregation are 'called' to come to the altar for prayer or a ministry rite, more room was needed for people to stand in the altar space. Now, without the altar rail, when congregants kneel to pray at the 'altar', they often kneel before the stairs in front of the platform that stretch across its length. Or, in more relaxed, less formal times of prayer, they kneel facing the first pew. This shows the generalization of the altar rail to the metaphoric concept of the altar, which is best symbolized now in the altar space.

responding to the sections of pews, left and right. It does not extend through the center. Rather, the space is open, creating an access to the platform and the pulpit. Although the altar (rail) has significance as a very important visual symbol, the image or metaphor of altar, which the rail creates, is even more influential. As a metaphor, it is packed with ritual significance within the Pentecostal tradition, as I have suggested above.

A class of objects, with apparently less religious significance than the Bible, the pulpit or the altar rail, is that of technical and musical instruments. Sound equipment—microphones, amplifiers, sound/light control boards, monitors, lighting equipment, projectors, screens and a variety of musical instrument—is integral to the establishment of the ritual context of each of the three churches. These instruments function to support and create a cultural space for the ritual. The presence of the equipment testifies to the incorporation of high-tech into the ritual field and thereby the liturgy. Perhaps, this is best seen in the musical instruments and the common use of the latest projection equipment at both the VVCF and L&L.[70]

When one enters the sanctuary of the L&L of VVCF, one sees a platform filled with musical technology. It reflects the contemporary rock concert stage with its maze of electric cords, monitors, guitars, synthesizers, microphones and other musical and technical devices. As the congregational singing begins, the worshipers do not reach for a hymnal. Instead, the 'worship chorus' appears on a large screen for all to see. During the 'worship' section of the service, the musical instruments with their players and the projected images of the lyrics dominate visually. Even the symbols of the pulpit, altar and the Bible are relativized during this segment of the service as the products of modern technology become ritual objects.

But perhaps the most significant and influential visual symbol in these Pentecostal worship services is the sight of fellow worshipers.

70. Pentecostals, since their beginnings, have used a variety of popular musical instruments in their rituals. Most frequently they have relied on the piano and the electric organ, while incorporating brass, woodwinds and percussion, and whatever the faithful may bring as an instrument of praise. This tradition is in full force in the CCC. Today, electronic keyboards, synthesizers and guitars merge their sounds with acoustic instruments to produce a popular contemporary sound, the remnant sound of the Pentecostal-style piano and organ are still often heard, particularly in Sunday night service.

Instead of sacred icons fashioned in wood and in plaster and intended to draw the faithful into worship, these congregants are encircled by fellow believers. Together they represent living, active, human, embodied icons. They fill the ritual space with visuals that draw one another into an awareness of God. From the worship leaders on the platform to the brother or sister across the aisle, Pentecostals influence each other's forms of worship, gestures and behaviors as they participate together in their ritual enactment. It is not that they are necessarily focusing on or actively watching each other. Rather, it is as though they see through their fellow worshipers as through windows. They look beyond; they see deeper. They recognize in each other their object of worship, their God. They realize these human icons are not God, yet the icon of a fellow worshiper helps. It acts as a lens through which the reflection of God is seen more clearly. Perhaps this notion of human icons in worship becomes more clear when it is recognized that Pentecostal ritualists in general are not statuesque. They move when they worship. Consequently, the kinesthetic dimension of the Pentecostal ritual field may best illustrate the iconic dynamic among fellow worshipers.

Kinesthetic Dimensions

The human body and its movement has another important iconic role in Pentecostal ritual: the kinesthetic (and tactile) dimensions of Pentecostal worship.[71] Enthusiastic Pentecostal ritualists have been labeled

---

71. See Lawrence E. Sullivan, 'Body Works: Knowledge of the Body in the Study of Religion', *History of Religions* 30.1 (1990), pp. 86-99, for a review of recent literature on the body; for the importance of the human body in ritual performance, see Bell, *Ritual Theory*, pp. 94-117; and Turner, *Forest of Symbols*, p. 90, Turner argues for the primacy of the body in ritual and in life in general.

Body movements and dance play a significant role in the rituals of the three Sea City churches. For the role of the kinesthetics (and dance) in worship see Doug Adams, *Congregational Dancing in Christian Worship* (Austin, TX: The Sharing Company, 1971); J.G. Davis (ed.), *Worship and Dance* (Birmingham: University of Birmingham, Institute for the Study of Worship and Religious Architecture, 1975) in which see especially W.J. Hollenweger, 'Dancing Documentaries: The Theological and Political Significance of Pentecostal Dancing', pp. 76-82; W.O.E. Oesterley, *The Sacred Dance: A Study in Comparative Folklore* (Cambridge: Cambridge University Press, 1923); *Religion and the Dance: A Report of the Consultation on the Dance* (New York: Department of Worship and the Arts, National Council of Churches, 1960); Geoffrey Stevenson and Judith Stevenson, *Steps of Faith: A Practical Introduction to Mime and Dance* (Eastbourne, Sussex: Kingsway, 1984);

'holy rollers'. Though derogatory, this epithet does relay a certain reality recognized even by detractors: a kinesthetic approach to worship.[72]

Contemporary educators, liturgists and other specialists have noted
the importance of kinesthetic to their respective fields. Pentecostals
have intuitively engaged in the kinesthetic. While perhaps they have not
explicitly spoken of their bodies and the gestural actions as icons of the
holy, they have in fact functioned within this understanding.

According to traditional Pentecostal ritual logic, God is expected
to move, but so are God's worshipers. Human physical movement
is closely tied to the movement of the Spirit. So, one does not praise
God with the mind (or spirit) alone. No, praise is to be more holistic,
expressed in motion as well as in words and thoughts. In the L&L
liturgy, for example, the people sway and even dance as they sing. They
typically clap to the music and applaud as a 'praise offering' at the
CCC. They raise their hands enacting celebration; join hands in prayer;
extend hands toward those in need at all three churches. At times they
fall 'under the power'. They spontaneously bow, kneel, stand and sit at
the VVCF, all as a part of their kinesthetic worship experience. Each
congregation moves even as God moves.[73]

Pentecostal/Charismatic gestures and movements in the liturgy convey a particular understanding of the movement of the Holy Spirit.
Their kinesthetic experience speaks of a spirituality that cooperates and
participates in the movements of God. These Pent/Char ritualists believe
that they experience and express the actions of God, the movements,
upon and through themselves. They speak of 'being moved by the
Spirit'. They can 'resist' or they can cooperate, even participate in
God's movings. Clearly, in the Pentecostal consciousness the kinesthetic dimension of worship is closely linked to the experience of God.

Margaret Taylor, *Look up and Live* (North Aurora, IL: The Sharing Company,
1953); Maria-Gabriele Wosien, *Sacred Dance: Encounter with the Gods* (New
York: Avon Books, 1974).

   72. See Land, 'Pentecostal Spirituality'.

   73. Even Pentecostal parlance conveys an experience of God that is fraught with
terms suggestive of the kinesthetic and tactile dimensions: 'I was moved', 'I felt the
Spirit', 'I know the touch of God', 'I felt warmth, like warm oil pouring over me',
'It was like electricity shooting through me'.

Summary

Even a brief sketch of a few of the elements of the Pentecostal ritual field reveals some of the values and aims of the ritual, which suggests a spirituality beyond the liturgy. Clearly the Pentecostal ritual field is no accident. It is both a conscious and intuitive effort to construct a sphere in which together a congregation most likely will *encounter* their God.

Experiencing God is the fundamental goal of the Pentecostal service. This experiencing or encountering God is often symbolized as a felt presence of the divine. The sense of the divine presence is a primary component, an aim, of Pent/Char spirituality. In the services this is evidenced by the use of 'Pentecostal icons', chiefly used to help the faithful 'come into the [felt] presence of God'. Pentecostal efforts to develop and maintain pathways into the presence point to the centrality of the mystical element in Pentecostal spirituality, the strong desire and claim to experience God directly and intimately.

Although I have focused here on the mystical encounter of God as primary to the shaping of the Pent/Char ritual field, clearly the encounter has a strong social dimension.[74] As one looks closely at the created corporate context in which Pentecostals experience their God, it is clear that they experience their God in a very social context. The Pentecostal ritual experience is not a solo affair, and each worshiper is greatly impacted and facilitated by fellow worshipers. Sounds, sights and movements, primarily produced by other ritualists, are not incidental to the (corporate) spirituality. In the Pentecostal ritual context, the presence of and interaction with fellow worshipers helps to intensify the rites and their effect on the ritualists. The social dimension of the Pentecostal ritual process is foundational to the Pentecostals' experience of God.[75] I will consider the social (liminal) dimension further in Chapter 6. But now I turn to consider the rites that make up the Pentecostal service.

74. The social dimension of the Pentecostal liturgy has been well explicated by Martin Marty. See Marty, *Nation of Behavers*, ch. 5, and *idem*, 'Pentecostalism in the Context of American Piety and Practice', in Vinson Synan (ed.), *Aspects of Pentecostal-Charismatic Origins* (Plainfield, NJ: Logos International, 1975), pp. 193-233.

75. Marty, *Nation of Behavers*, p. 114, has rightly discerned the social dimension of the Pentecostal rites. He asserts, for example, that the Pentecostal ritual 'behavior is highly social', though 'the experience must be personally appropriated'.

Chapter 4

PENTECOSTAL FOUNDATIONAL/PROCESSUAL RITES, MICRORITES AND CHARISMATIC RITES

Rituals enfold the secrets of Pentecostal spirituality. To comprehend the Pentecostal ethos one must consider the core ritual, the worship service. Obviously the spirituality of Pentecostals includes more than their liturgical rites can contain. Private devotions, personal witness, individual experiences with God and a plethora of pietistic practices flourish apart from the Sunday services. Nonetheless, the fact remains that at the heart of the Pent/Char spirituality, both corporate and individual, lies the liturgy.[1] The spiritual life of Pentecostals centers in the worship service, which grants vital understanding of the characteristic qualities comprising the overall spirituality.[2]

In the previous chapters, I have sought to sketch some of the contexts, the frames, within which an emerging Pentecostal spirituality occurs. I have depicted the development of the Pentecostal movement in the twentieth century, I have portrayed the broad outlines of three specific congregations and I have sought to describe some of the significant elements and dynamics of the ritual field that frame the experience of the ritual. In this present chapter, I will seek, first, to describe the *foundational/processual* rites that provide the basic structure of the core

1. Bruner, *A Theology of the Holy Spirit*, p. 22, rightly understands the central role of the Pentecostal liturgy when he describes it as 'the experiences of the many [that] merge into the one and by this confluence the power of the Spirit is felt in multiplication'. Marty, *Nation of Behavers*, p. 114, agrees, as does White, *Protestant Worship*, pp. 192-208, and others. Hollenweger describes the importance of Pentecostal liturgy and its dynamics within the category of 'a genuine oral liturgy'. See his *Pentecostalism*, esp. ch. 21.

2. Terms such as ritual, liturgy and rites seem foreign to Pentecostal communicants. When used such terms are employed to describe the religious practices of others, not their own. But to the alert outsider, ritual is ever observable among Pentecostals. See Appendixes A and B on Pentecostal macrorituals and rites.

Pent/Char ritual (i.e. the liturgy), and, secondly, I will briefly highlight some of the component rites, which I have called *microrites* (e.g. practices, behaviors, gestures) contained by the foundational rites. The foundational/processual rites together with their components, the microrites, constitute the complete ritual.[3] Following our discussion of the foundational/processual rites and the microrites that inhabit them, I will give special attention to the *charismatic rites* as particular examples of microrites and as characteristic practices traditionally attached to the Pent/Char ritual and to Pentecostal spirituality in general. This will then allow me, in succeeding chapters to consider Pentecostal rites as they are oriented and embodied by ritual modes of sensibility (Chapter 5) and finally to consider some of the consequences of these elements and dynamics of Pent/Char ritual (Chapter 6), before I summarize my understanding of Pentecostal spirituality (Chapter 7). I am now ready to reflect upon the foundational/processual rites and their microrites.[4]

3.   These terms, 'rites, practices, behaviors and gestures' are used in a sense similar to that of Bellah and associates' usage of 'practices' (*Habits*). 'Practices are shared activities that are not undertaken as means to an end but are ethically good in themselves (thus close to praxis in Aristotle's sense). A genuine community...is constituted by such practices. Genuine practices are almost always practices of commitment.' These practices 'define the community as a way of life...they define the patterns of loyalty and obligation that keep the community alive' (pp. 154, 334). See also Bell, *Ritual Theory*, pp. 69-93, where she presents a theory of 'practice', features of practice and then compares them to the concept of ritualization.

4.   While I have considered many modes of presentation for this chapter, I am most indebted to the models advanced in, Victor Turner, '*Mukanda*: The Rite of Circumcision', in *idem, Forest of Symbols*, pp. 151-279. Ruel Tyson, Jr, James L. Peacock and Daniel W. Patterson (eds.), *Diversities of Gifts: Field Studies in Southern Religion* (Chicago: University of Illinois Press, 1988); Geertz, *Interpretation of Cultures*; Barbara G. Myerhoff, 'A Death in Due Time: Construction of Self and Culture in Ritual Drama', in John J. MacAloon (ed.), *Rites, Drama, Festival, Spectacle: Rehearsals toward a Theory of Cultural Performance* (Philadelphia: Institute for the Study of Human Issues, 1984), pp. 149-78; Margaret M. Kelleher, 'The Communion Rite: A Study of Roman Catholic Liturgical Performance', *Journal of Ritual Studies* 5.2 (Summer 1991), pp. 99-122; Grimes, 'Ritual Criticism of a Catholic Liturgical Evaluation' and 'Ritual Criticism of a Modernized Mystery Play', both in *Ritual Criticism*, pp. 28-62, 89-108.

The Foundational/Processual Rites of the Ritual

Overall, Notre Dame Professor of Liturgy James White was correct when he described the Pentecostal worship service as less structured and less sequential than most Christian liturgies.

> The Pentecostal tradition is strangely free from the compulsion to get from A to Z in any service and may meander from Z to F and then on to O and T. In the process, a variety of gifts may be shared by the congregation… The Spirit blows where it wills and uses whom it chooses.[5]

However, upon close examination certain patterns that structure Pent/ Char worship service do emerge.[6] True 'the Spirit may blow where it wills', and a fair amount of meandering takes place during the performing of numerous microrites and the sharing of a 'variety of gifts', yet in the three churches of this study I located a fundamental structure within the typical service.[7] This foundational pattern emerges in a processual form within the service. The foundational/processual pattern consists of three primary rites: the rite of worship and praise, the rite of the pastoral message and the rite of altar/response[8] (each of these three primary or foundational rites consisting of a potential series or cluster of other more or less interchangeable 'microrites', practices, behaviors, and gestures).[9]

5.   White, *Protestant Worship*, p. 192.

6.   Menzies, *Anointed to Serve*, pp. 344-52, discusses changes in the Pentecostal worship service post-World War II. For an analysis of more recent changes in the ritual, see Poloma, *Crossroads*, esp. ch. 11.

7.   Once I had located this triadic pattern as typical in each of my three Sea City churches, I looked for it in other Pent/Char congregational settings. I discovered the triadic pattern, with some variations, in each of the 20 other churches and church settings (e.g. congregational meetings, chapel services, camp meetings, retreats), I observed. These 20 congregational settings were mostly in northern California (four were western New York and two in Ontario, Canada) and the majority were Assemblies of God (one Pentecostal/Charismatic ecumenical setting, one Calvary Chapel, one Foursquare gospel, three 'non-denominational' Pent/Char).

8.   I discovered this triadic liturgical form during my field studies, but later I became aware of what James F. White identifies as the American Frontier tradition's three-part service, 'preliminaries', 'preaching' and 'harvest'. No doubt this American format has had an influence on the underpinnings of the Pentecostal service, though White says that the Frontier tradition, unlike the Pentecostal tradition, relied on a 'carefully prepared and familiar structure' (*Protestant Worship*, p. 192, and see ch. 10 for a description of the America Frontier tradition).

9.   See Appendix B for a categorical listing of microrites.

Also, sets of gathering and dispersing practices and a series of transitional rites within this foundational ritual procession help ground and join together the three primary rites, much like mortar when poured as a base and further applied as an adhesive for the building blocks. Together these functions of the foundational/processual rites help to maintain the overall structure of the liturgical ritual of the Pentecostal service. It is proper to speak, then, of five foundational/processual rites—the three primary 'building block' rites, gathering/dispersing rites and transitional rites—of the main ritual. A rite can be understood as any act or set of acts, actions or activities widely recognized, sanctioned and handed down by the faith community.[10] The present discussion will follow the contours of the foundational/processual rites while attempting to consider other rites and practices (microrites) that may occur within the boundaries of each of these five foundational categories. Although in many cases, the microrites can occur within more than just one foundational rite (e.g. healing rites, as a microrite, can occur either in the first or third primary rite, i.e. the rite of praise and worship or the rite of altar/response). I will introduce the microrites into the discussion within the category or phase of the ritual that seems most appropriate. Here is an outline of the foundational/processual rites:

Foundational/Processual Rites in Pentecostal Ritual

Gathering and greeting

        RITE OF WORSHIP AND PRAISE

        Transitional rites

        RITE OF PASTORAL MESSAGE

        Transition

10. This basic understanding of 'rite' relies on Ronald Grimes's definition. Grimes defines a rite as 'a set of actions widely recognized by members of a culture'. He further explains that they are 'differentiated (compartmentalized, segregated) from ordinary behavior'. Typically, Grimes and others classify them as 'other' than ordinary experience and assigned a place discrete from such activities. 'A rite often acts as part of some larger whole, a ritual system or ritual tradition that includes other rites as well' (*Ritual Criticism*, pp. 9-10).

RITE OF ALTAR/RESPONSE

Transition

Farewells and dispersing[11]

Gathering and Greeting

Before the ritual formally begins, important preparations and practices occur that help to secure the success of the ritual. Preparations to the physical facilities begin well before the service, but then final preparations commence 15–20 minutes prior to service time: technicians set the lights and ready the sound system, the worship team meets for a sound check and for prayer (they have practiced during the week), and make other last minute preparations.[12] The sanctuary stands ready for the ritualists to arrive.

Other than the ministers and liturgical leaders (e.g. worship team and instrumentalists and band), the 'greeters' arrive first. The greeters station themselves at the main entrances to the church in order to greet formally and give a 'bulletin' (a worship folder containing congregational announcements and highlights of the service, including a place for sermon notes, but no formal written order of the liturgy) to the congregants as they arrive.

But the formal greeters constitute only a small part of the greeting and gathering that begins in this pre-service period. As people are met at the door they begin their greeting practices with the formal greeters. Often others join in and a cluster of people gathers. Soon, several clusters congeal, first in back of the sanctuary, then in the aisles and the seating area. As they meet they normally embrace or shake hands; they begin to 'chat' and 'warm up' to one another. These greeting and gathering rites prepare them to worship *together*. Worship furnishes a communal and very social activity for these Pentecostals. As a result they do not normally enter into their sanctuaries, sit down quietly and prepare

11. This structural pattern and the procedure can vary in exceptional services (e.g. the pastoral message might be eliminated or the rite of altar response and the pastoral message may be reversed in order). Spontaneities or planned alterations characterize such variation. Nonetheless, I discerned this fundamental structure and procedure in hundreds of services observed in my field research, in all three of the churches of this study and in other Pent/Char churches during 'surveys' of more than 20 other churches. See n. 6 above.

12. At the CCC the choir is central in the preparation process.

themselves for the service in quiet meditation. They socially prepare themselves. Their social interaction helps to ready them for affectively intense worship rites, rites that require a high degree of participation, a deep level of commitment and a high degree of personal vulnerability. With such potent rites and a certain amount of peer expectation, these Pentecostal ritualists need to feel comfortable with one another. They want to 'feel at home' unthreatened, secure in the ritual milieu, so their greeting and gathering practices help (re)establish the atmosphere necessary for them to enter into the ritual uninhibited. Their greeting and gathering practices then function to prepare the ritualists and create a conducive atmosphere for the ritual performance that follows.

At the CCC sometimes an informal organ prelude initiates the service, but, as with the other two churches, the sounds one hears during the gathering and greeting are the strains of folks 'catching up' on how the others are doing. Though much of it seems 'small talk', one senses a true and deep relating, a sharing of life and loving responses. At the L&L people so enjoy this gathering and greeting time that the worship leader sometimes finds it difficult to get their attention in order to begin the service. And even after the service begins, the greeting continues. One-third to one-half arrive late. They merge into the congregation, but usually not without stopping and talking to others in the back of the auditorium; before finding their place they will pause to hug or shake hands with those in the nearby seats. The music of the congregational singing covers the sounds of their greetings, but even the 'late comers' 'warm up' before they begin to worship.

The Rite of Worship and Praise
'Worship' has become a folk term among Pentecostals and Charismatics. All three churches speak of 'worship' when referring to the first main phase of the church service. That is to say, congregants generally use the term 'worship' in a more restricted sense than it is used among other Christians. For instance, seldom during the field study did I hear the whole Sunday liturgy referred to as a worship service. While the verb worship at times connotes the general adoration of God, among many contemporary Pentecostals a noun form of the word, worship, has developed; it is understood within their subculture. 'The worship' nearly always referred only to the first 20–35 minutes of the service.[13] An

13. Apparently, this restricted connotation, though enjoying widespread usage among North American Pentecostals, is a relatively new coloring for the term. It

illustration of the point inheres in the words of one of the worship leaders at the CCC. He frequently signals the beginning of the service by
coming to the pulpit and saying, 'Let us pray before we begin to
worship'. Even prayer to him was not a part of 'the worship'.

From song service to worship. Perhaps in describing the worship and
praise rite best one must first note its revivalistic Pentecostal predeces-
sor the 'song service' or the so-called 'preliminaries'. The early twentieth-century Pentecostals drew heavily from the American frontier revival and Wesleyan-holiness traditions. The song service was bequeathed
from the frontier revivalism as the initial phase of the revival service
that included gospel songs and hymns as a preliminary activity that
would orient the congregation toward the main moment in the service,
the evangelistic preaching.[14]

Some contemporary Pentecostals still admit the function of the worship as preparatory to the sermon. For example, when we interviewed
Carl, a college student and member of the VVCF, he insisted that the
'correct' sequence for the service specifies, 'the worship first, then the
teaching. The worship prepares the heart of the people for the word'
[pastoral message]. Notwithstanding this member's point, the worship
and praise rite shows signs of innovation. It no longer remains a mere
preliminary moment. With the advent of the Charismatic renewal came
a reorientation toward explicit adoration of God. This adoration springs
from the newer genre of worship choruses that have emerged and now
dominate the congregational music in all three of these churches.[15]

A description of the rite of worship and praise. At this point a concrete
example would be fitting. Here, I will draw upon our field notes to describe a customary Sunday morning worship rite at the L&L church.
While variations in style exist between the worship and praise rites at

---

seems to have emerged along with the adapted forms of worship in the Charismatic
renewal of the 1970s and 1980s. Pastor Ralston of the CCC, in a sermon during
1992, spoke of the transformation of the Pentecostal 'Song Service' to the neo-
Pentecostal 'Worship'.

14. See White, *Protestant Worship*, pp. 150-91.

15. Worship choruses comprise the vast majority of the congregational music
sung. Only infrequently are more traditional hymns or even gospel songs sung
during the worship in any of the three churches.

the L&L, VVCF and CCC, a great commonality abounds among this foundational rite as performed in these three churches.

A wide range of symbolic-expressive behaviors (i.e. micorites) mark the worship/praise rites.[16] It can begin rather abruptly: 'Good morning, why don't you find a seat and we'll begin,' the worship leader gently prods. About half of the folks in the meeting room have already taken seats and probably engaged in greeting and talking to friends sitting near by. The other half stands in the back or the isles in clusters joyfully gabbing. Most do move to their seats following the worship leader's request and attention shifts as the worship team begins the first song. The upbeat rhythm of guitars accompanied by keyboards and other band and orchestral instruments replaces the sounds of greeting. The service begins.

As much as any period of the service the worship time bears the imprint of Pent/Char spirituality. It denotes a time of expressive, some-what free-flowing, even experimental, ritualizing. The participatory worship characteristically accommodates a democratic dimension. It allows for individual-personal expressions and experience but subsists within an all important social (communal) context.[17]

With the chords of the first song many spontaneously stand. It is reminiscent of the contemporary rock concert, where fans endeavor to become more actively involved in the music by standing and engaging themselves kinesthetically in the music.[18] They clap to the beat, sway with the rhythm and may sign with their hands[19] or raise them as acts of

16. Potentially, the ritual practices and certain constellations of microrites during the worship and praise rite at the three churches are the most distinguishable as Pentecostal. The form of the sermon and the altar/response times are generally well within the American Evangelical tradition, albeit adapted.

17. See Marty, *Nation of Behavers*, ch. 5, and *idem*, 'Pentecostalism', for the social dimensions and social behaviors. For a brief but reliable description of a praise service see Meredith B. McGuire, *Pentecostal Catholics: Power, Charisma, and Order in a Religious Movement* (Philadelphia: Temple University Press, 1982), pp. 79-80.

18. This description reflects the worship and praise rites at the L&L and VVCF more than the CCC.

19. At the L&L some congregants use a form of the American sign language signs during the singing of some congregational songs. At times there will be a person or two on the platform along with the worship team 'leading' the signing (although most of the congregation does not sign along). Their flowing motions have a dance quality about them. Signing is a form of kinesthetic worship

praise. They sing the chosen songs with eagerness and enthusiasm. It appears, from the beginning of the service, that the whole of the embodied self is absorbed into the worship.

The worship team, the musicians who lead the singing (the 'worship') from the platform, to a large extent shape the tone and atmosphere of the rite. The selected music (songs), the order of the songs, the manner in which musicians play and spontaneously rearrange (or repeat) the songs moves the congregation into a progression of worship attitudes and modes of sensibility.[20] The musical context sets up a framework within which a range of expressions are deemed appropriate.

If the music begins, as it frequently does, with an upbeat, celebrative set of songs, the congregation may stand, clap, sign and dance as they sing their joyous chorus. In the wake of each song and before the team begins the next song, worshipers will often make spontaneous short verbal praises, such as 'Praise the Lord'. Sometimes the worship leader will pause between songs to allow the people to express verbal praises. The team may even signal the appropriateness of the moment by modeling verbal praises as they conclude a song. With eyes closed and hands lifted, members of the team may speak out phrases of praise, while other team members strum guitar chords, providing a kind of musical background to the emerging 'concert praise'. These moments of concert praise may persist a few seconds or extend for a couple of minutes. They usually adhere to certain patterns of phrases, though this certainly varies among individuals. Some may voice 'Thank you Jesus,' or 'Glory to God,' or 'Hallelujah'. Others pray their own spontaneous prayer/praise in more sentence forms: 'I thank you, Father, for your blessings on us this week.' Still others may employ glossolalia as praise. A single individual may incorporate a combination of all these forms. Simultaneously and together, each of the congregants voices his or her praises. During the most celebrative mode of the worship rite some even shout, others whisper, while most speak their prayers at a conversational level. This range of vocal prayers constitutes the cacophony of praise characteristic of the three churches.

Most often the celebratory praise moves toward, or alternates with, a more contemplative style of worship. The musical accompaniment of the team shifts, refocuses the style and content of the choruses and

expression at the L&L. It is not for the benefit of the deaf, as there are no deaf in the L&L congregation.

20. Ritual modes of sensibility will be discussed at length in Chapter 5.

modifies the verbal expression. The service progresses to a more meditative, reflective moment. The tone and the words of the songs help to move the worshipers into a more 'intimate communion'. This mode of worship appears to the outside observer in great contrast to the more outward, praise-filled, festive-type expressions that preceded it. Many of the same gestures and physical expressions, though toned down, continue in this contemplative mode. Appropriate verbalizations are now gently whispered.

Potentially, coupled with these moments of meditative worship, a range of other modes and attitude may emerge. For instance, a variety of verbal charisms, forms of mutual ministry, need sharing, testimonials and prayerful interacting may be expressed or enacted. Often people begin (usually with the direction of the worship leader) to pray for one another, particularly regarding a felt need. This can occur one on one or in small groups. At times, the leader will ask if someone has 'a word'.[21] Almost always an individual responds affirmatively to this. It may be a testimony from the week past, or an exhortation to the congregation. It might be seen as a prophetic word, or it might be a message in tongues and interpretation. Following this movement (progressive or alternating) of celebratory praise and contemplative worship with moments of word gifts, the service normally comes into a major transitional time where other rites are enacted. I will discuss them shortly, but now a few reflections on the rite of worship and praise.

The expressions of various ritual practices (and other cultural symbols) in a variety of configurations signal different sub-themes and dramatize different values and beliefs. But at the center of the variety exists the belief among the congregants that they are actually experiencing the presence of God in an intimate, immediate, mystical way. Such understanding grounds and propels the ritual expressions.

The salient belief that God by God's Spirit *acts, involves* and *concerns* God's self with the contemporary world and its people both within the church and in the workaday world underlies all the ritual expres-

---

21. 'Words' can be given spontaneously, without the leaders request, at the L&L. At the CCC they are seldom asked for, and occur almost always spontaneously, without any verbal directive from the worship leader, though members learn the 'appropriate' moments and signals for such words. At the VVCF spontaneous utterances directed to the whole congregation are never appropriate during the worship and praise rite. Individuals may, of course, make their own utterances (prayers) as a part of the concert praise.

sions. Furthermore, the assumption of Pentecostals that God acts in the human realm is not confined to their reading of the New Testament. They argue that God's actions are documented in their experience of the holy. Their experiences, they believe, mirror the kinds of experiences reported in the New Testament and reveal God's connection to and concern with people in the contemporary age.

Transitional Rites

A quiet pause after five to eight congregational choruses and songs commonly signals the conclusion of worship and praise rite. As a reflective mood pervades the sanctuary, the musicians gently put down their instruments, the vocalists of the worship team slowly back away from their microphones and the entire team slips out of sight. The congregation, many of whom have been standing, begins to sit as they realize that the rite of worship and praise, usually about 20–35 minutes, is now complete.

The first major transition of the service immediately follows the first primary rite (worship and praise). The transition may consist of several practices and microrites, thus I have called it the period of 'transitional rites'. Together, these transitional rites function to both connect and separate the first primary rite (rite of worship and praise) and the second primary rite (the pastoral message). This period is an 'in between time', a time when there is a pause in 'the action'. The first rite is emotionally engaging and highly participatory. It is intense, as can be the rite of pastoral message to come. The ritual pause inherent in the transitional practices allows a certain amount of relaxation among the congregants.[22] Both the first and second primary rites are taut, like the tension on a bowstring, but in the transitional rites the tension is relaxed, the string of the ritual is loosened. The potent drama of the ritual gives way to more commonplace things, practices I have called, the pastoral 'bridge' prayer, pastoral 'warm-up', congregational 'business', and musical presentations.

When the worship team leaves the platform, the pastor, usually the

---

22. See Gary B. McGee, 'Leaving Room for Sacred Pauses', *Advance* 28 (January 1992), pp. 8-9. McGee, a Pentecostal historian, addresses the need for what he calls 'sacred pause' in the Pentecostal ritual. He implies that the pause, I am calling the transitional time, is not adequate. He argues that the influence of the neo-Pentecostal worship has created a tightly fitted series of worship choruses that lack pauses for reflections and potential gift ministries.

senior pastor, makes his first official appearance.[23] He comes to help mark the end of the first phase and to bridge into the next.[24] Often in a conversational tone, he will begin to 'just talk' with the congregation. Moving away from the pulpit and sometimes off the platform, he engages them in a 'conversation' (they may or may not actually speak back). Frequently, the conversation draws from a symbol in the worship and praise time, just completed. Perhaps, he uses a phase from the previous song as a symbol to connect an event from the past week (possibly a current international, national or local event) to the liturgy. Often, symbols and concepts raised by the pastor give a hint of his message to come (in the next rite).

The pastor will normally lead in a time of prayer during these transitional rites. The prayer may follow immediately upon the completion of the rite of worship and praise or may follow his time of 'conversation' with the congregation. And though he will typically shape the structure and style in which the prayer will be prayed, it need not be a 'solo' prayer (e.g. the pastor doing all the vocal praying). He might, following a time of prayer requests, ask others to lead out in prayer, or he might involve the entire congregation in praying for one another, in circles, small groups or pairs. Often a time of petitionary prayer transpires.

Another set of practices typical to all three of our churches during these transitional rites is what I call 'congregational business'. Of course, there is an offering, a collection taken,[25] and at some time during this transition announcements of coming congregational events are either pointed out to be read in the bulletin (given by the official greeters) or are announced by a congregational leader who has particular interest in the event. Sometimes the announcements take the form of a testimony, giving personal reason, for example, why men should come to the upcoming men's retreat based on what personal spiritual value the retreat has to the speaker. Other testimonials, not connected to announcements, may be given during this time period. These testimonies

---

23. At the L&L and VVCF the senior pastors sit with the congregation during the rite of worship and praise; there are no chairs on their platforms. At the CCC, however, the whole pastoral staff sits on the platform through the service. Thus, at the CCC the senior pastor is visible during the first rite.

24. The use of the masculine personal pronoun, here, and subsequently, reflects the fact that in all three of these churches the *senior* pastor is male.

25. We have noted above the differences in offering taking among the three churches.

may be more formal, somewhat prepared and by request of the pastor, or they may be spontaneous and extemporaneous.

The transitional rites have traditionally included musical presentations, vocal and instrumental 'special music'. At times these presentations are made during the offering and/or they immediately preceded the pastor's sermon.[26] When the pastor returns to the pulpit after such a musical presentation, or following an announcement or a testimonial, this signals the completion of the transition and the beginning of second primary rite.

The Rite of the Pastoral Message and other Speech Acts as Rites
Preaching: From focal point to partner. Some evidence suggests that the earliest Pentecostals of this century valued the rites of praise and worship equally with the sermon.[27] However, the apparent influence of much of the Evangelical tradition and that of the tradition of American frontier liturgical format of 'preliminaries' and then the sermon as the main event had an effect on the typical Pentecostal service during the middle decades of the twentieth century. The neo-Pentecostal influences upon the ritual in general have been felt during the 1960s and subsequently. While preaching remains *a* focal point in the service (not *the* focal point), the renewed emphasis on the 'worship' (with its revitalized neo-Pentecostal forms) and a subtle rejection of the term 'preliminaries', symbolizes the revaluing of the rite of worship and praise. The worship and praise rite then has become a primary rite, just as preaching is a primary rite. In the three churches, no longer is the 'song service' merely 'preliminaries' and subservient to a sermon.

In these three churches today the role of the rite of pastoral message within the overall ritual process compares to that of partnership. The pastor's message unites with the rites of worship and praise and altar/

26. 'Special music' presented to the congregation reflects a part of the older Pentecostal tradition of transitions. It always plays a part of the transitional rites at the CCC and is almost never incorporated into the rite at the L&L or VVCF.

27. See Roger G. Robins, 'The Rule of the Holy Spirit in Early Pentecostalism: Order in the Courts', an unpublished paper presented to the Sixteenth Annual Meeting of the Society for Pentecostal Studies, 13–15 November 1986, at Southern California College, Costa Mesa, California; and early accounts of the Azusa Street revival, Bartleman, *Azusa Street*; Fred T. Corum (ed.), *Like as of Fire* (Wilmington, MA: Fred Corum, n.d.) (reprints of *The Apostolic Faith*, paper of the Azusa Street Revival).

response. One might say that the three are co-equal in the liturgies. Each has value, each has legitimacy and involves expression to God and edification for the congregation. In other words, the preaching/ teaching cannot be regarded as the sole or even most important reason for the service.[28] Thus, instead of the singular focus of the service being the preaching, in all three of the churches, and especially the L&L and VVCF, the two newer churches, the preaching functions in equal part- nership with the worship and praise rites and altar rites.[29]

One aspect of the partnership necessitates the obvious coupling between the sermon and the altar/response. The rites of the pastoral message and the altar/response equally provide a context for the divine– human interaction. The pastoral message is seen as word of God and the rite of altar/response is the congregation's opportunity to respond in a focused way to that word. These two fundamental rites serve as macro (speech) acts, one a word from God the other a 'word' (action) from the congregation. This interchange is analogous to the divine–human inter- action of the rite of worship and praise. However, the dimensions or duration of the interaction embody a primary difference. In the rite of worship and praise there is a frequent alternation between the inter- locutors, while in pastoral message as a kind of focused macro 'divine' speech act one expects macro (congregational) human response. These two 'words' comprise one complete interchange. In this way, the pas- toral message and the altar/response are related. Together, they are linked to the rite of worship and praise in the overall 'conversation', of the ritual process as structured by the foundational/processual rites.

Characteristics of the pastoral message rite. The three churches share at least three important characteristics within the pastoral message rite. First, it expresses the world view of the congregation, that is, the mes- sage helps, in all three of the churches, to give voice to a common definition of the 'things that matter most'.[30]

---

28. This is demonstrated in some services being designated as a 'worship and praise service'. In such a service little or no preaching is required. To come together to 'worship' is seen as valid even without the rite of preaching.

29. There are in these churches three foci in a typical service, not one focal point.

30. Margaret M. Poloma cites fellow sociologist Meredith McGuire, who asserts from her first-hand analysis that the prophetic (e.g. pastoral message) 'is significant in developing and maintaining a common definition of the situation' in neo-

Secondly, the preaching enables a 're-experiencing of a biblical text'.[31] Nearly all sermons, in all three churches, are rooted in biblical texts, but the text seldom comes across as merely a past event. Current application holds primacy over its historical significance. Each of our three pastors attempts to guide his congregation to a reappropriation of the text in a way that suggests an immediate meaning of the biblical text. This facilitates the experiential dimension of the worship service and seeks to send the ritualist into the world with an experience of a text that will continue to affect their life, ethics and world view.

A third characteristic of the rite of pastoral message identifies it as a prophetic pronouncement, directed and empowered by the Holy Spirit.[32] Here, I use the term 'prophetic' in the sense of speaking God's word to others. While the preaching/teaching style varies among the three pastors, in each case the pastoral message presumably 'comes from God'.[33] Consequently, these three congregations spend a considerable amount of time on this rite.[34] And in most cases they are highly engaged in and attentive to the rite, which attests to the message's prophetic appeal.

Other speech acts as rites. The prophetic dimension is integral to the Pentecostal ritual and its spirituality. Often, Pentecostals are as anxious

Pentecostal settings (Poloma, *Crossroads*, p. 193). See also McGuire, *Pentecostal Catholics*, pp. 93-105.

31. Following Paul Ricoeur, Joseph Byrd describes the hermeneutical concept of 're-experiencing a text'. Byrd suggests that the Pentecostal preacher facilitates a re-experiencing of a biblical text by reaching for an immediate experience for their listeners ('Paul Ricoeur's Hermeneutical Theory and Pentecostal Proclamation', *Pneuma* 15 [Autumn 1993]). See also Joseph Byrd, 'Formulation of a Classical Pentecostal Homiletic in Dialogue with Contemporary Protestant Homiletics' (PhD dissertation, Southern Baptist Theological Seminary, 1990).

32. See Ray H. Hughes, 'Preaching: A Pentecostal Perspective', in *DPCM*, pp. 722-24. Another often used term in our three churches, especially the VVCF, is 'anointed'. This can be applied to preaching (i.e. 'anointed preaching'). This designates preaching that goes beyond learned biblical study and exposition. It refers to the dimension of the Spirit and the recognized influence of the Spirit on the messenger, the message and the audience.

33. This does not mean that the congregation receives the message uncritically. Members check their Bibles and their understanding of the tradition to measure the pastor's words. But in the end, most of the time, they agree that it is 'the word'.

34. In each of the three churches the amount of time given to the sermon is longer than most non-Pentecostal churches. At the CCC and L&L an average length is 30–40 minutes, while at the VVCF it is often a little longer.

to speak for God as they are to hear from God. They practice their message-giving on one another. The sermon represents only one instance of message-giving in the ritual, albeit the most extended and most exclusive.[35] Less extended and exclusive speech acts, acts of communication, also function as (micro)rites with a prophetic dimension within the Pentecostal ritual. Testimonials, sharings, exhortations, sacred expletive, oral prayer, prophetic speech, other charismatic utterances, even quasi- or non-language 'speech', such as shouts, are available, open to all members as acts of communicating with the congregation. These speech acts function as rites within the overall ritual and together with the sermon they not only give voice to their God and to God's people, they work to seal congregational commitment to the divine and to the faith community.[36]

The Rite of Altar/Response

'The altar/response' constitutes the third primary, foundational/processual rite. I have chosen this combined term to reflect both the tradition of the 'altar call' and the explicit focus on congregational response typically apparent in all three churches during the last section of the Sunday ritual.[37] This final foundational and primary practice fundamentally functions as a rite that calls for an explicit response.[38] The main structure and tenor of the response is most often determined by the senior

35. Preaching in these three churches is the most exclusive speech act or means of communication in the ritual. Most other forms of communication in the rites are more democratic, open to all congregants. However, the sermon remains limited to the pastor or his chosen representative (often a guest speaker or an elder in the congregation).

36. Because many of the speech acts have a recognizable pattern (i.e. they represent a genre) and fit the definition of rites, the community encourages them as practices that add to the overall ritual. They all function to shape and sustain the faith community as acts of intensification and of commitment. See Bellah *et al.*, *Habits*, for a discussion of acts or 'practices of commitment' and their function within a community (*Habits* throughout, esp., pp. 154, 157, 251-52).

37. Though the extended form of the altar/response occurs in the Sunday morning services in all three of our churches, it commonly occurs in the Sunday evening service at the VVCF and CCC.

38. Within the rite of altar/response numerous other rites maybe incorporated. For example, rites of healing, possession rites (see Grimes, *Ritual Criticism*, p. 236) and rites of passage and intensification are all common within the altar/response.

pastor.[39] At the conclusion of the preaching, frequently after a brief 'transition,'[40] the pastor calls for some kind of response from members of the congregation.[41] The requested response usually focuses on a specific point of the pastoral message or on a more general topic or need. Or, given the opportunity, parishioners may respond to a particular inner 'prompting of the Spirit' that they individually sense. Alternatively, they may be 'moved' by a charismatic word shared by a congregant. In all cases, the rite depends on acts of response by ritualists, facilitated by the pastor.

Forms of the rite of altar/response. Classical Pentecostals have not only used the altar as a symbol of the place of initial conversion as did the revivalist, but they have followed their Wesleyan–holiness forebears who sought to use the altar as a place for the sacrifices of prayers, (various) life commitments and reorientation, and a waiting on mystical experiences.[42] The Pentecostal rites show clearly the incorporation with adaptation of each of these forms of altar/response. These Pent/Char responses, centered in the imagery of the altar, may suggest a Pentecostal propensity for creativity, adaptation and for employing a range of responses.[43]

39. Even when the senior pastor does not give the pastoral message, for example, on the occasion of a guest speaker, the pastor will normally conduct the rite of altar/response. The 'guest' preacher will finish their sermon and 'turn it back' to the pastor. The pastor will then proceed with the altar rite as he or she determines.

40. This transition may be nothing more than a short prayer, organ interlude or a congregational hymn. A congregational member may verbalize a charismatic word.

41. Of course, this too fulfills a part of the American Protestant revivalistic Evangelical heritage. 'Altar calls' have been developed to an 'art form' within the Evangelical tradition, but Pentecostals have adapted them to their own purposes. Contemporary Pentecostal adaptations of the Evangelical altar call (and the earlier 'Pentecostalization' of the rite) include a variety of responses to felt needs which represent an opportunity for 'ministry' characterized by various prayer and healing rites.

42. In the American Wesleyan–holiness tradition the most typical mystical experience at the altar was called variously 'entire sanctification', 'second work of grace', 'Christian perfection', 'holiness' and 'pure love'.

Within this tradition, Phoebe Palmer's nineteenth-century, Methodist-revivalist 'altar theology' helped to pave the way for the Pentecostal adaptations that would follow. See Charles E. White, 'Phoebe Worrall Palmer', in *DCA*, pp. 860-61.

43. The breadth of responses indicates the openness of these Pentecostals to the state of the human conditions as they see it. They recognize and seek to address

I have recognized a variety of forms of altar/response rites in my field research.[44] There are both abbreviated and extended forms.[45] The abbreviated form includes a simple benediction, a pastoral prayer (either a general prayer or a specific prayer, e.g. with a call for hands, then a concluding prayer) or a congregant 'closes in prayer'. The extended altar/response forms fit into three overlapping categories, first, various altar calls that function as rites of passage and/or rites of intensification (e.g. calls for conversion, for Christian recommitment or dedication, for Spirit baptism).[46]

through many different methods and styles of 'ministry', the need of the congregation and of humanity in general. Implicit in the responses is a belief that support and help are needed and available within the rite.

44. In addition to the 'forms' and styles of altar/response rites, I have observed a variety of modes of sensibility that oriented these different forms of the rite. In the next chapter I will discuss, more directly and in greater detail, Pent/Char ritual modes of sensibility and their role in the liturgy and general spirituality. Here, I only wish to note that the rite of altar/response, in its various forms, may be oriented by numerous modes, each one potentially affecting the tenor of the rite. I have often observed, for example, a dominant contemplative sensibility in the CCC altar times, though I have seen celebrative, ceremonial and improvisational sensibilities (and a combination of these together) in evidence too. The ritual mode of sensibility most frequently observed at the VVCF altar/response rites appears as a transcendental efficacy that specifically orients their rites of healing toward a pragmatic end. Whereas the abbreviated forms of altar/response typical of the L&L are often infused with a penitent mode of sensibility, particularly when the pastor calls for conversions to Christ.

45. Altar/response rites not only vary considerably among the three congregations, they vary weekly within the same church. The VVCF tends to have a lengthy response even in Sunday morning service. Their rite of altar/response is seen primarily as a time of 'ministry', often involving elaborate healing rites. On the other hand the L&L and CCC frequently have an abbreviated altar/response, sometimes only a benediction. When this is the case, the altar/response functions at an earlier time of the service. Often it is incorporated into the rite of worship and praise. The sequence is not sacrosanct for either of these two churches. The VVCF's altar/responses is sequentially more set than it is in the other two churches. While variations exist within the altar rite itself at the VVCF, sometimes emphasizing healing, other times focusing on charismatic 'words', the altar time always acts as a 'finale' for the service.

46. The symbol of the altar represents a sacred space where certain rites of passages are accomplished. For instance, it was a place of 'tarrying' in the holiness heritage. The Pentecostals have used it as a tarrying place for the baptism in the Holy Spirit or as a place of prayer for a recommitment, a deepening of one's faith

General times of prayer 'around the altars' signify a second category of extended altar/responses. This category normally involves most or a sizeable minority of the congregation. This rite includes a level of intensification for individuals who participate, congregants recognize it very much as a social gathering, a time of corporate prayer. As ritualists meet together around the altars for prayer they demonstrate their common commitment to God and one another. They exhibit a rite of solidarity.

Rites of ministry and healing comprise the third category of extended altar/response. These too may take a variety of forms (e.g. various healing rites and ways of praying for needs), but the rites of ministry explicitly aim at ministering to and praying for felt needs (e.g. physical, emotional, spiritual, relational, even financial) that congregants and visitors present. No felt need seems to be out of bounds during this ministry time, when Pentecostal ritualists minister in prayer to one another.[47]

This form of the altar rite (i.e. ministry/healing centered), particularly at the VVCF, has an empowering effect. From the time of the transition following the pastoral message, expectations rise. The service moves towards its climax. The congregation, looks for direction from the pastor with anxious anticipation. He gives the call and people respond, they come forward for healing. Healing teams quickly follow and begin to minister the rites. Among the watching congregation, the healing team members and the church members being prayed for, expectations remain high. One 25-year-old man commented following a healing service at the VVCF,

> When I've been prayed for at other churches, they just prayed and sent me on my way. I don't think they really expected anything to happen.

life, or a place and time to be prayed for by others for healing or other life issues (see below). In each case the altar space symbolizes the place of transformation (and intensification), and the rite, acted out in sincerity, accomplishes the transformation.

47. For a sociological look at contemporary healing rites, 'alternative healing' methods, and particularly Pent/Char healing rites as a more holistic orientation to healing (in contrast to the 'disease orientation of modern medicine'), see McGuire, *Ritual Healing*. McGuire recognizes in the alternative healing rites meaning-producing qualities generally absent in the medical model. She also demonstrates the sense of order and empowerment that can be the result of the rites. Her findings are generally consistent with my own.

> But at the Vineyard, when they pray for you, say for healing, they really
> expect something to happen. They ask you if something is happening.
> They'll keep on praying and interviewing you. They expect healing.

These remarks imply, along with the sense of expectation, a sense of empowerment. The altar rites that I observed seemed often to empower the ritualists. The empowerment influences the sense of divine participation in the rites. Also ritualists associate it with the renewed sense of meaning generated by the participation in the rite. The sense of meaning helps to shape and give order to the spirituality of the ritualists, those who come to be prayed for, and those who perform the rites of healing. The congregation similarly benefits as they too join in prayer.

Understanding the altar rites. The altar/response rites in their various forms among these three churches are fundamentally symbols of responsiveness to God, and of solidarity among congregants. As I have indicated, the Pentecostal service is not only about God, it attempts an interaction with God. The altar/response rites clearly indicate this desired interchange. Whether a healing rite, for example, during which the ritualist hopes for a divine 'touch', or whether a rite of intensification encouraging a response to God with a renewed life consecration, or a general prayer time around the altars, in the altar rites the Pent/Char ritualists seek to respond to and thus interact with the divine.

On the other hand, these altar rites also allow an opportunity for congregational commitment to one another, to the community. The openness and responsiveness of the congregants to their God, often reflects an open sensitivity to each other. Many altar times fundamentally signify a praying for and ministering to each other, ritualist to ritualist, in an egalitarian fashion. Owing to the common forms, levels of commitment, similar expectations and mutual participation a sense of solidarity occurs in the midst of and following the altar/response.[48]

Transition, farewells and dispersing. The final transition in the Pent/ Char liturgy follows the altar/response and actually serves to conclude

---

48. The altar/response is one example of a Pent/Char rite whose consequence is social (communal) solidarity. Donald Gelpi reflects on an analogous idea when he argues, that a function of Spirit baptism is 'its ability to bind Christians together in a charismatic community of mutual service' (*The Divine Mother: A Trinitarian Theology of the Holy Spirit* [Lanham, MD: University Press of America, 1984]).

the service formally. Often a pastor prays a brief prayer of benediction.[49] At the CCC the conclusion entails almost always the final phrases of the Lord's prayer, sung victoriously with full organ accompaniment, 'For thine is the kingdom and the power and the glory forever. Amen'. With the last note of the 'Amen' congregants begin to disperse.

In all three of the congregations, following the formal ending of the liturgy, people begin rather lengthy sets of farewell and dispersing rites. While many exit the sanctuary after only bidding farewell to a few of their fellow congregants, possibly one-half of the people seem in no hurry.[50] They cluster together in the aisles, the back of the sanctuary, the foyer and the parking lot and begin animated conversations with friends. (Some pause to pray, laying a hand on the other's shoulder, bowing their heads and softly speaking a petition for a 'brother' or 'sister'). These dispersing practices may continue for 10–20 minutes, while children appear from their Sunday school and Children's church services. Kids begin to play, run around outside and sometimes even in the sanctuary (the sacred space has become mundane again, even the kids know it) as their parents 'fellowship'. These farewell and dispersing practices round out the ritual, a ritual performed with God by a community of persons linked in a common spirituality.

Having considered the foundational/processual rites with many of the attending microrites, I now turn our focus to one set of microrites that are particularly characteristic of the Pentecostal ritual and its supporting spirituality, the charismatic rites.

49. A pastoral 'commissioning to the world' often marks the conclusion of the services at the L&L. Pastor Markowitz may, for example, exhort or remind his congregation of the responsibility to the world, 'take the good news you have experienced here and share it with those in need'. The formal end of the VVCF is often a very unceremonious announcement (e.g. 'don't forget tonight [referring to the evening service], we'll see you then').

50. Though there are variations among the three Sea City churches, due to the physical arrangements of each of the buildings and the 'congregational personality' unique to each, the time spent and gestures show similarity among the three.

The Charismatic Rites

'Charismatic' and 'charismatic rite' are slippery terms. The words 'charismatic' and 'charisma' can have a variety of connotations among Pentecostals. So, when using charismatic to classify various rites, I admit that it is not a fixed category. Rather, here I will use the term 'charismatic rite' descriptively and heuristically. The Greek word *charismata* as used in the New Testament connotes graces, favors or gifts. It was of course introduced in its singular form *charisma*, into the social sciences by Max Weber and has been used in popular English parlance as well.[51] Pentecostals, however, most often refer to the category of *charismata* as 'gifts of the Spirit'. Though they derive their understanding of gifts of the Spirit from numerous biblical texts, the most basic understanding of the *charismata* comes from the Pauline list of charismata given in 1 Cor. 12.1-11. This text with subsequent verses sketches what have been called by Pentecostals 'the nine gifts of the Spirit', word of wisdom, word of knowledge, faith, healing(s), miracles, prophecy, discernment of spirits, tongues and interpretation of tongues.[52]

While the Pauline text speaks of 'workings' (*energemata*) of the Spirit, for example, 1 Cor. 12.6, and the Pentecostals in the three churches speak of 'manifestations of' or 'operations of' the gifts of the Spirit, neither Paul nor these Pentecostal congregants use the term 'rites' of the Spirit or 'charismatic rites'. So why did I choose this term? Because, in my view, the understanding, experience and expression of the *charismata* in these three churches fit within the overall definition of rites, 'practices widely recognized, sanctioned, and handed down by the faith community'. While some variation exists between the three churches, each congregation recognizes certain charismatic practices as legitimate

---

51. For a brief but insightful description of the variety of connotations of *charisma* see McGuire, *Pentecostal Catholics*, pp. 43-48.

52. I have greatly simplified the discussion here. I do not intend to enter in to a detailed analysis of the charisms, nor, even to discuss the charisms in general as they relate to Pentecostalism. Rather, I aim to present a preliminary and foundational classification of the charisms as experienced and expressed in the Pent/Char liturgies of our three churches.

For examples of Pentecostal and Charismatic theological constructs of the charisms, see Gelpi, *Charism and Sacrament*, and *idem, Committed Worship*. For a brief explanation, see J. Ramsey Michaels, 'Gifts of the Spirit', in *DPCM*, pp. 332-34; also, in *DPCM*, see articles on each of the Pauline charisms.

within the context of liturgical ritual. Generally, congregants perceive these charismatic rites as an especially appropriate part of particular foundational rites. For instance, quiet tongues speech is appropriate during corporate prayer within the rite of worship and praise in all three churches. Or, at the VVCF, congregants expectantly hoped for discernment and word of knowledge, especially in the healing rites that are a part of the rite of altar/response.

To understand the charismatic rites within the Pent/Char ritual better, here, I will consider first a classification of the charismatic rites and second, criteria with which the congregations assess a rite as charismatic or not.

A Classification of the Charismatic Rites

Our field research has lead us to conceive of the charismatic rites as expressed in the three churches in five basic categories, charismatic speech acts, insights, actions, demonstrations and improvisations. Here I will briefly sketch the contours of these categories with some examples of the rites within each category.

Charismatic speech acts. In classical Pentecostal congregations, such as the CCC, charismatic speech acts often are referred to as 'utterances' (e.g. an 'utterance in tongues'). In neo-Pentecostal congregations the generic term 'words' are understood as several kinds of charismatic speech acts. For example, a liturgical leader in a L&L service asked on one occasion, 'Does anyone have a *word* for us at this time?' This use of the term 'word' normally means a charismatic speech act. In this case the speech acts that were considered appropriate were those recognized as a 'prophetic word', 'a message in tongues' (and an interpretation of the message), a 'word of wisdom' or a 'word of knowledge'. All of these, though seldom distinguished from one another (except for tongues), other than the generic 'word', are believed to be Pauline charisms. I classify other speech acts as potentially charismatic rites.[53] They include concert or individual praise, sacred explicative, concert or individual intercessory/petitionary prayer, exhortations, testimonies, messages and sermons.

---

53. I use the term 'potentially' because the following speech acts, though in most cases are recognized as legitimate in the liturgy in all three of the churches, they are not in every case perceived to be charismatic. Shortly, I will discuss the perceptions of rites as charismatic or not.

Charismatic insights. These connect most often to some other charismatic rite, especially an action. For example, at the VVCF the gifts of discernment, knowledge and wisdom typically function as rites linked to their healing rites. Those praying often hope to discern clearly the needs of the person being prayed for. Reports not uncommon at the VVCF claim incidents of 'supernatural knowledge' and insightful wisdom from the Holy Spirit concerning persons' lives and needs during healing rites. This seems also relatively common in the home fellowship meetings of the VVCF and to a more limited extent in some of the home groups at the CCC. In the home groups these rites of charismatic insight subsist loosely tied to healing rites. They may occur as a part of simply 'praying for one another'.

Charismatic actions and behaviors. These may include the rites connected to prayers for healing (e.g. laying on of hands, anointing with oil, holding hands, reaching out toward one in need) and to other behaviors that are often recognized as charismatic. Behaviors and gestures that are potentially regarded as charismatic include standing, kneeling, bowing, swaying, hopping, jumping, dancing, signing (like sign language), 'praise offering' (applause), 'falling in the Spirit'.

Charismatic demonstrations. I call the perceived (supernatural) 'workings' (*energemata*) of the Spirit 'charismatic demonstrations'. By that I mean those manifestations that the congregation assigns as clearly supernatural (to them), such as 'working of miracles' or what is often generically referred to as 'signs and wonders'. Most of these designate healings that are determined to be divine in origin. Members of the VVCF especially seek to be involved in these types of charismatic demonstrations. They believe that such demonstrations are manifestations of the power of God that will help to convince non-believers.

Charismatic improvizations. Technically, what I am calling 'charismatic improvizations' do not pertain to rites. While a rite embodies a recognizable form of an act, a practice that is known to the congregation, a charismatic improvisation is sometimes a spontaneous innovation to a recognized rite.[54] Such an act might be called a quasi- or pre-rite, having not yet attained a recognized form. The 'rite' of charismatic

---

54. For a discussion of an analogous concept that Grimes calls 'ritualizing', see Grimes, *Beginnings*, pp. 55-56; and *idem*, *Ritual Criticism*, pp. 9-11.

improvisation can innovate on an already recognized charismatic rite (e.g. individual tongues speech becomes congregational tongues singing) or the innovation itself might be perceived as a charismatic impulse (i.e. 'a prompting by the Spirit'), in which case, even if the rite that sustained the innovation was not at the beginning a charismatic rite, by nature of the 'charismatic' improvisation the rite becomes charismatic. For example, liturgical dance becomes a charismatic rite when the dancers sense the impulse of the Spirit and the congregation recognizes the 'touch of the Spirit' upon the dance. The dynamics of charismatic improvisations suggest that the boundary between rites considered charismatic and those believed not is flexible and not always clear-cut.

Charismatic Criteria

My field research leads me to believe that a number of practices can be perceived as 'more or less' charismatic. Some explicit, implicit and intuitive criteria provide foundation to the judgment of the congregation. I have attempted to sort out through participant observation, questioning, interviewing and dialogue with congregants, the main criteria for determining a rite's charismatic nature. While variation emerges between the three congregations, and no doubt among individuals within each church, it seems clear that each of the three congregations employs the following criteria when recognizing a practice as 'charismatic'.

A speech act, insight, action, demonstration or improvisation may be considered a 'charismatic' rite if it (to some extent) fulfills the following conditions:

1. It is *'in line' with Scripture*, that is, both its form and its content must not violate the Bible. If the form is thought to be a manifestation of a biblical charism, it can be accepted as charismatic. A charismatic rite by definition must be recognizable, although an adaptation and/or an innovation in the forms. Once perceived by the congregation, for example, to be one of the Pauline charisms, it is then charismatic. But more important than a biblical form is a biblical content. Minimally, a charismatic utterance must not violate or conflict with the community's understanding of the Scripture if it is to be seen as authentically charismatic.

2. It is seen as a result of a *direct impulse of the Spirit*, that is, that at least one member of the congregation senses a stimulus

that they understand to be from the Spirit and acts upon it.[55]

3. It is perceived by the congregation as an act *deriving from the Spirit* (i.e. the act has a discernable 'supernatural' origin, it is beyond the natural).

4. It is an act that is recognized by the congregation as a manifestation *by one who is at the time 'in the Spirit'*. When the person is recognized as 'in the Spirit' or 'anointed' then their acts are considered charismatic.

5. It, by its nature or manifestation, *heightens the sense or awareness of the Spirit's presence*.

6. If a respected spiritual leader, one who exercises wisdom and practices spiritual discernment (e.g. the pastor) gives a signal that authenticates a charismatic act, congregants will be strongly influenced toward recognizing the rite as charismatic.[56]

Any one of these criteria can authenticate an act as charismatic. When more than one criterion functions (successfully applied) then the recognition of the rite as charismatic is even more assured.

Charismatic rites are important to our congregations, in part because they are thought to reflect the actions of God. Several ritualists recognize one ritualist performing a charismatic rite, the performer to some extent reflects the divine. Thus, a charismatic speech act manifests God's word, charismatic insight sees through God's eyes, charismatic actions manifest the movements of God and charismatic demonstrations (e.g. 'working of miracles') equal God working God's wonders. Charismatic rites make up an important piece of the Pentecostal puzzle I call Pent/Char spirituality. They demonstrate, as do other dimensions of the ritual, a high regard for the recognition of and participation in what is believed to be the immediate presence and actions of Holy.

To summarize, I have considered the procession of the typical ritual of the three Sea City churches. I have shown how the three primary rites together with the transitional rites (and the gathering and dispersing practices) make up what I have described as the foundational/

---

55. Numbers 2 through 5 are in some way connected to what I have called below an ecstatic mode of sensibility. Here, suffice it to say that, if the congregation recognizes a practice or rite as performed with an ecstatic sensibility, the congregation may more readily recognize the rite as charismatic. See Chapter 5 for a discussion of the Pent/Char ritual mode of ecstacy.

56. For a fine extended treatment of 'Pentecostal discernment', see Parker, *Led by the Spirit*.

processual rites. These rites give the ritual its fundamental structure. This fundamental structure serves as a framework within which the microrites emerge spontaneously or intentionally. In either case, a variety of microrites configure to give the ritual its internal shape. Consequently, the multitude of potential component practices, gestures, acts and actions (i.e., the microrites), fitted within the fundamental structure (i.e., the foundational/processual rites), help to account for the perception of the ritual as flexible, and for the sensation of freedom. (Two characteristics valued in Pentecostal spirituality.) The microrites are not mere 'seasoning' that stimulate the Pentecostal tastes and senses. Instead, the microrites together in their various assortments and configurations provide the basic ingredients that make up Pentecostalism, even as they constitute the elements of the liturgy.

Erving Goffman has called the service as a whole a 'focused gathering', that is, a gathering in which 'a set of persons engrossed in a common flow of activity and relating to one another in terms of that flow', enact the rites.[57] In such a ritual gathering a fundamental dramatization occurs in which the Pentecostal ritualists form and discover their own temperament and spirituality, individually and corporately, at the same time.[58] The 'common flow' that Goffman portrays is in the Pentecostal service a result of the common participation in the configuration of rites, but the rites are shaped not only by structural patterns, but they become fundamentally oriented and animated by certain modes of sensibility. I am now ready to consider these Pent/Char ritual modes of sensibility.

57. Cited in Geertz, *Interpretation of Cultures*, p. 424.

58. See Geertz, *Interpretation of Cultures*, pp. 437, 451. Geertz attempts to demonstrate that such rituals are shaped by and shape the enactor and enable the ritualist to 'see his own subjectivity'; as a result of the ritual participation, ritual, he asserts, 'opens his subjectivity to himself' (p. 450).

Chapter 5

MODES OF PENTECOSTAL RITUAL SENSIBILITY

As I prepare to introduce the modes of Pentecostal sensibility, let me retrace my steps to this point. I began my investigation by considering some of the contexts, within which Pentecostalism has emerged. I sketched the origins and development of the twentieth-century America Pentecostal movement and surveyed three denominations that emerged within the movement. I then narrowed the scope to consider the three specific Sea City congregations in which I did my field research. In Chapter 3 I described some of the significant elements and dynamics of the ritual field that frame and participate in the experience of the ritual. I focused upon six chosen components of the ritual field: time, space, identity, sight, sounds and movement. Then in Chapter 4 I described the typical liturgical structure and process of the three Sea City churches. I located what I called the foundational/processual rites and I highlighted some of the component rites, which I named 'microrites', giving special attention to the charismatic rites. These rites together constitute the complete ritual.

I focus in this chapter on Pentecostal ritual *modes of sensibility*.[1] As *embodied attitudes*, the modes of ritual sensibility help orient and animate each of the various Pent/Char rites, actions and acts, including the charismata, within the Pentecostal ritual. Within Pentecostal ritual (and probably within other Christian ritual expressions), the rites, as structural and processual practices, help to provide the dimension of organizational design to the liturgy. However, the embodied attitudes, ritual sensibilities, are not only important to the general success of the ritual,

---

1. By 'sensibility' I mean an embodied attitude that is the result of abilities to feel or perceive, as in a receptiveness to impression or an affective responsiveness toward something. Ritual sensibilities both orient and animate a spirituality's beliefs and practices. My understanding of sensibility overlaps Steven Land's category of 'Pentecostal Affections' (see his *Pentecostal Spirituality*, esp. ch. 3).

they are particularly responsible for helping to animate the rites. It is through the modes of ritual sensibilities that the Pentecostal practices are enacted and experienced.[2] The realm of ritual sensibilities has often been neglected in the analysis of ritual, causing one leading ritologist recently to 'call' for studies that would treat the embodied attitudes of ritualists with the care this dimension of ritual deserves.[3] In my investigation of ritual sensibility, I have conceived of this ritual dimension as related to, though not necessarily contained within, the structure of the rites. I believe that the modes of ritual sensibility interact with the rites, that is, a dynamic affect mediates between the acts and the attitudes, the rites and the sensibilities. In this chapter I will build upon a structural/ processual understanding of the Pentecostal rites found in the previous

2.   Donald Gelpi has noted that one of the difficulties of liturgical reform has been that, while concerned church leaders have done a service for the church in revising, restructuring and rearranging the rites, liturgies in local parishes are not routinely vitalized by reforms. 'Liturgical renewal requires much more than ritual reform' (Gelpi, *Committed Worship*, ch. 1). Gelpi asserts that, in addition to the need of ritual revisions, there is a fundamental need for conversion. In other words, to revitalize the ritual the people themselves need to participate in a revitalizing process. Gelpi's comprehensive construct for the dimensions and dynamic of the human conversion process deserves careful consideration by those interested in ritual performance and reform. Here, I only raise the issue of conversion to suggest the link between the dimensions of conversion (e.g. affective, intellectual, moral, religious, sociopolitical) and the modes of sensibility in the Pentecostal ritual. In this chapter, I will propose that the Pentecostal rites and practices as presented in Chapter 4 are animated by particular embodied attitudes. These human sensibilities are greatly affected by the conversion process as Gelpi conceives it. Consequently, the vitality of the Pentecostal (and certainly other religious traditions) ritual is directly impacted not only by the modes of sensibility, as I will present in this chapter, but by the dynamics of the conversion process that shapes the sensibilities. See Donald L. Gelpi, 'The Liturgical Reforms of Vatican II: The Unfinished Revolution', in *idem, Grace as Transmuted Experience and Social Process, and Other Essays in North American Theology* (Lanham, MD: University Press of America, 1988), pp. 141-67; *idem, Committed Worship*. For a concise presentation of Gelpi's construct of conversion see 'Personal and Political Conversion: Foundations for a Theology of Liberation', in *idem, Grace as Transmuted Experience*, pp. 97-139; for a more exhaustive treatment, see his *Experiencing God*.

3.   Ronald Grimes asserts that 'there is a pressing need in ritual studies for a set of distinctions among types of ritual sensibility. The usual distinctions...are insufficient.' Grimes believes that the distinctions made among rituals should be attentive to the 'sensibilities or embodied attitudes that may arise in the course of a ritual' (*Beginnings*, p. 36).

chapter as I seek to clarify the modes of ritual sensibility most prevalent in the rituals of the three Pent/Char Sea City churches.[4]

From my fieldwork and subsequent analysis, I have identified at least seven modes or ideal types of ritual sensibility that pervade Pentecostal services.[5] Even a cursory look at these seven modes can help illuminate some of the features of the Pentecostal ritual and reveal an essential affective component of Pentecostal spirituality.

Explanation of Modes of Sensibility

The modes of sensibility are not so much types of ritual or rites as *embodied attitudes, sensibilities, affections* with which ritualists perform and experience ritual. The modes of Pentecostal ritual sensibility act as both the 'filters' through which worshipers experience and express their rites (i.e. the modes of sensibility *orient* the ritualists toward the rites) and as *animators* of the Pentecostal rites.

Various sensibilities may arise in the midst of ritual or in the course of a particular rite. Theoretically, any rite or practice could be matched with any mode of embodied attitude, though some sensibilities seem more appropriate to particular rites than do other sensibilities. For example, a more penitent attitude might be more appropriate to the altar call rite aimed at 'backslidden' members than a sensibility of celebration. Modes seldom exist as pure as the ideal types. They often mix together. For instance, the modal sensibility of celebration might mix with the mode of ecstacy. If, however, one specific modal sensibility dominates, then I can speak of it, for example, as a 'rite of celebration', indicating the dominant or primary embodied attitude or orientation expressed and experienced within that particular practice.

During my field research and subsequent analysis, I have come to distinguish the following modes of ritual sensibility within Pentecostal services: celebration, contemplation, transcendental efficacy, penitent/purgation, ecstacy, improvisation (ritualization) and ceremony.[6] In the

---

4.   For a fuller discussion of the Pentecostal rites and their structure, see Chapter 4.

5.   Although examples of an 'ideal type' (a singular, unmixed sensibility) of a Pentecostal ritual mode of sensibility may be uncommon in the actual practice of the rites (most often the modes co-exist, even mix), the 'ideal' or 'pure' category can fulfill a heuristic function.

6.   Grimes identifies a series of modal categories. Although his categories are

first part of this chapter, I will describe each of the seven modes of sensibility in turn and seek to explain and give brief examples of how each mode functions as a dimension of the Pent/Char rites. Following the explication of these seven Pent/Char modes, the second part of the chapter will illustrate my conception of the dual axes of Pent/Char rites and Pent/Char modes of sensibility.

Mode of Celebration

I address the ritual mode of celebration as the first mode of sensibility. It occupies a central place in Pentecostal ritual and worship.[7] Almost from the very beginning of the services in the three churches, an attitude of celebration typically prevails. Perhaps the broadest range of characteristically Pentecostal expressions occur within the celebration mode in the ritual.

Often leaders reserve the beginning of the Pentecostal service for a celebrative mode of worship. The worship leader asks, 'Are you ready to worship?' There is a short prayer, whereupon the music begins. It is an 'up-beat' song. Most if not all the congregation stand and sing praises as they celebrate their gathering and their God. Believers move to the celebrative music, some raise hands in praise, others lift their heads heavenward with smiles. Still others sway or dance in delight.

The ritual mode of celebration, as an ideal type, takes root in the

---

not meant to apply to Pentecostal ritual (they are broad and seek to encompass types of sensibilities in varied, even universal ritual settings), his general insight suggests application for Pentecostal ritual. In the identification, description and analysis of Pentecostal sensibilities, I have used Grimes's foundational insight. However, my set of seven modes of ritual sensibilities reflects an extension, a significant rearrangement and conceptual adaptation of Grimes's categories, in order to make them specifically applicable to the Pentecostal rites. For Ronald Grimes's categorization of modes present in ritual see *Beginnings*, pp. 35-51, for examples of his modal conception used as a framework for interpreting particular rituals see the same book, pp. 101-13, 221-31, and in the case studies of his *Ritual Criticism*, pp. 7-144.

7.   The emphasis on the mode of celebration connects to or in part arises from the aspect of the American culture that Bellah *et al.*, *Habits*, have called 'the expressive culture'. This subcultural category is often linked to particular cultural expressions (e.g. the arts). See also Bellah *et al.*, *The Good Society*; Steve Tipton's, *Getting Saved from the Sixties: Moral Meaning in Conversion and Cultural Change* (Berkeley: University of California Press, 1982).

action and attitude of *play*.[8] Celebration contains little or no religious bargaining, nor pursues any specific result. The rooting in play and lack of 'practical' emphasis place this mode in sharp contrast to other Pentecostal sensibilities that animate other forms of prayer, forms and sensibilities wherein there is a pragmatic consequence expected.

The celebrative mode embodies an attitude characterized by expressiveness and a quality of spontaneity.[9] Pentecostals praise and worship in this mode with no ulterior motive, utilitarian results are not sought. Instead, the people, with play-like abandonment, praise their God with expressive words and actions. In general, this mode portrays the kind of joyous attitude often experienced in festal folk celebrations.

When people begin to detach themselves from ordinary pragmatic matters of daily life, initiation of the play of the celebrative mode takes place. Because contemporary Pentecostal worship services often begin in this mode, the sensibility itself functions to separate the Pentecostal liturgical worship from the world of the commonplace (the mundane). Often, the worship leader encourages the congregation with, 'Let's shut out all the influences of the week, all the distractions of work and family, and worship the Lord'. Celebration then, with its play-like quality, helps to set a boundary within which the worship of the community emerges. So, in a sense, play, that is, playful celebration, distinguishes all of Pentecostal ritual.

Mode of Transcendental Efficacy
While the celebrative mode of Pentecostal ritual is characterized by a playful, expressive, spontaneous and free sensibility, the ritual service as a whole is normally balanced by a mode of sensibility called 'tran-

8.   Grimes, *Beginnings*, pp. 35-51, and *idem*, *Ritual Criticism*, p. 151.

9.   The celebrative quality of Pentecostal worship allows for an expressive, creative moment. Pentecostal people are often encouraged to make spontaneous, creative expressions of praise. Such moments of innovation might be thought of within the category of *improvization*. The freedom of improvization avoids chaotic worship by remaining within the boundaries of Pentecostal ritual themes. Just as improvization in music has a freedom and playful attitude and yet remains attached to a melodic theme and to certain patterns within the music, so Pentecostal ritual improvization remains connected to basic worship themes and patterns within Pentecostal rites. This kind of creative impulse helps to keep Pentecostal ritual vital and dynamic. Pentecostal ritual improvization, particularly within the celebrative mode, is a ritualizing mechanism that helps to renew the ritual avoiding static rites. See the section on 'Improvizational Mode' later in this chapter, pp. 188-89.

scendental efficacy'. The transcendental efficacious mode lies at one end of the spectrum of ritual attitudes and the mode of celebration lies at the other. Transcendental efficacy refers to an attitude that participates in 'pragmatic ritual work', particularly in relationship to a transcendental reality (i.e. God) and to the power of that transcendental reality to produce an effect. This mode, in contrast to the Pentecostal celebrative mode, functions with practical goals. A sense of utilitarianism and instrumentalism further characterizes it.[10] Among Pentecostals, rites performed in the transcendental efficacious mode strike a note of expectancy. When Pentecostals pray in this mode they expect an answer. Unlike the sensibility of celebration that may freely play, enjoying and experiencing the meaning of symbols, the mode of efficacy employs the symbols, declaring how things work by working them. The mode of efficacy reveals an attitude that is more concerned with consequence than meaning.

Thus, a ritual action with a transcendental reference that accomplishes or seeks to accomplish a hoped-for empirical result characterizes this mode of sensibility. The three churches often designate this orientation as 'ministry'.[11] Rites of and prayers for healing, miracles, Spirit baptism and 'intercessory prayer' exemplify this pragmatic mode of sensibility within the Pentecostal services, rites and spirituality.[12]

The rite of altar/response clearly demonstrates the pragmatic dimension of Pentecostal spirituality. Often the final phase of the Pentecostal liturgy; the altar/response can mean a time of praying for or supporting

10. See Grimes, *Ritual Criticism*, p. 151. Speaking of a mode analogous to transcendental efficacy, Grimes asserts that 'the manipulation of symbolic means to achieve material ends' is in contrast to the 'playful freedom typical of celebration'.

11. 'Ministry time' is the designation given the rite of altar/response (see Chapter 4) at the VVCF. Unlike the CCC and L&L, the VVCF uses the altar response rite almost exclusively for 'ministry', particularly rites of healing. Consequently, their altar/response is nearly always oriented by the mode of transcendental efficacy.

12. Prayers of 'intercession', often called 'intercessory prayer' (i.e. intense prayers within which the congregants see themselves as interceding between God and the needs of another, or pressing global needs), is a rite that is very much a part of the Pentecostal tradition. It is a rite that I observed to be most often oriented by the mode of transcendental efficacy. This type of prayer most often emerged at midweek prayer meetings (at the VVCF), periodically around the altars during the altar/response (at the CCC) and sometimes briefly during prayers during the Sunday liturgy's rite of worship and praise (at the L&L and CCC).

in other ways persons who have responded to a 'word' in the sermon or to another impulse from the Spirit. Frequently, healing rites and other ministries unfold during the altar/response. The ritual sensibility of transcendental efficacy then often dominates the altar/response.

Transcendental efficacy demonstrates an attitude that vitalizes Pentecostal actions, especially those acts seen as empowered ministry. Ritualists believe and state continually in Pentecostal services that God desires to minister to people's needs, even the ordinary, daily personal needs. Understandably then, ritualists orient themselves towards ministry. Sensitized to one another's needs, they look for opportunities to act upon this sensibility. They make themselves available as instruments or channels of the Holy Spirit in order to do the work of the ministry—to serve God and humankind.[13]

Mode of Contemplation

Contemplation forms a third distinct ritual mode of sensibility that I have identified as fundamental to the Pentecostal service.[14] A deep receptivity and a sense of openness to God characterizes the contemplative ritual mode. This mode shapes the Pentecostal ethos. In the rites of the Pentecostal service and as an ideal for all of life, Pentecostal people seek to 'be open to the work of the Holy Spirit'.[15] They hold as an ideal and actively cultivate *docility* before their God.[16] In the Pentecostal service the contemplative mode may not be a sustained attitude

13. This attitude often strongly shapes the Pentecostal service. Pentecostals usually incorporate rites of ministry (e.g. healing rites) as a part of their ritual worship service. Ritualists often exercise the Charismata, spiritual gifts, within the transcendental efficacy mode of sensibility. Furthermore they hope for gifts of faith, healing, and miracles and often exercise them within this mode. I have also observed gifts, recognized as discernment and knowledge, animated by the transcendental efficacious orientation as a part of a rite of healing.

14. I do not use 'contemplation' in a restrictive, traditional or theological sense.

15. Spiritual gifts, the charismata, may also operate with a sensibility of contemplation. Perhaps most suited to this contemplative orientation are tongues (for 'contemplative' prayers), discernment (for perceiving God's promptings), wisdom and knowledge (as a kind of hearing in the waiting mode) and 'words' of wisdom, knowledge and prophecy (as 'voice' of God to those docilely waiting and listening). These make up a few of the possibilities for the 'gifts' operating within the contemplative mode.

16. On the concept of 'docility' as central to charismatic experience, see Gelpi, *Charism and Sacrament*, and *Experiencing God*.

that permeates the entire service, but this embodied attitude does frequently appear as the dominant congregational mode during specific moments or seasons of the service. During my field research, during nearly every service attended, a contemplative sensibility emerged during 'the worship', (the congregational singing during the first phase of the ritual). Usually, the dominant celebrative mode precedes a dominant contemplative mode. Both were integrally linked to the music, particularly to the genre of the 'worship chorus'. Often the contemplative mode emerged again as dominant near the close of the service, during the altar/response phase.

The Pentecostal contemplative worship mode of sensibility has a mediating function among the other ritual modes. It helps to place in relationship the modes of celebration and transcendental efficacy. The contemplative attitude aids the alternation between these two primary Pentecostal modes of sensibility. The mode of contemplation itself approaches the divine in a reverent interrogative mood. While the mode of celebration actively *plays* and the mode of transcendental efficacy engages in *ritual work* toward its pragmatic goal, the contemplative mode attentively *waits*. The 'tarry until' attitude of the Pentecostal mode of contemplation generally holds sway, that is, it waits as a preparation for what it cannot control. In each of the other two modes there is a sense of at least some human control, but in the mode of contemplation the aware congregation participates in the understanding that ultimately it seeks the action and presence of the other, the one that cannot be controlled. So any symbolic manipulation aims at fostering an expectant docility that waits and listens. This docile waiting balances the free play of celebration and the pragmatic ritual work of the efficacious mode.

Penitent (Purgative) Mode

Although I seldom heard the terms 'penitent' or 'purgative' in any of the three churches during my fieldwork, there were moments during particular services when these terms seem best to describe the mood, the dominant attitude of the congregation. When I use the term penitent mode to describe an orientation within the Pent/Char ritual, I mean a sensibility characterized by contrition, repentance, remorse, sorrow, lamenting or grieving.

If the mode of penitence becomes dominant in a service, it likely emerges during the altar/response rite. Depending on the genre of altar call, the penitent mode might be the most appropriate attitude.[17] On the other hand, when a penitent mode arises and dominates during one of the worship and praise rites, it seems in principle odd, because the celebrative and contemplative modes characteristically orient the rite of worship and praise. Thus, it might be reasoned that a penitent sensibility would be inconsistent. However, I observed a service at the L&L where, during the worship and praise rite, a very natural flow occurred from the celebrative to the contemplative mode (which is quite normal) and then into the penitent mode.[18] Typically, however, I found that the penitent mode seldom dominated during the ritual and when it did, it did not persist.[19]

Mode of Transcendental Ecstacy
Here I mean a range of sensibilities wherein the ritualists believe that they are having an experience, performing rites or manifesting behavior that is directly influenced by their God.[20] Through my field studies, it seems possible to distinguish styles and degrees of transcendental

17. The altar/response, particularly at the CCC, can be a time to 'get right with God'. This most often, in their ritual expression, necessitates a penitent attitude. While it is seldom that the whole congregation responds to this genre of altar call, the penitent mode prevails for all, while some, in particular, respond.

18. I also discovered during interviews that some individuals often experience a penitent sensibility during the worship/praise rite, even when it is not the dominant mode. One young man, a congregant from the VVCF, told me that 'Sometimes during the worship [rite] I feel like I need to repent and be right with God'. This statement, and other similar sentiments I heard during interviews, seem to reflect the flexibility within these early rites. They allow individuals not only to participate in the general course along which the congregations move via their rites and their dominant modal sensibilities, but also permits individuals to sense personally an interaction with the divine and respond appropriately. It might also be an indication of the lack of a prayer of confession near the beginning of the Pent/Char service.

19. The exception to brief occurrences of a dominant penitent mode was during special services. For example, the midweek prayer meetings at the VVCF has more of a propensity for a penitent sensibility than even the altar/response rites at the same church (they were almost always dominated by a transcendental efficacy).

20. On 'ecstacy' and the related topic of mysticism, see I.M. Lewis, *Ecstatic Religion: An Anthropological Study of Spirit Possession and Shamanism* (Baltimore: Penguin Books, 1971); Evelyn Underhill, *Mysticism* (New York: New American Library, 12th edn, 1974 [1911]); R.C. Zaehner, *Zen, Drugs, and Mysticism* (New York: Pantheon Books, 1972).

ecstacy.[21] More mild forms have a sense of being 'inspired' to speak or act. In the more dramatic forms, sometimes there is the sense of being acted upon or seized by the (transcendental) divine. In both extremes, and the degrees between, ritualists believe that the Holy Spirit has to some extent infused them or acted upon them. Such experiences are perceived as being a direct (mystical) experience of the divine. The styles in which ritualists respond to this range of ecstatic experiences also vary from individual to individual and also among congregations. In general, however, the style in the three churches in recent times seems to have been 'toned down'. That is, even in the more salient types of this mode, ritualists generally do not radically change their appearance or mannerisms. This particularly fits the ritualists in the two younger churches, the VVCF and L&L. In the VVCF, for instance, ritualists seem to work at speaking conversationally, making only slight alterations in vocal tones and intonations, when giving a prophetic word. On the other hand, an outsider observing the congregation during the worship and praise rite at either of these two churches would immediately note the differences from 'normal' everyday behavior. The gestures and facial appearances might suggest some kind of ecstatic experience.[22]

Symbolically the role of the transcendental ecstatic mode shapes the Pent/Char mentality. For Pentecostals, ecstacy is a sign, though not infallible, of the Spirit's presence and of interaction with the Spirit. Much of what is considered charismatic or distinctively Pentecostal in some way connects to this transcendent ecstatic mode of sensibility. For the openness to this orientation underlies Pentecostal liturgy and spirituality. Ritualists express 'openness to the Holy Spirit', leading to an authentic Pent/Char ritual. They must believe in the possibility of infusion with the Spirit's power and life. They believe in direct inner influence (e.g. 'anointing') that affects their performance of the rites and changes their perception of and their actions in the world.[23]

---

21. For an analogous treatment, that is, of 'degrees of...imputed divine authorship', see McGuire, *Pentecostal Catholics*, pp. 110-12.

22. As with other modes of sensibility, this one, transcendental ecstacy, can be combined with another mode. For example, I often observed an apparent mix of both the celebrative and the contemplative modes, particularly during the rite of worship and praise.

23. See the discussion in Chapter 4 on the charismatic rites and perceiving the Spirit's influence. Though the ecstatic mode, as defined here, need not be the

Mode of Ceremony

This mode of sensibility shows more intentionality than the other sensibilities of the Pent/Char ritual. Orientation toward the rites requires surrender of at least some individual idiosyncracies and independence to the larger liturgical task and to the ritual leader. The empowered leader directs, even controls, the liturgical forms dominated by this sensibility.[24]

The mode of ceremony usually pertains more to the rites and liturgies of mainline Christianity and to forms of civil religion than to Pentecostalism. It is true Pentecostals intentionally avoid that pomp of ceremony, however, the ceremonial mode does arise in each of these three churches.[25] Although there has been a conscious avoidance of them, ceremonial sensibilities do facilitate at least some of the Pent/Char rites. Typically, an orientation to ceremony dominates three rites, the transitional rites (i.e. the offering, announcements, special music, pastoral prayer), the 'sacraments' (i.e. the eucharist and the initiation rites—baby dedications and baptisms) and the sermon.

Normally, the sermon or pastoral message rite represents the most sustained ceremonial orientation in all of the three churches.[26] As I noted, the ceremonial mode invites the participants to submit their own idiosyncracies to the larger group's tasks. A ceremonial attitude, one in which the individual congregants surrender to some extent their independence to the larger cause of teaching or proclamation of the message, governs the Pentecostal preaching rite, even with its participatory nature. Consequently, power is more centralized as the power of the group is understood and contained within the boundaries of their recognized ritual leader. While ceremony does dominate the pastoral message

exclusive embodied attitude in the performance of what I have called 'charismatic rites' and practices, it does in most cases affect the orientation.

24. See Grimes, *Beginnings*, pp. 41-42.

25. The 'pomp of ceremony' is more radically minimized at the VVCF. For example, the offering (collection) has no music, and generally the pastor talks or makes church announcements while the usher takes the collection. Likewise, the Eucharist lacks even the minimal ceremonial sense that many Pent/Char churches give to it.

26. In some special rituals (not the normal Sunday liturgy) there is a sustained dominant ceremonial mode of sensibility throughout the entire service. These services are often connected more to the elements of 'civil religion'. For example, the CCC has an annual Thanksgiving eve service. It is dominated throughout by the ceremonial mode. See Bellah, 'Civil Religion in America'.

as well as the transitional rites and the sacraments in these three Pent/
Char churches, spontaneity and improvization often affect even these
practices.

Improvizational Mode (Ritualization)

As I have indicated above, ritual is best understood as a dynamic phenomenon. 'Ritualizing' connotes the activity of cultivating or inventing
rites.[27] A rite by definition gains its status through the recognition of the
community or congregation. The Pent/Char mode of improvization
comes to light as a sensibility that is characterized by a creative innovation within the 'theme', that is the common form of a particular rite
or ritual gesture. The ritual sensibility of improvization can refer to the
spontaneous dimension inherent in the Pentecostal service. A more or
less guided spontaneity exists typically within the established patterns
of the community's rites,[28] much as musical improvisation adheres to
the underlining theme of the composition.[29]

The improvization orientation toward the rites remains at the foundation of all the Pent/Char modes of sensibility that I have identified.
Along with any one of them, engagement of this mode becomes possible. The sensibility of improvization can usually mix with another
mode of sensibility.[30] Perhaps this possibility exists, as Grimes asserts,

27. Grimes, *Ritual Criticism*, p. 10. The concept of the Pent/Char mode of
improvization employs elements of the insight of Grimes into the primary ritual
mode that he identifies, ritualization.

28. The pastor or ritual leader often guides or leads in the improvizational
mode. Of course, if a rite is to be effectively performed, it requires that the other
ritualists follow the lead of the pastor's improvizing and participate in the improvizational mode. The liturgical leader not only acts to stimulate improvization but
functions as a boundary for the emerging expression, guiding the form lest it
become detached from the 'theme'. See below, n. 35, for an example of congregational improvization guided by a ritual leader.

29. Grimes refers to such a 'rite' during its process of emergent innovation as a
quasi-rite or a pre-rite (if it is on track toward recognition) (see Grimes, *Beginnings*,
pp. 36-39 and 53-68). Harvey Cox in his *Fire from Heaven* takes another tack. In a
creative and nuanced treatment of Pentecostal Spirituality, Cox juxtaposes Pentecostalism and jazz. He notes a variety of commonalities, including the dynamics of
improvization in both Pentecostal worship and jazz (see pp. 143-57).

30. Improvization as a mode of sensitivity frequently connects to another mode.
For example, the improvizational mode often works with the celebrative mode in
the worship rite at the L&L. The improvizational mode appears also in the preaching and leadership roles of ritual leaders during key moments in the ritual. All three

because of a grounding in the 'biogenetic and psychosomatic' human reality.[31] My field research seems to bear this out, for example, I often heard ritualists appeal to such phrases as 'being moved', 'feel prompted' or 'sense the Lord is saying' as explanations of a particular action. These expressions rely on psychosomatically informed dynamics. So Grimes is apparently correct when he insists that ritual action, particularly that effected by the improvizational mode, is fundamentally a return to nature and body.[32]

This completes the descriptive explanation of my understanding of the seven ritual modes of Pent/Char sensibility. Now, in the second part of the chapter I will illustrate my image of the dual axes of Pent/Char rites and Pent/Char modes of sensibility.

Rites and Modes: Dual Axes

I portray my understanding of the modes of sensibility and rites of the Pentecostal ritual as two dimensions, each on its own axis. I aim in this section of the chapter to illustrate these dual axes and thereby to show the relational dynamic within the Pent/Char ritual between the ritual practices and modes of sensibility. First, I will give illustrations of how two microrites (the raising of hands and tongues speech) relationally interpenetrate with a variety of modes of sensibility. I will then present a chart, also as an illustration of the connection between the Pent/Char rites and the ritual modes.

Two Illustrations

To help explain how the Pent/Char ritual modes of sensibility affect the Pentecostal practices, I will first look at a simple gesture very common during the Pentecostal liturgy, *the raising of hands*.[33] I will use this example to illustrate how other gestures, and more complex rites, may

pastors prepare sermons with detailed outlined notes, but each shows evidence in his weekly sermon of improvizing within the moment. This can be seen when comparing the multiple services and the variation of the same sermon with the same notes.

31. Grimes, *Beginnings*, p. 36.

32. Grimes, *Beginnings* and *Ritual Criticism*.

33. For an excellent discussion of religious ritual gestures, see Ann Hawthorne, 'Introduction—Method and Spirit: Studying the Diversity of Gestures in Religion', in Tyson, Peacock and Patterson (eds.), *Diversities of Gifts*, pp. 3-20.

potentially be enacted with, and oriented by a variety of modes of sensibility, and to suggest that the meaning of a particular rite, action or physical gesture changes in accord with the mode of sensibility. Secondly, I will consider a speech act, a charismatic speech act, *glossolalia* and how it is similarly oriented by the particular mode of sensibility in which it is performed.

The raising of hands. This is often considered a trademark of Pentecostal worship.[34] Outstretched arms with lifted hands in the liturgies of the three churches can express a broad range of experiences. This breadth is supported by a range of ritual sensibilities. Thus, one gesture (i.e. the raising of hands) has the ability to express numerous and differing experiences, it can have varied meanings, each one animated by at least one ritual mode of sensibility. For example, individuals, often extend hands high to express praise to God in a celebrative mode. Sometimes, in a more ecstatic sensibility, hands are lifted and waved as an expression of the ecstacy. Lifting hands, with palms up, often expresses an openness to God, a vulnerability and receptivity and is frequently accompanied by an embodied attitude of contemplation. The lifted hands and bowed heads as an act of contrition may express the penitent mode. The mode of transcendental efficacy also animates hands to be lifted. For instance, in healing rites I observed, typically, a ritualist would place one hand on the person being prayed for and lift his or her own other hand heavenward. This can express a reaching out to God while touching one in need. An offering of oneself as a conduit for healing power, an 'instrument for God's work'. Of course, the liturgical leaders at times lift their hands as a sign of blessing and this happens in a more ceremonial mode. With these examples, it becomes clearer how a simple act or gesture may be employed variously and with many modes of sensibility.

Glossolalia. My second example is also a characteristic Pent/Char rite, the charismatic speech act of *glossolalia.* Here, I want to illustrate how

---

34. As I observed hundreds of Pentecostal services in my field studies, it was quite clear how important ritual gestures are within the Pentecostal liturgy, particularly those made with the use of the ritualists' hands. Not only the lifting of arms and hands widespread, but the laying on of hands in healing rites, holding hands in prayer, reaching out, extending a hand toward another in need, signing in songs (sign language-like) and other hand gestures are prevalent.

a particular speech act within the Pent/Char liturgy, even as a gestural activity, can be preformed with the variety of orienting modes of sensibility. We want also to suggest with this example how sensibilities may overlap or be combined.

Speaking in tongues has a variety of expressions in Pentecostal services. As I have defined the ecstatic mode above, I would claim that glossolalia is expressed in the Pent/Char mode of ecstacy. Pentecostal congregants when explaining tongues often quote Acts 2.4, that 'the Spirit gave them utterance'. By this, they understand that the Spirit enables or empowers the person to speak in tongues. They do not deny the human element, on the contrary, tongues is recognized as a close interaction between the Spirit and the human. However, tongues speech in our three churches is seldom trance-like. Normally, one senses that she or he is being inspired or aided by the divine in the tongues speech. Yet, ritualists seem very self-conscious and aware of their part in the act of speaking in tongues. The glossolalia prayers seem to add to the consciousness of the presence of the Spirit. In short, the fundamental mode of sensibility within which the enactment of tongues speech takes place is the mode of ecstacy. However, that fundamental orientation combined with other dominant modes shapes the experience and the meaning of tongues speech in a variety of ways.

Congregants perceive the rite or practice of tongues speech in the Pent/Char liturgy as a type of prayer. Thus, a prayer of celebration (in tongues) takes place in the celebration modes, a joyful, even play-like expression of celebration, often an expression of praise 'in the Spirit'. In the contemplative sensibility tongues act as a tool of 'reflective' though not logical meditation, a prayer of quiet openness to the Spirit's work, a speech act that symbolizes docility. Glossolalia, as part of the healing rites, might signal the transcendental efficacious mode. Tongues speech combined with vernacular prayers becomes part of the rite that seeks efficacious ends. Even the penitent sensibility may guide and give meaning to tongues speech. Not uncommonly, a repentant Pentecostal may pray penitent prayers around the altar aided by glossolalia. So-called 'message in tongues' among classical Pentecostals have a ritual sequence, a pattern that is ceremonial in nature. Depending on the congregational norms, the message may only be given during certain appropriate moments in the service, and it has an expected range of lengths that should not be violated. In the L&L and CCC a few seconds in length would not be considered a 'message'. If an utterance meant for the whole congregation and not private prayer exceeded a few minutes, the congregation would become uncomfortable and the pastor would likely interrupt the 'message'. A message of 'legitimate' length is however normally followed by a short quiet pause, until someone gives an interpretation. This sequence and pattern varies somewhat among congregations, but within each congregation there is a standard ceremonial way, known to the ritualists of that congregation, in which a message in tongues is to be given and interpreted. So, the Pent/Char sensibility of ceremony provides a modal boundary for the message in tongues rites.

Having noted the strength of sequence and pattern within the use of tongues in a ceremonial mode, it is important to add that the mode of improvization often animates the use of tongues. Personal tongues speech, of course has patterns of practice both within and outside of the liturgy, but individuals report variations, perhaps due to an improvizational impulse, within the practices of their 'prayer languages'. Also, an orientation to improvization in the use of tongues may continue within a liturgy.[35]

---

35. An example of improvization with glossolalia emerged in the wake of the Charismatic movement of the 1970s. Prior to the Charismatic renewal, classical Pentecostals reported 'singing in tongues' on occasion, but in many congregations it was rare, and when it occurred it was often dramatically ecstatic and normally involved a single individual. Charismatic improvization popularized the general practice of tongues singing (perhaps they revitalized it, since it may have been more wide spread early in the Pentecostal movement). A particular improvization with tongues occurred in a service the author attended. A guest speaker closed his sermon in prayer and as a part of the altar/response he asked people to sing a familiar chorus with him. The congregation did. Then he said, 'Now let's all sing together in our prayer languages' (tongues). Clearly, by the hesitant response of the congregation, this was unknown to them. The speaker was drawing upon two common practices (singing a worship chorus and tongues speech) to create a new practice. But soon the majority of the congregants picked up the melody (of the chorus) and began to sing in tongues. Together the ritualists moved into a sensibility of improvization. Many spoke later of the experience as liberating. It was at least a variation on a theme that moved the use of tongues not only into singing for these congregants, but made it a more corporate activity. See Donald A. Johns, 'Singing in Tongues', in *DPCM*, p. 788. Also commentaries on 1 Cor. 14.15, 'I will sing with my S/spirit…'

Chart of Dual Axes

Rites	Modes of Sensibility						
	Celebrative	Contemplative	Efficacious	Penitent	Ecstatic	Ceremonial	Improvisation
Foundational							
Worship and praise	1	1	3	2	2	3	3
Pastoral message	4	3	3	2	2	1	2
Altar response	4	1	1	1	2	2	3
Microrites							
Charismatic rites							
Tongues	1	1	2, 3	2, 3	1	1	3
Kinesthetic Rites							
Raising hands	1	1	2	2	1	2	2
Dance	1	1	4	3	2	1	1
Acts of response							
Healing rites	4	2	1	2	2	1	3

To provide one more illustration of the interaction of Pent/Char ritual modes of sensibilities and rites, I present a chart that shows two axes (rites and modes) and how selected rites may be animated by the modes. I have not included all rites, rather, I have selected representative rites to exemplify my point; namely that the rites may be oriented by and experienced through a variety modes of sensibility. These modes most easily attain recognition when they dominate during the performance of a rite. The chart reflects the field studies, in which I discovered general patterns of modal dominance among the rites in the three churches. I have ranked modal dominance on a scale of '1–4': 1 = often a sustained dominant mode; 2 = often momentary dominance; 3 = sometimes dominant, at least briefly; 4 = rarely, if ever dominant. For a more complete list of Pent/Char rites see Appendix B.

Conclusion

The seven Pentecostal modes of ritual sensibility that I have sought to explicate in this chapter are integral to the ritual of the three Sea City churches and to their broader spirituality. This description of Pentecostal modes, though incomplete, does point out several elements important to an understanding of Pentecostal spirituality. In general, Pentecostal worship practices, rites, remain not merely as structured exercises preformed by detached individuals to accomplish religious obligations. They are not generally forms of 'ritualism'. While the Pentecostal rites do maintain a structure—a structure important to the performance of the ritual—a structural analysis alone cannot yield an adequate understanding of the Pent/Char ritual and its spirituality. To understand the character of the rites one must penetrate the embodied attitudes or sensibilities that animate and mediate the experience of the rites. Human beings embody these sensibilities while enacting their religious practices according to the particular modal orientation that they bring to the rites.

It might be argued that Pentecostal ritual remains vital and authentic to the extent that its rites are infused with appropriate and spirited sensibilities that embody and enact the congregation's experience. The alternative suggests a ritual that may have suitable structure but little life or meaning, owing to mechanical involvement that lacks the authenticity of appropriately engaged sensibilities. The vitality of Pentecostal ritual has less to do with the structure of the ritual than the embodied attitudes, the orientation, with which congregants engage in the rites as structured. Salient sensibilities appropriately applied can help to produce what Pent/Char ritualists claim is for them, vital and authentic ritual performance.

In particular, I would suggest three specific insights into Pentecostal spirituality from the analysis of the Pentecostal ritual modes of sensibility. First, the emphasis on celebration points to a fundamental characteristic of Pentecostal spirituality—a spontaneous, joy-filled, *playfulness*. This playfulness encourages improvization within creative moments and produces an innovative spirituality. Secondly, Pentecostal spirituality has a strong element of *pragmatism* oriented to demonstrations of power particularly for purposes of ministry (though the demonstrations of power are fundamentally symbolic of the presence and interaction of the divine). Lastly, the dimension of Pentecostal spirituality revealed in the embodied attitude that I have designated 'contemplation' contains a *deep receptivity*, a particular kind of vulnerability to God that is encouraged by Pentecostals. Their spirituality values a docility before God. I turn now from the modes of sensibility with which the rites are enacted and through which the rites are experienced to consider some of the consequences of Pentecostal ritual process.

Chapter 6

EXPRESSIVE AND EFFICACIOUS ROLES OF THE
PENTECOSTAL/CHARISMATIC RITUAL PROCESS

Ritual works for Pentecostals. They depend on it. In fact, authentic rituals vitalize Pentecostal spirituality. As I have stated, the Pent/Char liturgical ritual helps to center the spirituality. Pentecostals rely heavily on their liturgies; the rites function as a kind of focal point for the overall spirituality. The ritual helps to express and create, to sustain as well as transform, the community and its spirituality. The Pent/Char ritual process provides its ritualists with the opportunity to express things that really matter. Ritual performs for Pentecostals an all important cultural-communicative role. But more than that, the Pent/Char ritual practices propel the community toward transformative consequences.

In this chapter I will be considering two primary roles of the Pent/Char ritual liturgy. First, I will approach the *expressive* character of the Pent/Char ritual. I want to reflect upon some of the ways in which the communicative dimension of ritual works within our Pentecostal communities, ways in which the ritual *expresses* the Pent/Char spirituality. Secondly, I will examine the *efficacious* character of the Pent/Char ritual. In the second section, I will consider some of the potential positive consequences of the Pent/Char liturgy.

Expressive/Dramaturgic Roles

It has long been recognized that ritual activities have an expressive, communicative, dimension. Social scientist Robert Wuthnow goes so far as to suggest that the entire symbolic or expressive aspect of culture might be considered as ritual.[1] While Wuthnow's generalization is

___

1. Wuthnow, *Meaning and Moral Order: Explorations in Cultural Analysis* (Berkeley: University of California Press, 1987), pp. 97-144. For Wuthnow, ritual

apparently unique, his emphasis on the communicative character of ritual action is not.[2] One of the most prominent metaphors used to characterize the expressive, communicative, nature of ritual practices is that
of performance. The analogy of drama and dramatic performance to
ritual actions has been used extensively by anthropologists and other
students of ritual.[3]

Ritologists have not always agreed on the content of the 'performance' of ritual, but they generally agree that ritual dramatizes, enacts,
materializes or performs a system of symbols.[4] In other words, ritual

is 'a symbolic-expressive aspect of behavior that communicates something about
social relations, often in a relatively dramatic or formal manner' (p. 109). Ritual is
taken to be 'an analytic dimension [of culture] that may be present to some degree
in all behavior'. Ritual 'emphasizes the communicative properties of behavior…[it]
often communicates more effectively because it conforms to certain stylized or
embellished patterns of behavior' (p. 109).

2.   Wuthnow believes that the 'essence of ritual lies in communication' (*Meaning and Moral Order*, p. 104). Other theorists fail to go as far as Wuthnow in his
claim that all symbolic-expressive behavior is ritual-like, yet many assert the importance of the communicative component of ritual. Examples of works that assume
and deal with the broader communicative dimension of ritual include Paul Ricoeur,
'The Model of the Text: Meaningful Action Considered as Text', in *idem*, *Hermeneutics*, pp. 197-221; Geertz, *Interpretation of Cultures*; Hans-Georg Gadamer,
Truth and Method (trans. Joel Weinsheimer and Donald G. Marshall; New York:
Crossroad, 2nd rev. edn, 1989); George E. Marcus and Michael M.J. Fischer,
Anthropology as Cultural Critique (Chicago: University of Chicago Press, 1986);
James W. Fernandez, 'The Performance of Ritual Metaphors', in J. David Sapir and
J. Christopher Crocker (eds.), *The Social Use of Metaphor: Essays on the Anthro-
pology of Rhetoric* (Philadelphia: University of Pennsylvania Press, 1977), pp. 100-
31.

3.   I have implicitly drawn from this tradition throughout the chapters of this
work. I am most dependant on the works of Victor Turner and Ronald L. Grimes,
though I am indebted to others that share the performance analogy. Examples of
others who use the performance metaphor include: Driver, *The Magic of Ritual*, esp.
pp. 79-130; Myerhoff, 'A Death in Due Time'; *idem*, *Number our Days*; Richard
Schechner, *Essays on Performance Theory, 1970–1976* (New York: Drama Book
Specialists, 1977); *idem*, 'The Future of Ritual', *Journal of Ritual Studies* 1 (1987),
pp. 5-33; Lawrence E. Sullivan, 'Sound and Senses: Toward a Hermeneutics of
Performance', *HR* 26.1 (1986), pp. 1-33; Stanley J. Tambiah, 'A Performative
Approach to Ritual', *Proceedings of the British Academy* 65 (1979), pp. 113-69.

4.   Though ritologists disagree on the 'content' (or the specific function) of
ritual, see the following as examples of ritual as dramatizing, enacting, material-
izing or performing a system of symbols (i.e. communication): A.R. Radcliff-

functions as a form of cultural communication that expresses some of the culture's symbols in symbolic actions. Thus, anthropologists such as Clifford Geertz and Victor Turner, for example, believe that ritual acts as a particular form of cultural performance that 'offers a special vantage point', a 'window' for observing the 'most important processes of cultural life'.[5] From this vantage point, one peers through the window of the liturgical rituals of the three Sea City churches. I will observe three expressive/dramaturgic aspects of the Pent/Char ritual as preformed in the liturgies of the CCC, L&L and VVCF: liturgy as expression of human concerns, liturgy as an expression of social structure and liturgy as expression of theological relationships.

Pent/Char Liturgy as Expression of Human Concerns
Throughout my field studies enthusiastic ritualists informed me that heartfelt, dramatic worship attracted them to a Pent/Char community. Ben, a new congregant of the L&L in his forties, explained that, while he sees himself as quite reserved, not given to 'much expression in worship', even somewhat 'inhibited', he claimed 'to be benefited by others' as they liberally expressed their worship. Ben volunteered that in other (Pentecostal) churches that he visited where 'less outward expression' characterized their rites, he felt more constrained even though their

Brown, *Taboo* (Cambridge: Cambridge University Press, 1939), pp. 30-32; Bronislaw Malinowski, 'Magic, Science, and Religion', in James Needham (ed.), *Science, Religion and Reality* (New York: Macmillan, 1925), pp. 17-29; Max Gluckman (ed.), 'Les rites de passage', in *idem, The Ritual of Social Relations* (Manchester: Manchester University Press, 1962), pp. 1-52; Edmund Leach, *Political Systems of Highland Burma* (Boston: Beacon Press, 1964), pp. 14-15; John W. Meyer and Brian Rowan, 'Institutionalized Organizations: Formal Structure as Myth and Ceremony', *American Journal of Sociology* 83 (1977), pp. 340-63; Turner, *Ritual Process*; Wuthnow, *Meaning and Moral Order, passim.*

    5.   Bell, *Ritual Theory*, p. 41. See Victor Turner, *From Ritual to Theater: The Human Seriousness of Play* (New York: Performing Arts Journal Publications, 1982), p. 82; and Geertz, *Interpretation of Cultures*, pp. 113-14, as cited by Bell, *Ritual Theory*, pp. 27-29, 41. Bell also notes the similar perspective of Theodore Jennings, 'On Ritual Knowledge', *JR* 62.1 (1982), pp. 111-27, who, she says, 'describes ritual as, first of all, a display to an observer (god, theorist, etc.) or observers (the community itself) and, second, as an epistemological project. Both of these dimensions of ritual act as a "point of contact" between the rite and the attempt by outside observers to grasp a "theoretical-critical understanding of it".' One is according to Jennings, 'invited' to watch, for ritual is a presentation for observers.

style paralleled his own.[6] Another new congregant, Sharon, a married woman in her early forties, told us that she visited numerous Sea City churches before coming to L&L. She complained 'they are too reserved', but here, she claimed, she discovered 'freer worship', obviously an attractive trait to her. Similarly, a 30-year old single visitor to the VVCF, Carlos, himself a Pentecostal, told us after the service that, while he enjoyed the liturgy, his church in a distant California city had more 'expressive worship'. These typical remarks show clearly the Pentecostals at our churches enjoy and are attracted to the communities in part because of a perceived 'freer', 'uninhibited', *'expressive'* worship experience.[7]

The Pent/Char liturgy becomes a medium for personal, sincere, genuinely open expressions, and a conduit of the community's concerns. Congregants, particularly during the rite of worship and praise, receive encouragement to make their worship very personal and deep. The ritual gives freedom within the boundaries of their particular ritual process to express a wide range of human sensibilities. They discover the opportunity to express in symbolic actions and words the things that matter most to them. As a result, the Pent/Char ritual creates a cultural domain for deeply felt expressions of human experiences.[8] Pentecostals consciously construct their liturgies to foster a wide range of diverse expressive practices that seek to dramatize a continuum of human affections, longings and convictions. For example, as discussed in Chapter 3, the rite of worship and praise affords worshipers the 'space' to express themselves. Not only are microrites and such practices as singing, concert prayer, sacred expletives and kinesthetic movement available as avenues of expression, but a range of modal sensitivities help to orient

6.   Other long-time members of L&L identified themselves as 'conservative worshipers', yet they sounded the same theme, demonstrative worship practices 'released' them to worship authentically.

7.   This *expressive* worship symbolizes to the congregants both sides of the 'conversation' that was discussed in Chapter 3. It symbolizes the opportunity of ritualists to express things of importance to God and to fellow believers and the 'freedom' symbolizes the opportunity for God to speak, for God to be expressive. The Spirit may move as the Spirit wills, according to Pentecostals. But they must remain 'open' to the Spirit's movings and not stifle God's actions among them with their structures or attitudes. They believe if they nurture sensitivity to the Spirit then they will not only perceive God's actions among them, but they may participate in those activities.

8.   See Chapter 3 for the creation and shaping of domains of the ritual field.

and animate these practices.[9] The combination of the practices with a variety of modes gives the worshipers a full spectrum of expressions with which to make known the concerns that represent their humanity.

Pentecostal/Charismatic Liturgy as an Expression of Social Structure
At least since the time of Emile Durkheim, students of culture have held that the rituals of a people reveal the social structures, identity, roles and relationships of the society.[10] Many contemporary ritologists continue to emphasize the role of ritual as a presentation of the group's social life, its structure and dynamics. For example, Geertz believes that the rituals portray 'the pattern of social interaction' of the society, Turner calls the ritual 'a social drama', while Grimes insists that in ritual the faithful 'enact social roles'.[11] In Chapter 3 I discussed the more structured liturgical identity/roles of the Pent/Char ritualists in the three churches. Here, I wish only to point out that the Pent/Char ritual often functions to clarify the social structure for the ritualists themselves by clarifying the role/identities, and that the liturgical roles performed in the ritual may actually alter identities.

First, the standardized roles enacted in the liturgy help to express identity/roles and thereby clarify the social structure. The dynamic manifestations of the ritual generally fit within the established liturgical roles as I have identified them. That is, most of the ritualists function within the established liturgical roles for the congregants, while their recognized leaders move within the three normal leadership patterns of facilitation/coordination, authority and expert specialization.[12] As these standardized role/identities function they clarify, sustain and reinforce the social boundaries. By that I mean that the pastor's identity emerges

9.   See Chapter 4 for a discussion of the Pent/Char modes of ritual sensibility.

10.   As examples of contemporary versions of ritual as expressing some aspect of social structure, see Douglas, *Natural Symbols*, for her view of 'symbolic boundaries'; Wuthnow, *Meaning and Moral Order*, who follows Douglas for his view of ritual and 'moral code/order', esp. Chs. 3 and 4; Leach, *Political Systems*, p. 14, who recognizes in ritual an explicit expression of 'social order'; and Margaret Mary Kelleher, 'Liturgical Theology: A Task and a Method', *Worship* 62.1 (January 1988), pp. 2-25, asserts the function of the liturgical ritual as structuring and transmitting 'relationships and expectations within the community' (p. 9).

11.   Geertz, *Interpretation of Cultures*, p. 144; Victor Turner, *Dramas, Fields, and Metaphors: Symbolic Action in Human Society* (Ithaca: NY: Cornell University Press, 1974); Ronald Grimes, 'Ritual Studies', in *EOR*, XII, pp. 422-25.

12.   See Chapter 3.

as they fill the role of pastoral and liturgical leader. Likewise, the worship team clarifies and establishes[13] its identity as it facilitates the worshippers. Congregants create and clarify their identities within the liturgical roles (i.e. worshipers, prophetic agents, care-giving ministers, responsive learners and active disciples) as they participate in the ritual action.[14] In other words, enactment of the Pent/Char ritual acts expedites the process of role/identity clarification assisting the community's expression and understanding of their on-going social structure.

Secondly, certain roles, particularly charismatic roles (i.e. 'prophetic agent', see Chapter 3) performed in the liturgy may function to impact, alter, even challenge a currently perceived identity of the liturgy.[15] Characteristic, spontaneous, charismatic liturgical leadership roles, perhaps best illustrate this modifying dynamic. In Chapter 3, I pointed out that in principle any member of the congregation can within a particular ritual framework emerge and function, at least briefly, as a liturgical leader. For example, while giving a charismatic prophecy, the prophesier directs the service, moving momentarily into a liturgical leadership role. Ideally any ritualist may serve the community in this manner. While Pentecostal ritual maintains 'space' for spontaneous interruptions, such interpolations may impact the perceived identities.

An extension of the example of the 'prophesier' might serve to illustrate how spontaneous charismatic manifestation may impact perceived identity within a Pent/Char community. If a variety of ritualists over time share charismatic words or prophecies within one congregation,

---

13. The word 'establish' might be misleading. Roles and identities are dynamic in the Pent/Char ritual. While sometimes persons fulfill a given role repeatedly (i.e. pastor, worship team member), and thus I speak of their role as established, the fact remains that roles and liturgical identities emerge, develop and change over time even when I designate them as established.

14. See Chapter 3 for a discussion of these liturgical role/identities.

15. While the Pentecostal 'charismatic roles' hint of Max Weber's characterization of the 'charisma', their functions can be seen as consistent with Victor Turner's vision of ritual's efficacy. Max Weber, *The Theory of Social and Economic Organization* (New York: Free Press, 1947); *idem, The Sociology of Religion* (trans. Ephraim Fischoff; Boston: Beacon Press, 4th edn, 1963); Turner, *Ritual Process*, and others. In this section of the present chapter I focus primarily on the expressive dimension of Pent/Char ritual. However, I insert here the point of potential modification, a 'shifting' of charismatic identities as germane to this stage of the discussion, for it helps to show how the expressive function of the ritual may also have an efficacious impact. I will consider further the efficacious aspects of the ritual below.

the congregants perceive the charismatic interjections as manifestations of a more or less 'random' selection by the Spirit of available and responsive ritualists. However, the congregation's judgment of the same ritualist being persistently 'used by the Spirit' may change. The ritualist's repeated role in charismatic words shifts his or her liturgical identity. The role of persistent prophetic agent produces an identity of a type of prophet. The same dynamic functions for the frequent manifestation of other charismatic gifts. Ritualists at the VVCF, for example, recognize one who often demonstrates an 'anointing' for performing healing rites as a healer of sorts. Their identities in the congregation thus shift.[16] Such shifts, alterations of identities, may challenge the patterns of leadership.

Spontaneous manifestations of charismatic leadership do at times challenge the more standard forms of leadership and authority. Such challenges can proceed in at least two particular streams. The result depends in part on the perceptions and responses of the challenge by the congregation and the authorized leadership. I characterize the first type of challenge as a power struggle, a 'power play'. In this type a ritualist is perceived as attempting through spontaneous charismatic leadership to undermine the structure of the leadership. In such a case the response varies (e.g. the official church leaders—elders, pastors—may privately confront the challenger), but essentially the response attempts to sustain the equilibrium of the congregational leadership.

The second type of challenge is perceived and dealt with differently. Understood as a challenge toward 'shared ministry', in this type the leadership and the congregation discerns within the spontaneous charismatic manifestation (of leadership) 'the anointing', a 'special gifting' or 'an office' needed to edify the faith community. Often the pastor, with the congregation's support, singles out such members and allows them

16. The shift in identity is not always in the same ('positive') direction. For instance, a ritualist may persist over time in charismatic manifestations that are not appreciated as fully appropriate by at least a portion of the congregation. This often results in the diminished appreciation of the individual's role within the community. The individual might be perceived as overly enthusiastic, or attempting to dominate the service at the expense of the other ritualists. Or the individual may be perceived to be 'not right on' or as 'missing the mark', that is, their manifestations are seen as not wholly authentic. While such ritualists are normally tolerated, they are not greatly respected. I located several examples of this phenomenon in the CCC. See the section on 'charismatic criteria' in Chapter 4, pp. 174-76.

to create a niche within the community's life to serve, to share in the ministry. Consequently, this type of challenge signals to the congregation a need for a type of ministry/leadership lacking or inadequately addressed in the congregation's existing social structure. Such charismatic expressions then function both to reveal and challenge the status quo of the social patterns. These kinds of manifestations operate as a ritual mechanism that can transform the perceived social roles/identities. Charismatic and other ritual expressions that reveal the social dimensions of the community are integrally linked to the community's theological understanding. I turn now to consider some of these theological relationships dramatized in the liturgy.

Pentecostal/Charismatic Liturgy as Expression of Theological Relationships

According to liturgical theologian Margaret Kelleher, a Christian liturgy presents a 'public spirituality, a vision of what it means to live as a member of the Christian community'.[17] If she is correct, the congregation functions as a 'corporate subject'. Together they implicitly set out in their liturgy a 'public spirituality'. That spirituality is a dramatic manifestation of what to them is fundamental to living as Christians. When the three Sea City churches are considered, this characterization of liturgies seems suggestive. For, as I looked closely at the liturgies over time in each of the churches, I came to perceive some fundamental theological implications. The liturgies point to the congregation's self-understanding, its principal reasons for being, its sense of mission.[18] The rituals of the Sea City churches express what it means to live and behave as Christian. The main theological functions of the liturgy are to celebrate (worship God), to edify the members and to send out the ritualists into the society with a mission. I understand these three purposes of the liturgy as corollaries to three primary theological relationships that illumine a three-pronged understanding of what it means to these churches to be and behave as Christian. Pentecostals understand Christianity relationally, that is, they grasp it experientially in the three basic relationships: the congregants' relationship with their God, the faith community's internal relationships and relationship to the 'world', their society and others.

17. Kelleher, 'Liturgical Theology', p. 7.
18. See Chapter 2.

Relationship to God. The most explicit purpose of the liturgy is to worship God. As I have repeatedly pointed out, worshiping God in the Pent/
Char liturgy means entering into a ritual dimension specifically set apart
for the experiencing of the divine presence. It is to relate to God in and
through the ritual practices of the Pentecostal service, to experience
God in a variety of modes of sensibility. The ritual as a whole composed
of rites and embodied attitudes expresses the divine–human relationship
as Pentecostals experience and comprehend it. And their experiential
comprehension of this primary relationship thrives only within a social
context.[19]

Relationship as community. Critics accuse Pentecostals of being overly
individualistic, but fail to recognize the Pent/Char liturgical spirituality's fundamental social orientation. The Sunday ritual at each of the
three churches portrays, ideally, a 'communion of the saints' an essentially social dynamic.[20] While all Christian liturgies enact social practices in varying degrees, the symbol and the experience of Spirit baptism (and other charismatic forms of worship) infuses the Pentecostal
services with a peculiar social force. Donald Gelpi referred to this
dynamic when he claimed that a 'consequence of Breath [Spirit] baptism [is] its ability to bind Christians together in a charismatic community'.[21] The shared consciousness of being a 'charismatic community'

19. Donald Gelpi argues that 'the enlightenment effected by [Spirit] baptism
transforms the Christian community into a social icon' of the divine (*Divine Mother*,
p. 183; see especially, pp. 206-208).

20. See below in this chapter for a discussion of liminality and communitas and
the role they play in production of the communal relationships in the Pent/Char
churches.

21. *Divine Mother*, p. 183. Gelpi's ideas converge here with Robert Bellah's.
Bellah and associates argue throughout *Habits* that the members of a society must
learn to speak the same cultural 'languages' in order to engage in the all important
cultural 'conversation', a conversation they insist is essential to the growth and sus-
tenance of a good society. Gelpi claims that a community, particularly a faith community, is dependent on the commitment of the individuals to the 'process of social
dialogue'. That 'a community comes to shared awareness of itself as a community
only when a certain number of fundamental conditions are met'. After he explicates
those conditions, Gelpi concludes, 'the Christian community will achieve full consciousness of itself as a religious community united in a common faith, hope, and
love only to the extent that its members share freely with one another Her [the
Spirit's] charismatic inspirations' (*Divine Mother*, p. 205, see pp. 202-206).

of Christian believers is apparently a salient force in each of the Sea City churches. The Pentecostal practices, the enactment of the rites, specifically help to raise the shared sense of community, a community that believes that its communion is as immediate with the Spirit as it is with the sisters and brothers.

The Pent/Char ritual enactments not only help to nourish the collective sense of being a charismatic community, they reinforce and assist the transmission of the community's beliefs.[22] To a large degree Pentecostals discover their communal spirituality in their ritualizing. They rehearse the Christian message in word and action in their liturgies. Learning the beliefs involves more than academic exercises. Pentecostals experience and enact their beliefs in the liturgy. The liturgical ritual is the great catechizing event in these three churches.[23] The transmission of the tradition is more dependant on liturgical action than on an external structured verbal catechesis. Thus, the ritual teaches what it means to live and behave as Christians in a faith community.

In sum, the Pent/Char rites express, and cultivate a particular type of community relationship. The three churches all exemplify what Gelpi

22. For examples of a society's or community's transmission of their tradition see Kelleher, 'Liturgical Theology', p. 9; Peter Berger and Thomas Luckmann, *The Social Construction of Reality* (New York: Doubleday, 1966); Tipton, *Getting Saved*, p. 237.

23. While Bible studies and sermons abound in the Sea City churches, formal catechesis is resisted. If one learns to be Pentecostal, it is in the corporate rites. Referring to this, one Pentecostal preacher exclaimed, 'It is better caught than taught'. Though formal Sunday school is considered absolutely necessary for children and teenagers, conversions, Spirit baptism and other fundamental Pentecostal experiences most typically transpire in youth services, or youth liturgies during a retreat or youth camp. The liturgical ritual, though adapted for the age group, consistently catechizes Pentecostals.

See Bridges-Johns, *Pentecostal Formation*, where she articulates the dynamics of Pentecostal catechesis and creates a paradigm for such a catechesis. Bridges-Johns recognizes that 'the setting for learning focuses on the worshipping community. As believers participated in the rituals of Pentecostal worship, they are incorporated, enculturated and apprenticed' (pp. 129-30). While identifying the centrality of the corporate worship in the formational processes, Bridges-Johns locates a unique approach to instruction inherent in Pentecostal spirituality. From native Pentecostal impulses and dynamics she develops a highly suggestive Pentecostal approach to group Bible study in four movements. This approach is rooted in and actualized within the context of the Pentecostal worshipping community and its liturgical rites (pp. 130-40).

calls the 'charismatic community', grounded in the common experience of Spirit baptism and other Pent/Char ritual actions. Their common experiences help to bind them together while reinforcing and relaying their beliefs and tradition. Because of the nature of their common charismatic experience, a 'mutual service', a form of edification, emerges within the liturgy, but the congregation's attention subsequently shifts from a self-centeredness toward forms of service to 'the world' to which they believe they have been commissioned.[24]

Relationship to the world: Mission. While I have argued that the liturgical ritual carries the central current of the community's spirituality in the three churches, none of these congregations fixates on its Sunday rites. Each looks beyond the corporate celebration of worship to service, mission in the world.[25] One of the congregants of the CCC, a long-time member of A/G, told us that 'service begins when church is over'.[26] With this he voiced an emphasis generally held in each of the Sea City Pentecostal churches, that the mission of the church 'is not contained within the four walls of the church building' or within the parameters of the corporate rites.[27]

24. An outcome of charismatic rites authentically enacted, according to Gelpi is the uniting of Christians together into a community of '*mutual service*' (*Divine Mother*, p. 183; emphasis mine).

25. In Chapter 7 I will consider 'mission(s)' as a primary symbol that acts as a metaphor for a dimension of Pent/Char spirituality.

26. 'Service begins when church is over' indicates the 'outward' look of Pentecostalism, an eye toward 'the world' and the mission to it. The phrase implies the movement from the liturgy, which is a central focusing ritual for Pent/Char spirituality (and more or less confined to the faith community), outward to the rest of life and its social interaction outside the community of faith. This dynamic is conveyed in Robert Bellah's understanding of the Eucharist as a 'focal action, a focal practice, that radiates out into the whole of our lives' ('Christian Faithfulness in a Pluralist World', in Frederic B. Burnham [ed.], *Postmodern Theology: Christian Faith in a Pluralist World* [San Francisco: HarperSanFrancisco, 1989], pp. 74-91 [85]). One Pentecostal put it, 'It's not how high you jump [in the ritual] but how straight you walk when you come down'. Exuberant worship is expected by Pentecostals, but service and ethical behavior beyond the confines of the ritual setting are required.

27. In each of the three churches I often heard this or similar remarks from the pulpit, indicating that the church is not contained by a building. The strong implication was that the church continued when dispersed and not involved in liturgy. As Pastor Ralston is fond of saying, 'The Church is the people', and the people as the

The Pent/Char liturgy includes implicit expressions of the mission beyond the faith community and its worship setting. The liturgical ritual points beyond itself to 'the world'.[28] Various liturgical leaders make frequent references during the transitional rites and the pastoral message to various forms of Christian service.[29] But at the heart of the Pentecostal fervor resides a strongly held evangelical vision for 'spreading the gospel'. 'Spreading the gospel' for Pastor Tom of the VVCF means feeding the hungry, caring for the poor, healing the sick and announcing the kingdom of God. Consequently, the VVCF encourages corporate and individual efforts and programs that aim toward the goals of this evangel. The CCC also represents mission to the world as spreading the gospel. Here too the conception of the pastor, Pat Ralston, sets the pattern. Ralston conceives of the Christian's role in the society as both disciple and citizen. Thus, the CCC urges its members to become involved in serving the civic community, through political, business, educational, charitable and other public arenas.[30] The true disciple, for Ralston, is the good citizen who shares his or her faith in

church have a mission, the mission is mostly accomplished beyond the liturgical ritual.

28. Members of these three churches go out of their way rhetorically to balance their enjoyment of and desire for the corporate worship experience with their understanding of the Christian duty of service to their neighbors.

29. Scarcely a week goes by in any of the three churches that the respective pastor or other liturgical leader does not refer to one or more of the following: (1) civic community involvement (e.g. participation in the local city council debates, helping the homeless, local relief efforts, the refurbishing and outfitting of a 'mercy-hospital' ship, gathering local support to assist with critical needs in developing countries; (2) an up-coming local outreach of the church that expects broad congregational involvement (e.g. VVCF feeding program, VVCF Mexico outreaches, CCC building projects in developing countries, L&L local evangelistic ministries); (3) recent 'ministry' by a member of the congregation (in testimonial form) to a 'neighbor' (the CCC uses this form to share the recent 'happenings' in their community of the faithful, the civic community and the VVCF emphasizes this form to highlight their understanding and expression of signs and wonders); (4) a missionary from the congregation (e.g. the L&L and CCC both have numerous congregants that service overseas as quasi-professional missionaries; they also support professional/vocational missionaries and mission agencies).

30. Ralston, for example, has led several community service programs that have not only garnered the support of numerous local churches, but have attracted the interest and support of a variety of civic service organizations, the business community and other public institutions.

active service to the community. The L&L, under the leadership of David Markowitz, emphasizes spreading the gospel by building strong families. The L&L seeks to serve families in the Sea City neighborhoods by providing a variety of counseling services, programs that distribute not only food and clothing but financial advisement and training for families and individuals. In each of these churches the liturgy looks beyond itself 'to spread the gospel', 'to serve the world'. Such serving reflects the Pent/Char understanding of the third fundamental Christian relationship, the 'relationship to the world'.[31]

The Pentecostal ritual affords its ritualists the opportunity to express things that matter most to them. Their liturgies dramatize human concerns, social role identity and theological relationships. Such expressive presentations, while symbolic, may also function with efficacious consequence. I now turn to examine some of the efficacious roles of the Pent/Char ritual.

Efficacious Roles: Some Consequences of Pentecostal Ritual

The second major category of roles, functions, of Pent/Char ritual focuses upon efficacious consequences. Pent/Char ritual is more than mere symbolic expressions that reveal and maintain static social and cultural values. True, as presented above, ritual does involve symbolic expressions, expressions that dramatize the social group's values. However, ritual also has an inherent power. One experiences an efficacy at work in authentic, vital ritual. Authentic Pent/Char ritual performance can transform its participants. As a potent agent of change, the Pent/Char ritual not only dramatizes, it animates transmutation.[32]

In this second section I will consider four efficacious dynamics or

31. Well within the larger Pent/Char tradition, these three churches all emphasize evangelization in their local community and globally. Little is explicitly spoken concerning learning *from* or receiving from 'the world' in Pent/Char churches. The emphasis when speaking of relationship to the world is on service, mission, *to* the world. For a view of Pentecostal understanding of the relationship to the world as symbolized, historically and theologically, in the concepts 'evangelization' and 'missions', see the following articles in the *DPCM*: L.G. McClung, Jr, 'Evangelism', pp. 284-88; *idem*, 'Missiology', pp. 607-609; Gary B. McGee, 'Missions, Overseas, (North American)', pp. 610-25.

32. For examples of studies dealing with the efficacy of ritual, see the writings of Turner, especially *Ritual Process, passim*; Myerhoff, *Number our Days*; *idem et al.*, 'Rites of Passage'; and Driver, *The Magic of Ritual*, pp. 131-91.

consequences of the Pent/Char ritual process: liminality, communitas, reflexivity and transformation. While drawing from the works of many students of ritual, I will utilize the ground-breaking work of noted anthropologist Victor Turner. The four categories reflect his thinking. I begin by considering liminality as both a matrix or context for efficacious ritual functions and a consequence of the ritual process itself.

Pentecostal Liminality: Matrix for the Positive Consequences
Liminality, a qualitative dimension of ritual process, facilitates efficacious outcomes of the ritual. Liminality itself is an efficacious consequence of the ritual process. As it itself is a result of the dynamics of the ritual, it bequeaths to the ritual community other gifts. I will examine these 'gifts' or positive consequences, shortly, but first I must consider liminality.

By liminality I mean the properties of ritual that are most distinct from the qualities, values, norms, rules of the prevailing society's social structure or status system by which the society defines and controls its institutions.[33] For Victor Turner, 'liminality' functions as a category or

33. Building on Arnold Van Gennep's conceptualization of rites of passage, Turner's work concentrated on the elements of the middle or 'liminal' phase. Turner recognized the liminal aspects within ritual forms other than rites of passage. People that participate in this 'in between', liminal, dimension of a ritual or live in a state of liminality are seen by Turner as a liminal people, for example, people who live, at least at times, on or across the social boundaries of the larger society. Liminal people have many things in common with the neophytes who participate in a rite of passage. These similarities reinforce the connection between the type of liminality experienced during a rite of passage and the liminality of those who stand on the boundaries of the prevailing structures of society and thus are in a liminal relationship to the society in general. Because such people are out of place according to the larger society and surrounded by mystery, they are often regarded as 'taboo', or, as anthropologist Mary Douglas has shown, 'polluted'. Despite their liminal position and taboo state, liminal people can frequently be sources of renewal, innovation and creativity. See Arnold Van Gennep, *The Rites of Passage* (trans. Monika B. Vizedom and Gabrielle L. Caffee; Chicago: University of Chicago Press, 1960); Turner, *Ritual Process*, pp. 94-130; Driver, *The Magic of Ritual*, pp. 158-62; Myerhoff *et al.*, 'Rites of Passage'. 'Taboo' and 'pollution' are discussed in Mary Douglas, *Purity and Danger: An Analysis of the Concepts of Pollution and Taboo* (New York: Ark Paperbacks, 1966), *passim*.

Although Bell, *Ritual Theory*, does not explicitly use Turner's category, liminality, her definition of ritualization echoes an analogous ideal, namely that ritualization, e.g. ritual actions, is distinguished from other social actions; it is 'cul-

domain within ritual, a dimension found in but not restricted to rites of passage or to a particular phase of ritual. Ritualists who participate in this domain participate in undifferentiated conditions that lie 'betwixt and between', or 'on the edge of' the limits and standards of society. The liminal conditions may consist of fleeting moments, intervals in the ritual that Turner calls 'moments in and out of time and in and out of secular social structure'.[34] Ritual liminality distances one from society's values and structures or suspends them temporarily. Such liminal conditions create an 'anti-structure'[35] that makes 'space' for something different to emerge. This anti-structural space makes 'room' for change and innovation.

Pentecostals participate in forms of ritual liminality. To some extent, the whole of the worship services of the three churches reflects a liminal quality. From the beginning of their services these Pentecostals seek to set themselves apart from the daily life they experience in their society. The service normally begins with enthusiastic celebratory singing, which marks the initial boundary of the ritual. As the rite of worship continues it often becomes quite contemplative, reflecting the mystical bent of the congregants and making it even more liminal. The practice of tongues speech, forms of praise and prayer, expectations and claims of divine intervention, together with a plethora of other behaviors and attitudes, also serve to move the services into liminal domains.

The liminal dimension of the Pentecostal ritual can be seen within some of the elements of the ritual that most clearly contrast the 'rules'

turally specific' and set apart as 'qualitatively distinct', i.e. 'sacred'. It would seem that Bell's definition of ritualization is more narrow than Turner's general understanding. However, her definition does seem to converge with the ritual in the liminal dimensions when she says, 'I will use the term "ritualization" to draw attention to the way in which certain social actions strategically distinguish themselves in relation to other actions... Ritualization is a way of acting that is designed and orchestrated to distinguish and privilege what is being done in comparison to other, usually more quotidian, activities. As such, ritualization is a matter of various culturally specific strategies for setting some activities off from others, for creating and privileging a qualitative distinction between the "sacred" and the "profane" and for ascribing such distinctions to realities thought to transcend the powers of human actors' (p. 74).

34. Turner, *Ritual Process*, p. 96.

35. Victor Turner's term 'anti-structure' does not mean 'no structure'. It is a kind of structure within a ritual, normally connected to the liminal dimension, that defines itself in contrast to the structure of the larger society.

of the society, rules that define normal behavior. In a real sense during the most liminal domains of the liturgy Pentecostals reject 'normal behavior'.[36] In its place there emerges a ritually acceptable code of conduct. These ritual behaviors (e.g. prophesying, ecstatic dancing, charismatic pronouncements and demonstrations, healing rites, and familial forms of affection) not readily acceptable in society are encouraged in Pentecostal ritual. Their liminal code of behavior and the communitas that often emerges represents an implicit critique of the society's rules and roles, but Pentecostals encourage such practices not only as a critique but also because of the effects such practices have on the ritual and the ritualists.

In Chapter 3, I described the ritual field as a created world meant to encourage Pentecostal worship, a context for divine encounter. While

36. This could be conceived of as characteristic of what Ernst Troeltsch designated as the *sect* type religion. Though American Pentecostals have in general moved significantly toward a Troeltschian *church* type of religion, liminal aspects of their ritual betray a sect dimension. This dimension allows for some of the Pentecostal creativity and experimentation. As Robert Bellah has pointed out, such sectarian dynamics 'may pull religion away from the public sphere', but the sectarian dimension 'may also be the *experimental staging ground* for new ideas and new social forms that may subsequently influence the culture and social focus of the society' [emphasis mine]. It might be argued that such is the general case with the Pentecostal (sectarian) movement, especially in its first half-century. As a liminal, sectarian movement it created an 'experimental staging ground' that produced new forms, social and religious, that subsequently influenced the culture, particularly, though not exclusively, through the Charismatic renewal. Though the renewal transmuted many of the cultural forms of the classical Pentecostal, it depended heavily upon the ideas experimented with and developed by the sect tradition of the Pentecostals.

I would contend that to a large extent the experimentation of the Pentecostal movement is integrally linked to its experimental liturgy, especially the liminal dimension of that liturgy. For in liminality Pentecostals have been freely inspired and motivated to create and condition the contours of the spirituality, often in opposition to the dominant cultural and religious forms and institutions. So, in effect, the liminality of the liturgy has contributed to the production of new forms and experiences that, while conceived in a sectarian-type setting, have now broadly influenced the religious landscape of even the most ideal church-type denominations in North American (and, for that matter, internationally). It has through these wider religious channels impacted the 'culture and the social focus of the society'. Troeltsch, *Social Teachings*; Robert N. Bellah, 'Introduction', in Mary Douglas and Steven M. Tipton (eds.), *Religion and America: Spirituality in a Secular Age* (Boston: Beacon Press, 1983 [1982]), pp. xi-xiii.

the liminality of the Pentecostal ritual field facilitates a sense of divine presence and communion, it also fosters the efficacious functions of the ritual, what I am calling the consequences. In short, Pentecostals encourage ritual liminality because they intuitively recognize that it helps to create the environment that acts as a matrix out of which other positive consequences can emerge. These consequences: communitas, reflexivity, and transformation, together with liminality are in a real sense *gifts* from ritual to the Pent/Char congregations.[37]

Creating Community through Communitas

To understand the ritual consequence of *communitas*, I look again to Turner, who first applied the term.[38] Turner described communitas as the relations among people under liminal conditions. During liminality the ritualists live outside the norms fixed by the social system. They live 'betwixt and between', in the 'interstices' of the prevailing structure states of the society. Partially because of this marginality and their common plight, a feeling of solidarity often arises among the liminal people. This unity and sense of oneness describes 'communitas'. A group bonding emerges as people within the matrix of ritual liminality share their common plight. The conditions and dynamics of a liminal phase can then facilitate the community building process.

Pentecostal ritual liminality and anti-structure often produce communitas. Within the liminality of the Pent/Char ritual, a direct, egalitarian encounter, a fellowship between people as people, frequently occurs. I have noted this dynamic above. Pentecostal ritual not only brings its people together in a physical assembly, it helps to unite them emotionally and spiritually. The performance of the Pentecostal rites, as much as anything else in their spirituality, creates and sustains the community of believers. There is a dynamic of community building at work in Pentecostal ritual.

This is partially because of the implicit call for a high level of mutual

37. Driver designates the ritual consequences as 'gifts', *The Magic of Ritual*, pp. 131-33.

38. For examples of Turner's ideas applied to Pentecostalism, see Bobby C. Alexander, 'Pentecostal Ritual Reconsidered: Anti-Structural Dimensions of Possession', *Journal of Ritual Studies* 3 (1985), pp. 109-28 (109); see also Alexander's *Victor Turner Revisited: Ritual as Social Change* (Academy Series, American Academy of Religion, 74; Atlanta: Scholars Press, 1991); and Cucchiari, 'Lords of the Culto', pp. 1-14.

participation in the Pentecostal liturgy. Pentecostal rites require a particular social interactiveness.[39] Ritualists expect one another to engage in the worship service, and spectators are essentially outsiders. This high level of participation in the rituals enhances the solidarity among those who perform the rites together.[40]

Feelings of union with other members of the congregation, especially during the more liminal phases of ritual, are typically reported by Pentecostal ritualists. The temporary suspension of the larger society's social and status structure during ritual liminality opens up the possibilities for new and different social relations and the resulting communitas. The liminal dimensions of Pent/Char ritual then become 'bearers of communitas', and communitas is a force for building and sustaining the Pentecostal community. So, communitas can be a consequence of Pentecostal ritual.[41]

Pentecostal Ritual Reflexivity
Another consequence of the Pentecostal rites and their orientation is *reflexivity*. By reflexivity we mean a self-conscious questioning, exami-

---

39. See above for consideration of the social dimensions of the liturgies in the Sea City faith communities. Also see, Marty, *Nation of Behavers*, pp. 113-14.

40. Since at least the time of Durkheim social scientists have recognized that mutual ritual performance reinforces the unity in the given community. This spirit of unity and mutual belonging is, according to Tom Driver, frequently the result of 'rituals of high energy' (see Driver, *The Magic of Ritual*, pp. 154, 164). The Pentecostal ritual performance is a symbolic expression of who the congregation is as a people. It expresses the group's self-identity and demonstrates its values and beliefs. This symbolic expression in turn acts to shape the identity, the common understanding of the community. Together, these dynamics strengthen solidarity.

41. During my field research the most poignant moments of spontaneous communitas occurred at the L&L during the worship and praise rite. A sense of deep community pervaded the congregation, especially after the more celebrative actions, during the quiet pauses. In contrast, at the CCC, I noted several times a pervasive sense of spontaneous communitas during the Sunday evening altar/response rite. When the response was for corporate congregational prayer 'around the altars' (not for healing rites or evangelical responses or any particular rite of passage, e.g. Spirit baptism), the sense of praying together as a community emerged. Strong emotional and spiritual bonding seemed evident. In these moments the congregation supported one another as they completed their 'formal' Sunday rites in a less structured setting. This period is apparently liminal in that it stands between the end of one week and the beginning of another. And often, when the congregation found itself together in such a moment, they experienced a spontaneous communitas.

nation and/or exploration that may arise within ritual liminality or within other marginal situations. The dominant society's categories, social boundaries and symbols can within liminality's anti-structure be questioned, altered, renewed or in other ways investigated. According to Turner, liminal qualities of ritual can help to free participants to become reflexive.[42]

Such reflexivity is encouraged among, even expected of, Pentecostal ritual participants. Reflexive awareness may occur at any moment within a Pentecostal service, or it may even pervade the entire service. The ritual parameters, the liminality of the Pentecostal ritual in particular permits, even stimulates, a free reflexivity. In a sense, the security and familiarity of the ritual context (and the possible communitas) facilitates a freedom to explore and question reflexively. Social and personal categories can be played with, inverted even suspended within the liminality of the Pentecostal service.[43]

In part, the reflexive consequence of the Pentecostal rites is a result of Pentecostal orientation to liturgical 'contemplation' (see Chapter 5). Rites experienced within the contemplative mode of sensibility are marked by an attitude of deep receptivity and docility toward God. In accord with this sensibility, the potential for an arousal of self-conscious questioning is actualized. In fact, ritual participants in each of the three churches repeatedly reported being moved to the edge of profound self-investigation and exploration. Such reflexivity frequently moves them toward moments of conversion and spiritual changes. The reflexive consequence is a gift of the Pentecostal ritual and a key to the last consequence, transformation.

42. The dynamics of reflexivity, however, are not necessarily confined to the safety of the ritual boundaries or to the liminal phase(s) alone. Turner saw that reflexivity could spread from the liminal conditions into the phase after the liminal period where the people are integrated back into the larger group and/or structured society. Herein lies the potential transformative force of the liminal reflexivity. According to Turner, liminal reflexivity is often responsible for producing transmutations of categories, symbols or values born in the liminal phase, carried into the regressive phase and finally into the larger social structure, so that elements of the anti-structure, shaped through reflexivity in the communitas of liminality, become transformative influences in the structured states of society, the states outside the ritual.

43. Myerhoff suggests that the underlying paradoxes of human life are exposed and accentuated in rituals where there is a certain safety within the familiar boundaries ('Rites of Passage', p. 382).

Transformation in a Pentecostal Mode

Victor Turner's work concerning the potential transformative function of ritual is especially informative to our Pentecostal ritual study. Turner's basic insight recognized in ritual a dynamic potential for transformation. He demonstrated that the ritual performance is not only dramaturgic, communicating the values of a community, but that the most vital work of ritual is to effect change. The transformative impact of ritual performance on its participants not only changes the individual ritualists, it impacts the broader life of the ritual community and the larger society beyond.[44]

Pentecostals have long claimed transformations during their rites. Characteristically, each of the Sea City congregations actively pursues transformation. They come together to be changed, transformed and they disperse in order to change their world. Their spirituality seeks conversions and transformations of individuals, of their communities of faith and of the world in general. But such transformations are the results of an empowerment. Ritualists speak of and seek the 'power of the Holy Spirit'. They claim that their lives and the world in general can be transformed only by the Spirit's power and by the Spirit-empowered people.[45]

44. Douglas, *Purity and Danger*. Also, Margaret M. Kelleher, 'Liturgy: An Ecclesial Act of Meaning', *Worship* 59.6 (November 1985), pp. 482-97. Margaret Kelleher, following Victor Turner and theologian Bernard Lonergan, recognizes the liturgical ritual as a 'form of ecclesial praxis' that in its actions 'manifest[s] and create[s] a self'. Here she speaks of a corporate self, a congregation, that is self-creating as it enacts its ritual, as it proclaims the Christian message in word and action. This 'process of mediating itself' is a form of what I have called transformation, for it describes a function of the ritual, wherein ritual goes beyond the mere communication of its community's beliefs and its social structures and transforms its participants.

45. This connection of ritual and empowerment is consistent with Emile Durkheim's claim that 'the believer who has communicated with his god is not merely a man who sees new truths of which the unbeliever is ignorant; he is a man who is stronger. He feels within him more force, either to endure the trials of existence, or to conquer them' (cited in Wuthnow, *Meaning and Moral Order*, p. 368, from Robert N. Bellah [ed.], *Emile Durkheim on Morality and Society* [Chicago: University of Chicago Press, 1973], p. 189). Robert Wuthnow follows the Durkheimian pattern in pointing out a stage of vulnerability for the ritualist prior to the sense of empowerment. This pattern is reflected in the Pent/Char ritual. As indicated in a previous chapter, the liturgies of the Sea City churches implicitly call for a high level of vulnerability, a 'docility before the Holy Spirit'. This vulnerability

In the liturgical rituals of the three churches, the pursuit of spiritual transformation clearly manifests itself. The desire for transformation drives nearly all Pent/Char ritual. This desire appears in the language and other symbols of Pentecostal ritual. Transformation symbols that permeate the rites, the testimonies, the songs, the sermonic illustrations and the altar calls, to name a few, express the language of transformation. The yearning for spiritual life brought about through conversions, Spirit baptisms, healings and other transformative experiences demonstrates the importance of transformation to a Pentecostal spirituality. Together these examples witness to the centrality of the transformed life, the converted lifestyle within our Sea City faith communities.[46]

The ritual role effecting transformation is integrally linked to the Pentecostal sensibility designated earlier as 'transcendental efficacy' (see Chapter 5). This mode of Pentecostal expression and experience is an orientation toward doing pragmatic ritual work. It is less concerned with the meaning of the attending symbols as with the effect. Transcendental efficacy embodies an attitude filled with expectancy that often animates rites and prayers for healing, conversion, Spirit baptism and others. This sensibility looks to God in anticipation of transformation while it seeks to do what it understands to be effective in the way of ritual work. Our ritualists know that their practice of the healing rites, for example, does not heal. 'God heals', they insist. But their ritual

and docility is not mere passivity, on the contrary, it requires an active responsiveness to the perceived impulses and word of the Spirit. It is in such vulnerability, linked to an active responsiveness, that empowerment is generated, according to Wuthnow. Thus the docility that often characterizes the rite of worship and praise and the active responses that are called for in, for instance, the rite of altar/response combine in a pattern that facilitate the sense of empowerment claimed by Pentecostals. (See Wuthnow, *Meaning and Moral Order*, pp. 138-40.) For a very different and quite nuanced perspective on the place of power in ritual see Bell, *Ritual Theory*, pp. 197-223.

46. The category of sense of divine presence and the category of divine transformation are co-joined in the Pent/Char spirituality.

The above claim that 'the desire for transformation' motivates most of Pent/Char ritual does not ignore ritual moments when particular sensibilities—such as a mode of celebration that reveals very little interest in transformation or any pragmatic goal—are dominant. While such 'moments' pervade Pent/Char worship, they do not negate the fundamental desire for transformation.

work, inspired by a mode of transcendental efficacy, is a kind of participation with God in the consequence of transformation.[47]

In summary, the Pent/Char ritual process functions both as an expressive, dramatic communication—of vital human concerns, community
social boundaries, and theological relationships—and as an efficacious
dynamic. In the efficacious ritual roles Pent/Char liturgy creates a liminal dimension that together with the ritual process, helps to produce a
uniquely ordered social group with its own beliefs that often has the
marks of communitas. The liminality of the ritual also works toward a
'space' for personal and collective reflexivity, which in turn provides a
basic stimulus toward transformation (namely personal conversions,
healings, empowerments, Spirit baptisms and dedications to missions)
consistent with Pentecostal understanding of the gospel and Christian
life. I turn now to the closing chapter to consider specifically the characteristic qualities of Pentecostal spirituality.

47. Pentecostals recognize that the transformation they seek is not the result of
their own works, but is through the gracious action of their God. They do, however,
participate in the process of their transformation(s). They come to (and shape) the
liminal context, they stimulate one another toward certain sensibilities of worship
that orient them toward God and toward an encounter with God. The encounter
itself, symbolized in the immediate presence of God, is communal, and it is responsible for effecting transformation.

Chapter 7

CHARACTERISTIC QUALITIES OF PENTECOSTAL/
CHARISMATIC SPIRITUALITY

This consideration of spirituality expressed in Pentecostalism has been
mediated through the lens of the rituals of three Sea City churches. It
began by giving the contexts of both the twentieth-century Pentecostal
movement and of each of the three congregations. Next it considered
elements of the ritual field that not only contextualize the Pent/Char
ritual drama but actually merge into the ritual process. It then sought to
identify and describe the typical structural procedure of the overall
ritual and its component rites. Also it located modes of sensibility that
orient and animate the performance of those rites. Lastly, it pointed out
some of the expressive and efficacious functions of the Pent/Char rites.
Throughout this work I have implicitly and explicitly drawn attention to
the characteristics of Pentecostal spirituality, particularly as expressed
and experienced in the rituals of the chosen churches. It remains for me
now to draw together these concepts and themes of Pent/Char spirituality. Thus, this concluding chapter will focus wholly upon the characteristic qualities of Pentecostal spirituality. In the Introduction to this
work I gave a general working definition of Christian spirituality. Now
after considering various aspects of Pentecostal ritual I specify *Pent/
Char* spirituality as a particular configuration of beliefs, practices and
sensibilities that put the believer in an on-going relationship to the
Spirit of God.[1]

---

1. No single treatment can possibly claim to encompass all of the varieties of
Pent/Char spiritualities even in North America, nor represent in detail the texture of
the experience of each group, let alone each individual Pentecostal. We recognize
the dilemma of generalization, but I believe that I can with some clarity focus on
the essential, elemental qualities that represent the core of Pent/Char spirituality (at
least within the three churches of this study). As a comparative device, I have also
considered the reflections of numerous scholars of Pentecostalism that bear directly

In order to explicate the major qualities of the Pent/Char spirituality I will proceed in two ways. First, I will suggest six selected emic or indigenous *ritual symbols*,[2] that function as primary factors (symbols)

on Pent/Char spirituality. The following are some of the works that I have considered and drawn from. Some of these will be specifically cited below. Barrett, 'Twentieth-Century Renewal'; Blumhofer, *Assemblies*, I, pp. 141-78; *idem*, ' "Pentecost in my Soul": Probing the Early Pentecostal Ethos', *Assemblies of God Heritage* (Spring 1989), pp. 13-14; Louis Bouyer, 'Some Charismatic Movements in the History of the Church', in Edward D. O'Connor (ed.), *The Pentecostal Movement in the Catholic Church* (Notre Dame, IN: Ave Maria Press, 1971), pp. 113-31; Burgess, McGee and Alexander, 'Introduction', pp. 1-6; Cox, *Fire from Heaven*; Charles Farah, 'America's Pentecostals: What They Believe', *CT* (16 October 1987), pp. 22, 24-26; Donald Gee, *Concerning Spiritual Gifts* (Springfield, MO: Gospel Publishing, 1972, [1937]); Gelpi, *Divine Mother*; *idem*, *Experiencing God*; Hocken, 'Charismatic Movement'; W.J. Hollenweger, 'The Pentecostals and the Charismatic Movement', in Cheslyn Jones *et al.* (eds.), *The Study of Spirituality* (New York: Oxford University Press, 1986), pp. 549-51; *idem*, *The Pentecostals*, esp. pp. 291-511; *idem*, *Pentecostalism*; Wayne Kraiss and Barbara Kraiss, 'The Changing Face of Worship', *Theology, News and Notes* (March 1991), pp. 7-11; Land, *Pentecostal Spirituality*; *idem*, 'Pentecostal Spirituality'; Kenneth Leech, *Soul Friend: The Practice of Christian Spirituality* (San Francisco: Harper & Row, 1977); Marty, *Nation of Behavers*, pp. 106-25; *idem*, 'Pentecostalism'; McClung, 'Evangelism'; McGee, 'Missions, Overseas'; Quebedeaux, *The New Charismatics II*, pp. 127-92; Robeck, Jr, 'Azusa Street Revival'; Robins, 'Pentecostal Movement'; *idem*, 'Pentecostals and the Apostolic Faith: Implications for Ecumenism', *Pneuma* 9 (1987), pp. 61-84; Spittler, 'The Pentecostal View'; *idem* (ed.), 'Spirituality'; *idem*, *Perspectives on the New Pentecostalism*; Vinson Synan (ed.), *Aspects of Pentecostal–Charismatic Origins* (Plainfield, NJ: Logos International, 1975); *idem*, 'Pentecostalism', pp. 31-49; Wacker, 'America's Pentecostals; *idem*, 'Function of Faith'; *idem*, 'Pentecostalism', pp. 933-45; White, *Protestant Worship*; J. Rodman Williams, *The Pentecostal Reality* (Plainfield, NJ: Logos International, 1972).

2.   Anthropologists often distinguish between *emic* and *etic* descriptions of culture, a distinction made first by K. Pike, *Language in Relation to a Unified Theory of the Structure of Human Behavior*, I (Glendale: Summer Institute of Linguistics, 1954), p. 8. An emic term is indigenous it is a term employed by the people of the culture. An *emic* analysis of a culture utilizes the folk terms and attempts to portray the culture and its meaningfulness as an insider understands it, whereas an etic analysis applies categories that the anthropologist finds helpful in describing the culture to outsiders. In this chapter I do not attempt to operate wholly within either of these types of analyses. However, in this first section especially, I do find it helpful to use prevalent emic/indigenous terms to describe aspects of Pent/Char spirituality.

within Pent/Char spirituality.[3] Each of these factors symbolizes a cluster of qualities, beliefs, practices and sensibilities connected to Pentecostal spirituality. Secondly, I will present a general outline of the characteristic qualities of Pent/Char spirituality within the organizing symbol of *experiencing God*. I begin by selecting six emic/indigenous ritual symbols.

Selected (Emic/Indigenous) Ritual Symbols: Elemental Factors of Pentecostal Spirituality

Throughout the previous chapters I have described and interpreted a variety of data concerning Pent/Char ritual symbols. In this first section of the present chapter, I select six fundamental indigenous symbols central to Pent/Char ritual and thus important to the understanding of Pentecostal spirituality in general. Here, I will consider them as elemental factors for understanding particular qualities of Pent/Char spirituality. I chose emic or folk terms, that is, familiar idiomatic concepts rooted in Pentecostal parlance. The following emic symbols commonly surface in each of the three faith communities and enjoy wide use among American Pentecostals: *leadership, worship, word, gifts, ministry* and *mission(s)*. I begin with the leadership factor.

Leadership

The symbol of leader within the Pent/Char ritual context suggest certain qualities about the leadership factor and the Pentecostal spirituality in general. In each of the three churches *leadership* functions as a powerful symbol. Here I will focus on five characteristics of leadership as experienced in a Pent/Char spirituality: leadership as spokesman or woman, as lay (non-specialist/expert), as spontaneous and recognized, as a responsive social dynamic and as boundary for order and ecstacy. Let us begin by looking at leadership as spokesperson.

Leadership as spokesperson and model. Much of leadership in the Pentecostal tradition emerges within the role of spokeswoman or spokes-

---

3. On 'select symbols' of a ritual, see Turner, *Forest of Symbols*, pp. 19-47, and Kelleher, 'The Communion Rite'; Paul Ricoeur, *The Symbolism of Evil* (trans. Emerson Buchanan; Boston: Beacon Press, 1967), esp., 'the primary symbols', pp. 3-157.

man.[4] As I have indicated above, the prophetic role is essentially open to any Pent/Char ritualist. Anyone who functions as a spokesperson for God leads, at least during the giving of their oracle. As a result of the prominent prophetic role in the Pent/Char tradition, the symbol of leadership conforms in part to the prophetic type. The prophetic role within the liturgy continues to shape the notion of leadership, specifically the role of the Pent/Char pastor. Though others may bear the message to the faithful, particularly during the ritual, the pastor must carry out the role of the prophet. Of course, the pastor often carries the burden of the prophet during the preaching rite. But in all these three churches the senior pastor also functions as the primary spokesperson for the divine during other rites. For example, at the VVCF, Pastor Tom gives most of the 'words of knowledge' that follow the sermon and precede the rites of healing. Similarly, at the CCC, Pastor Ralston most often gives the interpretation to a message in tongues.

But leadership means more than anointed utterances. The boundaries of leadership include other functions and other types. For example, worship teams at the VVCF and L&L are primarily the leaders of the first phase of the ritual process. Members of the teams do not normally lead by giving verbal directions or announcements. Rather, they model and facilitate worship and praise.[5] They, as a team, symbolize leadership in their actions and demeanor during the worship and praise rite.

Leadership as lay (non-specialist/expert). Elders and deacons also represent leadership in the Sunday ritual. Though the role of elders and deacons varies from church to church, normally they are all lay and not part of the professional staff of the church. Their leadership is more a leadership within the congregational life of the church, but they are also

---

4.   In the history of the Pentecostal movement, spokes*women* have played a prominent and significant role. Aimee Semple McPherson and Kathryn Kuhlman represent only two or the most well known. But as specialists (i.e. preachers, evangelists, teachers, missionaries) or lay, women have spoken from within the Pentecostal tradition, usually to their own local congregations. Their congregations believed them to be speaking on behalf of God.

5.   They represent leadership as a team, as opposed to individual leadership. For example, on the first visit to the L&L I did not recognize that there is a 'head' of the team. During the worship rite the team of four vocalists and several instruments seem to be one unit—a true team. Upon further investigation, it became clear that one was the principal leader, but the sense of multiple leadership in the form of a team continues even after one knows who primarily directs.

recognizable symbols of leadership within the ritual context to the discerning eye. Their presence is felt. Often they greet visitors, serve as ushers, make announcements, help serve communion, pray for the sick, minister around the altars during prayer times, teach, even preach from the pulpit. Elders and deacons represent the importance and the prominence of lay leadership in Pent/Char spirituality.

Leadership as spontaneous and legitimate. As indicated, leadership is not limited to the standard established roles (e.g. pastor, elder, deacon, worship team). Spontaneous leadership may emerge through almost any member of the congregation, as one 'moved by the Holy Spirit' takes action.[6] However, the mere action does not assure a resulting leadership identity. A spontaneous action must be legitimized, emerging acts of leadership must be recognized. To be legitimate it must be recognized as 'from God' or 'The Spirit' and it must be 'in order' or appropriate to the moment in the service. In other words, to be legitimated, the congregation (and the established leadership) must discern the burgeoning leadership's charismatic qualifications.[7] The congregation must see a spontaneous act of leadership as 'anointed' or 'operating in the gifts'. If they are Spirit anointed and properly operating in the gifts of the Spirit, they must be recognized as 'moving out' during an appropriate moment in the service and with an appropriate tone or else they will be seen as 'not in order'. The congregation and the established leadership must believe in the appropriateness of spontaneous charismatic leadership.

Leadership as legitimated by a responsive social dynamic. It is clear that spontaneous leadership, while available to any individual ritualist, depends on a corporate legitimation and recognition. In this dynamic even the spontaneous charisms have a social dimension.[8] Thus, the Pent/Char symbol of leadership speaks of the social functions of the

6.   The Pent/Char understanding of charismatic 'leadings' and 'giftings' yields a potential for a variety of leadership roles and styles both in the ritual and in the larger Pent/Char communities. For both the established leaders (e.g. pastors) and spontaneous leaders are expected to move and lead according to the Spirit's guidance. The resulting leadership roles will vary according to the individual leader and the particular situation.

7.   See Chapter 4, 'Charismatic Criteria'.

8.   For an informative view of charismatic leadership as social, see Peter Worsely, *The Trumpet Shall Sound* (New York: Schocken Books, 2nd edn, 1968), esp. the 'Introduction'.

spirituality. Certainly, spontaneous charismatic eruptions may symbolize the immediacy of the divine and the docility of the emerging leader, but they also reveal the complex social dynamic of discernment that either recognizes an action as legitimate or not.

This social dynamic of leadership also emerges in a quality of responsiveness within the liturgical ritual. Leadership provides a symbol for the *responsive/relational quality* of the Pent/Char spirituality. A dialogical relationship defines the interaction between leader(s) and followers in the ritual setting.[9] A sense of responsiveness characterizes the whole ritual.[10] The expressive actions of liturgical leaders almost always, either explicitly or implicitly, call for and expect a congregational response. For example, worship teams lead in a manner that will elicit a maximum responsive form of worshipful singing; the pastoral message seeks a response—often an immediate one; calls for healing and commissioning rites also invoke congregational responses as do various charismatic words. Pentecostals use leadership roles to rouse responses from liturgists to their God. Fundamentally, liturgical leadership metaphorically stands for the divine leadership. Pentecostals consciously seek to reply to the voice of the Spirit, to respond to the 'leading of the Spirit', both in the ritual and beyond.

Leadership as a boundary: Order and ecstacy. Finally, the Pent/Char ritual leadership symbolizes a basic binary opposition: order/ecstacy.[11]

---

9.   Victor Turner, Mary Douglas and other anthropologists consider inherent 'binary oppositions' that often define a symbol. A sampling of binary oppositions within the ritual leadership symbol suggests that the variety of the leadership roles each has a responsive congregational role: pastor/people; prophet/listeners; priestly/needy; teacher/learners; exhorter/responders; worship leaders/responsive worshippers; facilitator/congregation; musicians/singing ritualists; word giver/word receivers; leader of a rite/participants in the rite; charismatic spontaneous leaders/discerning followers. See Turner, *Ritual Process*, p. 106, for an example, and Douglas's *Purity and Danger* for extended illustrations.

10.   For a study that recognized the unique responsiveness of Pent/Char spirituality, see Cucchiari, 'Lords of the Culto'.

11.   Anthropologists at least since Claude Levi-Strauss express distinctions and tensions within a culture by locating binary oppositions or discriminations. Victor Turner uses this method to contrast liminality and status system. See Turner, *Ritual Process*, pp. 106-107. For other example of this technique see Mary Douglas's use of symbolic boundaries in cultural analysis in *Purity and Danger* and Wuthnow, *Meaning and Moral Order*, esp. pp. 66-96.

The Pentecostal service maintains a leadership balance in part through a dynamic tension between order and ecstacy. An individual ritual leader, particularly the pastor, functions as a symbol of both order and ecstacy. Pastoral leadership must fulfill the congregation's expectations that they can lead them into forms of group ecstacy. On the other hand, the pastor remains responsible for maintaining the boundaries that provide order. As I have mentioned, there are various leaders and potential leaders in any of the liturgies of the three churches. This variety of leaders must incorporate the order/ecstacy tension, as the individual pastor must.

Though it is not always recognized, the Pent/Char ritual leaders are surrounded by signs of order. In the discussion of the ritual field, in Chapter 3, I identified ritual objects associated with the symbol of leader: pulpit, platform space, altar space, microphone, musical instruments and other technological instruments. These symbolic objects help to create the field in which the ritual proceeds. These symbolic objects and spaces, together with the leader(s), interact to give shape and order to the ritual experience.

How is this tension of order and ecstasy understood in the leadership symbol? As I have said, the Pentecostal congregation recognizes the leader as one who follows God's Spirit. As the follower of God, they must be 'in tune' with the Spirit. Pentecostals ardently believe in a divine order (as opposed to a merely human order that is insensitive to God's design), and they insist that to follow the Spirit authentically one must participate in the divine order. Thus, leadership must discern order with sensitivity to the Spirit and the people. The people may be led into ecstasy but it must reflect the Spirit's order. Most often the established leadership in these churches functions as a boundary for ecstacy, a symbol of orderliness. In this way the pastor in the liturgy functions somewhat analogously to the early Rebbes of Hasidism.[12]

---

12. The Rebbe, especially in Jewish Hasidism, was a very charismatic leader who lead his followers in high states of ecstacy. He functioned, however, as an ordering boundary. The symbol of the Rebbe (or Zaddik) was a firm boundary, his leadership was absolute and quite domineering. But within the well-defined, firm boundaries of his leadership the Hasidim were granted greater flexibility and freedom in their worship and life-styles than other contemporary Jewish groups. The Hasidic ecstacy could be approached with a sense of abandon because their Leader provided such secure and dependable boundaries. As long as the group was within his boundary they were free. On Hasidism and the Zaddik or Rebbe, see Louis Jacobs, *Hasidic Prayer* (Oxford: Oxford University Press, 1972); Ada Rapoport-Albert, 'God and the Zaddik as the Two Focal Points of Hasidic Worship', *HR* 18

Thus, what may appear as disorder even chaos in the Pentecostal ritual to the non-Pentecostal or the non-discerning, represents a godly order to the Pentecostal believer, an order that includes the 'interruptions' in the human plan, an order that provides for ecstacy within its boundaries. For the Pentecostal the symbol of leadership represents both order and ecstacy. I turn now to consider the other main elemental factors of Pent/Char spirituality, beginning with 'worship'.[13]

Worship
This represents a set of meanings configured by Pentecostals. Their understanding and practice of worship lies at the heart of their ritual and spirituality. For example, throughout our field research we continually heard the term, 'I come for the worship', or ' "Vineyard" has the best worship,' or, 'Worship is the most important part of our service'.

Pentecostals understand worship as having three main connotations: (1) Worship as *a way of Christian life*, particularly outside of the church services and activities. All of life is seen as worship, as an expression, a gift, offered to God. (2) Worship as *the entire liturgy*, the whole of the Pentecostal service. (3) Worship as a *specific* portion, aspect, or *rite* within the overall liturgy. While all three of these connotations contain a Pentecostal understanding of the symbol, here, however, I will draw mainly from the third. I will consider these dimensions of worship as experimental in the worship and praise rite: worship as encounter with hierophany, as attentiveness to God, and as yielding a sensitivity to human need.

(1978), pp. 269-325; Gershom G. Scholem, *Major Trends in Jewish Mysticism* (New York: Schocken Books, 1941), ch. 9. See also Mary Douglas's conceptualization of boundaries in her categories of 'grid' and 'group' in *Natural Symbols*.

13. The leadership symbol is central to an understanding of the other elemental factors of Pent/Char spirituality that I have selected: worship, word, gifts, ministry, and mission. The dynamics between the leadership symbol and these other main symbols are based on the congregations' values. The leader of Pentecostal worship is perceived as embodying the values of the community. In some ways the leaders symbolize the community in total, its values and potentials. Leaders help to model the ideals of the community in worship. Their roles in worship, word, charisms, ministries, and outreach help to demonstrate the possibilities within each symbol. The potential for transformation and (re)ordering of the community are in part recognized in the symbol of leadership. The leadership symbol, then, helps to shape the common vision and guide the worshipers toward that vision.

Encounter with hierophany.[14] Among the Sea City congregants, 'worship' is another way of saying 'presence of God'. Worship functions as a code term. It refers to the encounter with the divine as mediated by a sense of the divine presence or power. Pentecostals believe strongly in the manifest presence of God. Their experience of the holy presence shapes them spiritually. In the liturgy the heightened awareness of this presence occurs often within the dimension they refer to as worship.

Pentecostals practice worship as both the experiencing (the immediate presence) of God and as the 'techniques', iconic ways into the presence of God.[15] Forms of musical expressions, including powerfully suggestive symbolic worship choruses and verbal and kinesthetic praise practices serve to 'trigger' a sense of close presence, a hierophany.[16] Within the milieu of hierophany, the Pentecostals encounter and experience the divine.[17] The rites then function as both experiences themselves and icons into particular forms of experience (e.g. hierophany).

The Pentecostal attitude toward worship is essential to understanding their practice of it.[18] For Pentecostals, worship is not strictly a human activity. Worship involves a deep communion between divinity and humanity, an encountering, a mutual experiencing. An attitude of expectancy shapes the practice of this communion. Believers expect God to come and meet with his people. Pentecostals believe that God alone inaugurates the experience by God's gracious acts and presence, con-

---

14. I understand hierophany here to mean an earthy manifestation of divine power.

15. See Chapter 3.

16. See Tipton, *Getting Saved*, for his understanding of a 'circle of reciprocally reinforcing links'. According to Tipton's study, the rites 'induce experiences. Experiences prove teachings. Teachings interpret experiences' (p. 237). Tipton recognized the centrality of experience to the groups he researched and he rightly notes the 'triggering' effect of rites, they 'induce experiences'. However, he seems to minimize the experiential dimension of rites themselves. In the treatment I recognize that while rites may function as a cause of another experience, they are themselves forms of experience.

17. Of course, Pentecostals believe in encountering and relating to their God outside of the hierophanic dimension. They often encourage each other with the verse 'we walk by faith and not by sight' (2 Cor. 5.7). To the Pentecostals this verse means that the Christian life is not based on 'sight' or manifestations of the divine. It is rather founded on faith in God. Nonetheless, hierophanies are appreciated as facilitating worship, particularly within the ritual setting.

18. See Jerry Shepperd, 'Worship', in *DPCM*, pp. 903-905.

gregants can only prepare themselves (through their iconic ways). Ritualists cannot force God's presence and movings. They can only prepare and wait for God's actions in the worshipers and then respond to the 'flow of the Spirit', when God's 'promptings' or 'stirrings' occur. The Spirit initiates, guides, facilitates and leads the worship. Pentecostals believe that God 'desires to meet with his people'. Thus, the Pentecostal approaches worship in an attitude of expectancy; God will encounter God's people. This understanding molds the style and structure of the ritual and informs the symbol of worship as a type of encounter with hierophany.

Worship as attentiveness to God. While the goals of encounter, experience, (and transformation) always predominate, worship embodies a kind of performance that attends closely to the divine. Particularly in the praise and worship rites, frequently at the beginning of the ritual, the Sea City Pentecostals see themselves as performing for the divine. God is the audience and the congregation is to perform the drama of praise. For, as they say, 'God inhabits the praises of his people.' This 'performance' for the ritualists represents a way of attending to God, a way of focusing on the divine, a 'ministry to God'.

Ministry unto God both differs from and connects with other aspects of 'ministry' in the Pentecostal worship economy. To perform acts directed toward God is understood as the ultimate in human expression. All other performance, or ministries, have secondary importance. According to a Pentecostal understanding, other ministries 'flow from worship'. The ministry of worship or attending to God functions as the foundational ministry. As a result Pentecostals root the other four selected symbols, word, gifts, ministry and missions, in their understanding of worship.

Worship as yielding a sensitivity to human need. Pentecostals claim that their forms of worship sensitize them to human needs and concerns. The priority of worshiping God, and thus maintaining a 'right relationship with God', they believe allows them a subsequent awareness of human needs. Pentecostals experience a self reflexivity, an empathy toward the needs of others, and a motivation to minister to others as a result of their worship. According to Pentecostals, the terms 'word', 'gifts' and 'missions' (see below) each represents human interaction enhanced by ritual worship and graced by the divine. God, they believe, 'desires to minister to peoples' needs' through the faithful and gifted ritualists. In worship the believers minister to God and then God in turn ministers in and through the believers to others.[19] For example, at the CCC, often during or immediately following the rite of worship and praise, a ritual leader will ask for prayer requests. From week to week it varies, but some form of prayer or healing rite will normally emerge at the end of the worship rite. Congregants may form circles of prayer, praying for one another's needs. Or, the pastor may call those who desire prayer for a need to come to the altar to be prayed for by the elders. Other times congregants may simply be asked to stand to signify a prayer request. Other ritualists will then come to pray with them. In each case, congregants reflect a sensitivity to human needs.

The Word
Pentecostals employ the term 'the word' to symbolize the belief that 'God speaks today,' as in the past, that is that God speaks to God's people even as God spoke in the biblical days. In the ritual, the symbol

---

19. Such rites point to the creative potential inherent in the Pent/Char practices and understanding of worship. The potential has both positive and negative possibilities. Positively, Pent/Char worship allows for enthusiastic, vital participation of all ritualists. It encourages each person to enter into a dramatic conversation with God mediated through a faith community, wherein worshipping Pentecostals become a people, a family, an interconnected, supportive, transformative community. The community seeks to reorder itself within its understanding of divine guidance, guidance from the Holy Spirit as understood in the worship context.

But there are of course potentially negative possibilities inherent in the Pentecostal practice and understanding of worship as well. One danger of a Pentecostal understanding of worship is that it can become too narrow. Pentecostals have in the past been intolerant to other forms of worship, Pentecostals can become fixated on their own icons and rites, revealing little appreciation for other possible symbolizations from historic Christianity or contemporary spiritualities. These potentially negative attitudes may work together to produce a form of Christian elitism (an oxymoron). Finally, the Pent/Char conception of worship is also ripe with the danger of self-deception. In the affectively charged dimension that Pentecostals call worship, human sensations and emotions are encouraged and are believed to help in the communicative process with the divine. The need rightly to discern an authentic 'move' of the Spirit is opposed to self deceiving impulses. The danger of assigning divine origins to neurotic impulses and behaviors always threatens in the absence of rigorous discerning practices. Our Sea City Pentecostals seem aware of these potentials, positive and negative, and apparently believe the risk is worth the taking. The benefits outweigh the negative possibilities.

of word functions as part of the divine–human 'conversation'. If praise and worship symbolize the human half of the conversation, then the word symbolizes the divine side of the dialogue. Pentecostals recognize the voice of God, the word, in biblical messages (e.g. sermons, teachings, exhortations), testimonial narratives and charismatic words.

The Bible and biblical messages. The Bible as word is seen as speaking to contemporary needs, sometimes in an overly simplistic interpretation, but always relevant in 'the now'. The pastoral message proclaims or teaches a 'biblical truth'. This biblical message places the word of God at the center of the service, between the worship and praise rite and the rite of altar response. Comforting or challenging, edifying or exhorting, directional or didactic, the pastoral message aims for biblical relevance. But in the Pentecostal ritual 'word' is not limited to sermons, teachings, or pastoral exhortations.

Testimonial narratives. God speaks in other moments of the ritual. The symbol of word extends to testimonies and narratives that place daily life as well as 'spiritual experiences' within a biblical/faith framework. These 'sharings' may occur in speech or song; they may take on a formal aim or be informally related, but authentic testimony that speaks out of human experience seeks to discern the works of God in the life of the faith community and world. Functioning in this way, testimony narratives provide a way of doing theology. Thus, the narratives both interpret the works of God and give voice to the words of God.[20]

Charismatic word(s). Perhaps the most dynamic dimension of the Pent/ Char understanding of 'word' is that of 'charismatic word(s)'. Aspects of these phenomena are referred to as 'gifts', 'utterances', 'words', 'prophecies', 'messages in tongues', 'word from the Lord', 'manifestation of the Spirit', etc. Not every charism or charismatic activity fits the category of word (e.g. gifts of healing are seen as actions of God and 'discernment of spirits' is seen as insight), but many charismatic manifestations in the ritual emerge within the classification, word (e.g. 'word of knowledge', 'word of wisdom').

Fundamentally, the word in Pentecostal parlance is a speaking forth in the name of the Lord. It gives voice to the divine under the impulse

20. See Land, *Pentecostal Spirituality*, esp. ch. 2, and his 'Pentecostal Spirituality', p. 485; and Cox, *Fire from Heaven*, ch. 7.

of the Spirit. Charismatic words vary. The style and form of such words vary with the context, the community, the personality of the speaker and the perceived need.[21] Frequently, a ritualist casts a word in a prophetic mode, with a 'thus saith the Lord' as a prelude or postscript. At other times a charismatic word's introduction takes a more cautious turn, 'I feel the Lord is saying…', a congregant begins. In either case there is an inherent risk. What if the 'prophesy' does not represent the word of God? What if the impulse to speak was not rightly discerned? What if the congregation does not 'receive' the word? These questions represent the risk faced by the would-be charismatic prophet. However, Pentecostal prophets face this risk with a belief that relies on the Spirit and on their own experience and knowledge of the Spirit's ways. Yet in the end the congregation must discern a charismatic word's appropriateness and validity.

While charismatic words ideally represent a word from God, the ideal is not always realized. Pentecostals test the words, because they recognize the room for error and the importance of the human dimension. One Pentecostal told us the story of a brother who felt he had a word from the Lord, but when he attempted to give it all he could say was, 'Be not ascared, for I am ascared sometimes too saith the Lord'. Sympathetic Pentecostals would neither ridicule this brother, nor would they accept the theology of his utterance. Charismatic words nonetheless are potentially edifying and at least at times Pent/Char spirituality is enriched by the word of God as mediated in charismatic vocalizations.[22]

21. Charismatic words vary in style and function within the same congregation as well as from congregation to congregation. The style of charismatic words at the L&L is that of a 'sharing': normally the presentation emerges as 'low key' during a pause in the worship rite. The CCC reflects a more traditional Pentecostal style, at times a charismatic word is given in a booming voice declaring, 'This is the word of the Lord'. The function of charismatic words also varies. For example, they are most often seen as encouragement, inspiration or exhortation for the whole congregation at the CCC and L&L. But, at the VVCF ritualists typically direct charismatic words to a single individual rather than to the congregation in general. This focus on the individual carries over into the ministries and healing rites that distinguish the VVCF. Here, 'healers' seek to give charismatic words as insight. Such insight is believed to assist in the healing process. Words are thus connected to the discerning process and the rites of healing.

22. Charismatic words may also occur as non-edifying, even destructive manifestations. This negative potential represents a continual pastoral concern.

The Gifts

Charismatic utterances are best understood within the symbol word, but the Pent/Char elemental symbol of 'the gifts' discloses charismatic *activity*. The gifts continue, as they have historically, to distinguish Pentecostal ritual from other Christian liturgies and to serve as a trademark of the overall spirituality. The manifestations of the gifts (especially the Pauline charisms) play prominently in the liturgies and congregational life of the Sea City churches. The gifts may be understood in part in the symbols of Spirit baptism, empowerment and edification.

Symbol of Spirit baptism. The CCC represents a classical Pentecostal view on the gifts. The gifts are understood by the CCC congregants as incorporated in the Spirit baptism, which is seen as a primary gift of the Spirit. In this view Spirit baptism or 'being filled with the Holy Spirit' represents a 'conversion-type' event subsequent to an initial Christian conversion. Spirit baptism does not symbolize a salvific, justifying event to Pentecostals. Rather, it represents a confirmation of the Spirit's presence in the believer's life and an empowerment or gifting. In this view, speaking in tongues evidences the initial event of baptism in the Spirit. Spirit baptism then occurs initially as an event and continues as the process popularly called the 'Spirit-filled life'. This process includes an openness to the Spirit's gifts and a willingness by the believer to operate within these gifts toward the edification of the body of Christ. Classical Pentecostal ideology continues to view Spirit baptism as the doorway into the larger more diverse experience and practice of charisms.[23]

Symbol of empowerment. The baptism in the Spirit is a symbol of empowerment. Spirit baptism is more than 'conversation' or an encountering with the divine. The Pentecostal baptism symbolizes an infusion of

23. Neo-Pentecostals and/or so-called third wavers often understand Spirit baptism in a less distinct fashion. For instance, baptism in the Spirit is less emphasized at the VVCF and the gifts are seen in a more dispersed, diffuse, baptistic way. Baptism in the Spirit is however taught by the national leadership of the Vineyard Christian Fellowship. See John Wimber's booklet and tape, *Power Points: A Basic Primer for Christians*, with accompanying tape 2, 'Baptism in the Spirit' (Anaheim, CA: Vineyard Ministries International, 1985). All believers have access to the gifts according to Pastor Tom (VVCF), though he seldom, if ever, mentions Spirit baptism. However, essentially, the same gifts are recognized and manifest by the congregation at the VVCF as at the CCC or L&L.

the divine, a union, with a resulting 'enduement with power'. Since Pentecostals seek and expect to do the work of God, modeling themselves after the early apostles after-pentecost, they acknowledge the need for empowerment. Spirit baptism then symbolizes an on-going experience of the Spirit, that is, an empowering experience that facilitates and supports the Pentecostal believer in her or his personal life and in serving God and humankind. While many Pentecostals expect the sign of tongues to accompany this experience, they do not reduce Spirit baptism to glossolalia. The charism of tongues represents only one of the expected phenomena to accompany the on-going life in the Spirit, the empowered life of the Spirit baptized believer.[24] So, while tongues may symbolize prayer to and presence of the divine, Spirit baptism as a gift represents the power and empowerment of the Spirit in a Pentecostal's spirituality.

Symbol of edification. Apart from Spirit baptism, the practice of the gifts, particularly in the ritual, reveals that the gifts function as symbols not only of empowerment but of edification. In each of the Sea City churches, the gifts function in a variety of ways, as media of edification. These Pentecostals frequently refer to edification as 'ministry'. Normally, this type of 'ministry' implies an orientation toward the members of faith community, an intention to fortify and renew, 'to edify the saints'.[25] Pentecostals believe then, that God grants gifts to believers for the benefit of the whole, so the church might be edified, 'strengthened and built up'. Thus, the term 'the gifts' points to at least three things: Spirit baptism, empowerment of individuals and edification of or ministry to the faith community. But ministry to the faith community cannot

---

24. Tongues as a charism may be considered a sign of Spirit baptism, but as a sign or 'evidence' it is distinguishable from the baptism or 'in-filling'. Tongues functions primarily as a form of prayer.

25. Gifts are not only oriented to the faith community's edification. As indicated above, the manifestation of the gifts may at times also direct attention toward God. This second orientation manifests in, for instance, an extensive use of the charisms within the worship and praise rites in all three of these churches. Pent/Char ritualists believe that their worshipful adoration, praise and communion are greatly facilitated by the practice of the gifts as instruments of praise (the prayer language, i.e. tongues prayer is perhaps most widespread in the 'gaps' in the liturgy). A third orientation sees the purpose for the gifts in part as facilitation for service outside of the church. In a general way, this is the understanding of Spirit baptism that I have presented.

be restricted to the medium of certain charismatic gifts. I now turn to the fifth emic term, 'ministry'.

Ministry

As I indicated in Chapter 6, *ministry* within the framework of Pent/Char spirituality occurs in three dimensions: ministry to God in worship, an edification ministry directed within the 'body of Christ' and ministry to the world. The symbolic center of the 'ministry' ideal lies in the second dimension, as I have just described the gift-edification. Ministry, especially in the liturgy, consists of the actions, prayers and other rites in which believers share and serve the needs of one another in 'the body'. Here I will consider the symbol of ministry (to the body) as a consideration of personal hunger and exigencies, as opportunity to serve and as a framework for the rites.

Consideration of personal hunger and exigencies. Much of the reason for a Pentecostal gathering can be understood in this ministry present in the ritual. In fact, Pentecostals have been criticized at times by other Christians for being too focused on the human dimension of the service (i.e. edifying the body) with a resulting neglect of worship and the focus on the divine. However, Pentecostals, in their own defense, point to the biblical Jesus, who they insist was intensely interested in addressing human needs. Consequently, Pentecostal ritualists, rather than avoiding the personal needs of members and visitors, seek out those in need and use the liturgical setting to address their personal troubles and concerns. The three churches represent examples of how Pentecostals consistently pursue opportunities to minister in the name of their God to human hungers, personal exigencies. For example, the senior pastors of each of the Sea City churches encourage their people to be alert to people's needs both inside and outside the church. Tom Allen, for instance, often exhorts his congregation to be attentive to the needs of friends and colleagues in the work place and the market. 'Offer to pray for them,' he instructs. 'They may think you're crazy, but you may be able to help them. Let Jesus work a miracle.'

Ministry as opportunity to serve. Ministry 'in and to the body' often takes place during the transitional rites at the CCC and L&L, and normally during the last phase of the service at the VVCF. For instance, the pastor will ask for those who have a need to raise a hand, or come forward to the altar, to indicate their needs so that they might be prayed for. This not only allows those in need to respond, but it provides an opportunity for friends and co-believers to serve, to minister. Normally, following the indication of a need, ritualists near those who raised hands or moved to the altars will move from their nearby seats in order to 'minister' in prayer to those in need. The 'ministers' will typically reach out and touch the one in need. They will take them by the hand or lay a hand on the shoulder. They may speak to them about their needs, and then will 'enter into prayer' on their behalf. The whole congregation will begin to pray together in 'concert', all ritualists voicing their prayers simultaneously. Those ritualists who have moved from their pews now cluster around the believer in need. In their circles of faith these ministers raise their voices in specific prayers for those in need. In this kind of prayer ministry, each congregant may become a minister, one who serves the needs of another. But Pentecostal ministry cannot be restricted to specific microrites. As I have just described, the symbol of ministry provides a lens through which to understand the primary rites and the ritual as a whole.[26]

Ministry as a framework for the rites. The symbol of ministry serves as a framing device for the primary rites of the Pent/Char service, particularly the rite of pastoral message and the altar/response rite. Certainly, the ministry of the word, that is, the pastoral message is seen by Pentecostals as 'ministry' that serves their needs. Pentecostals speak of being 'fed by the word'. The close attention of the members, in each of the three churches to the teaching or sermon seems to indicate the importance and sense of relevance to life the ministry of the word has to the parishioners.

But ministry is perhaps seen in its most salient form around the altars, often as a climax to the rest of the ritual. Healing rites are most prevalent during this time. Pentecostals attempt to minister to the 'whole person'. Physical conditions are dealt with, though not exclusively. During ministry times around the altars, they pray diligently for any dimension of felt need. No need is out of bounds or inappropriate. Any need can be discussed, discerned and dealt with in prayer, counsel and action. While each of the Sea City churches designs its liturgy to minister to people's needs, at the VVCF, the 'ministry time' has become

26. See Appendix B for a list of microrites. Also, for a discussion of the primary rites, that is, the foundational/processual rites, see Chapter 4.

their trademark.[27] At the VVCF the whole service aims toward 'the ministry'. For the VVCF the ministry time is their version of the altar/ response rite. The first two foundation and processual rites, the worship/ praise rite and the pastoral message rite, build upon each other in order to arrive at a climactic ministry time. Congregants expect the opportunity to be prayed for, cared for, ministered to, and at the VVCF the third phase of the service is nearly always the designated period for 'ministry'.

Pentecostal spirituality characterizes ministry as a giving and receiving of empathic understanding, a concerned touch, heartfelt prayer and appropriate action by people who deeply care for one another. But Pent/ Char concern extends outward, beyond the liturgy, to where the symbol of ministry shifts to the symbol of missions.

Mission(s)

The indigenous symbol *missions* connotes an orientation to the world or to the society as distinct from the church. In Chapter 6 I discussed 'relationship to the world' as one of three theological relationships that the Pent/Char liturgy expresses. Here I want only to highlight the importance of the term missions as expressing an integral dimension of Pent/Char spirituality. To our Pentecostals 'mission(s)' means ministry beyond the faith community, called to accomplish God's purposes, gifted service and distribution of resources.

Ministry beyond the faith community. As argued above, although the ritual is one of the best windows of insight into Pentecostal spirituality, the Pent/Char liturgy does not contain the whole of the spirituality. Edified and transformed by their rituals, Pentecostals push past the limits of the liturgy and seek to move beyond their faith communities. They are, though, 'launched' by and from the community. Within the faith community Pentecostals train and equip themselves to meet their mission. They 'experiment' with charisms and ministries, all with an eye toward missions. They want effectively to meet and to 'minister to the world'. Of course, such language seems lofty, but the symbol of missions pervades the consciousness of the Sea City congregations.[28]

27. For some concrete examples of this rite, see Chapters 4 and 5.

28. Pentecostals stand within the Protestant missionary movement of the past two centuries. Like other American Evangelicals, Pentecostals seek to reach their world with the gospel. In fact, according to noted missiological researcher and

Called to accomplish God's purposes. The language of 'reaching the world' sounds so idealistic, in part because it draws on an understanding of being called by God to become involved in God's purposes. The Sea City Pentecostals not only appropriate to themselves Christ's commission to his disciples to 'go into all the world and proclaim the gospel' (Mk 16.15), they believe that God 'raised them up' for this period of history.[29] They feel called to 'this generation'. They have a mission: to spread the gospel in their society and around the world. As a result of their sense of mission, the spirituality of Pentecostals seeks to 'equip' toward the accomplishment of their missions' goals. Part of the equipping process, they believe, is accomplished by the Holy Spirit. According to Pentecostals, the Spirit leads into missions, the Spirit gifts for missions and the Spirit enlightens the understanding concerning missions, that is, its aims and methods. Pentecostals discover themselves, and their spirituality in the context of God's purposes, God's will. Missions for Pentecostals not only gives a reason for being, it takes them beyond themselves and their own concerns to consider the needs of others.

Gifted service. Their emphasis on the Holy Spirit's role in outreach most distinguishes the Pentecostal understanding of missions. The Spirit is 'the Great Evangelist' in Pentecostal belief, and God's Spirit 'is active in the world today', assert the Pentecostals. The Spirit 'draws men and women to Jesus'. It then remains for believers to 'work with the Spirit' in gifted service. Pentecostals regard the charisms of the

Vatican consultant David B. Barrett, Pentecostals as a group have produced more than one-quarter of the world's five million 'full time Christian workers' and missionaries. Pent/Char churches have financially supported missionary efforts around the world at a level disproportionate to their size. See Barrett, 'Twentieth-Century Renewal'; *idem*, 'Annual Statistical Table'; and *idem*, *World Christian Encyclopedia* (New York: Oxford University Press, 1982).

29. From the beginning of the American Pentecostal movement the Pentecostals have had a belief that they were 'raised up' by God in their time to be a missionary movement. Drawing on the rich Lucan imagery in the New Testament book of Acts, Pentecostals apply to themselves Christ's prophecy 'you shall receive power when the Holy Spirit comes upon you, and you shall be my witnesses...to the ends of the earth' (Acts 1.8 RSV) See McClung, 'Missiology'; McGee, 'Missions, Overseas'; *idem*, 'Azusa Street Revival'; Menzies, *Anointed to Serve*, pp. 242-54; Blumhofer, *Assemblies*, II, pp. 166-67; Anderson, *Vision of the Disinherited*, p. 72; Hollenweger, *The Pentecostals*, pp. 63-69.

Spirit as 'tools' for doing the 'work of the ministry in the world'. This form of gifted service seeks to take the forms of ministry expressed in the liturgy and within the faith community and extend them into a broader arena. For most of the Sea City congregants this means using their spiritual gifts in daily life.[30] But for many it means stepping out into forms of service overseas.[31]

Distribution of resources. Finally, the symbol of missions means a distribution of resources. According to statistician and missiologist David Barrett, Pentecostals in general give a higher portion of their resources to missions than other Christian groups.[32] The CCC, for example, seeks to give 25 percent of their church income to missions. But each of the three Sea City churches 'invests' heavily of their time, energy and financial resources in mission projects. The distribution of their resources into various missions provides a way of giving 'unselfishly'. Missions dollars do not pay the salaries of the pastors, nor the church utility bill, nor other important and legitimate expenditures that benefit the congregation's members. Missions funds seek only to benefit others, those beyond the faith community. Thus, missions means unselfish distribution of resources. Pentecostals seek to utilize their resource and their gifts to extend the good news. In this sense Pent/Char spirituality is an Evangelical spirituality.

Having now considered these primary, selected, indigenous symbols from within the Pentecostal ethos and spirituality, I turn now to the second descriptive approach to the qualities of Pentecostal spirituality.

Experience of God: Outlining the Pentecostal/Charismatic Spirituality

I have considered six indigenous symbolic terms that disclose characteristic qualities of Pent/Char spirituality.[33] Inherent to each of these

---

30. A typical remark linking the gifts and ministry follows, 'I encourage you to push past the [Spirit] baptism, push past gifts and move on into the actualization of ministry in Christ's name, ministering in the world—in his name'. Here Vineyard Ministry leader prods his congregation to actualize ministry. The gifts function to actualize the Pentecostal mission. Wimber, *Power Points: A Basic Primer for Christians*.

31. The symbol of missionary, though altered in connotation, continues to serve Pentecostals as the paradigmatic symbol of the committed and called Christian.

32. Barrett, 'Twentieth-Century Renewal'.

33. Following Donald Gelpi I have chosen the (edic/analytic) category *experi-*

selected primary symbols is the fundamental binary opposition or distinction of human/divine. In this second part of the present chapter, I want to address this distinction in Pent/Char spirituality within the foundational category of the human *experience of God* as understood within Pent/Char spirituality.[34] The following sketches a general outline of the characteristic qualities of Pent/Char spirituality under the organizing, symbolic rubric of experiencing God. I categorize the qualities under main headings: experiencing God mystically as supernatural, experiencing God in a communal context, experiencing God as an empowering Spirit and commissioning Lord, and experiencing God as creative.

Experiencing God Mystically as Supernatural

As I have considered the ritual and rites of the Pent/Char churches of this study, I have been confronted with highly expressive forms of worship. I have discovered practices richly dramaturgic. I have classified, identified and described the modes of sensibility in the ritual. And, I asserted a fundamental supposition that these ritual expressions are rooted in a spirituality, a spirituality that expresses itself and is nourished by its rites and rituals. I have assumed that the performance of the rites is an encompassing experience, one that includes the elements of the ritual field, and, according to Pentecostals, one that grounds itself as a human experience of the divine. Pentecostals assign all that is ultimately holy and supernatural to the divine one, their God. I shall now consider this cluster of qualitative characteristics under two main headings: experiential/mystical and supernatural.

Experiential/mystical. As noted earlier, the category of experience is foundational to understanding the spirituality of Pentecostals. One way to approach this important quality is situating it within the Christian mystical tradition. Though Pentecostals seem largely unaware, they

ence of God as a central organizing symbol by which to consider spirituality. Gelpi's adroit use of this category produced a philosophically sensitive theology of 'human emergence' within the North American tradition. See especially Gelpi, *Experiencing God*, and *idem*, 'On Perceiving the Human Condition North Americanly: A Strategy for Theological Inculturation', in *idem*, *Grace as Transmuted Experience*, pp. 1-40.

34. Similarly, one might think of the six selected symbols, explicated above, as ways in which Pentecostals experience God. For example, they experience God in their leadership, their worship, the word, the gifts, their forms of ministry and in mission(s).

participate in a rich heritage of Christian mysticism. Evelyn Underhill describes mysticism as

> the direct intuition or experience of God; and the mystic as a person who has, to a greater or less degree, such a direct experience—one whose religion and life are centered, not merely on an accepted belief or practice, but on that which he regards as first-hand personal knowledge.[35]

The Christian mystic, she continues 'is one for whom God and Christ are not merely objects of belief, but living facts experimentally known at first-hand; and mysticism [is then for the mystic]...a life based on this conscious communion with God'.[36] Underhill's definition accurately characterizes the members as a type within the three churches studied.

In a very real sense the Sunday services of all three of the churches are designed to provide a context for a mystical *encounter*, an experience with the divine. This encounter is mediated by the sense of the immediate divine presence. The primary rites of worship/praise and altar/response are particularly structured to sensitize the congregants to the presence of the divine and to stimulate a conscious experience of God. The worship and praise rite especially functions as a framing context for certain mystical-type experiences of God. At least in part, the apparent goal of the worship service is to allow the worshipers to have a heightened sense of the presence of the divine. The gestures, ritual actions and symbols all function within this context to speak of the manifest presence.

Within the contemplative mode of sensibility described in Chapter 5, the Pentecostals seek a mystical sense of the divine presence. When a worship leader says, 'Let's enter into the presence of the Lord,' it is not heard as mere rhetoric. The congregation expects to have a keen awareness of divine presence. The mode of sensibility called celebration is frequently used to facilitate the process of entering into the presence. Its music and ritual actions function as Pent/Char icons, as windows into

---

35. Evelyn Underhill, *Mystics of the Church* (Wilton, CN: Morehouse–Barlow: 1925), p. 10.

36. Underhill, *Mystics of the Church*, p. 10. Also by Underhill on the Christian mystical tradition, see *The Essentials of Mysticism and Other Essays* (New York: E.P. Dutton, 1960 [1920]); *idem, Mysticism*; *idem, Practical Mysticism* (New York: E.P. Dutton, 1915); also see R.C. Zaehner, *Mysticism, Sacred and Profane: An Inquiry into Some Varieties of Praeternatural Experience* (Oxford: Clarendon Press, 1957).

the reality of the divine. Normally, the celebrative mode melts into the mode of contemplation in which an even more salient sense of the divine is felt.

A young man from the VVCF wanted us to understand his experience. As we questioned him concerning the contemplative mode within the worship rite, he emphasized the sense of *'being'*. 'Worship is more than just preparation for the sermon,' he insisted, 'it is a time of just being, not doing or even worshiping, but being.' This experience of being in the presence of God is fundamental to the Pent/Char spirituality. Although the trademark of Pentecostalism has been seen in active, even boisterous rites, beneath such manifestations is an essential belief in the experience of the presence of their God.

Complementary to the sense of immediate presence, the experience of the divine is expressed as a *responsive spirituality*. Pent/Char congregants respond not only to the sense and other symbols of divine presence, they participate in a responsive relationship with the symbolic elements that signify the actions of the Spirit. The Pentecostal service models a kind of dialogic relationship between God and humans that is espoused as normative for the Christian life by Pentecostals. The rite of altar/response illustrates the kind of responsiveness that occurs continually throughout the rites. Ritualists respond individually and as a group, they respond 'in their hearts' and in their actions. But passivity has little place in Pent/Char spirituality and Pentecostals actively pursue a spirituality characterized by a responsiveness to their God.[37]

Emphasis on the supernatural. When observing, listening to or participating in, even at a cursory level, the liturgical rites of the churches studied here, the emphasis on the supernatural is unmistakable.[38] The entire ritual assumes the awareness of the presence of God in a general sense, if not the in-breaking of the Spirit in a 'supernatural way'.[39]

---

37. Examples of responsiveness (the dialogic relationship between congregants and their God) can be seen both in speech acts and actions of Pentecostals. Their language illustrates the point. They speak of: 'hearing from God'/'speaking to God', of being 'touched by God'/'touching God', 'meeting with God'.

38. The supernatural emphasis has been a hallmark trait from the very beginning of the Pentecostal movement. See Wacker, 'Functions of Faith', for a discussion on the 'thoroughly supernaturalistic conceptual horizon' that characterized early Pentecostalism.

39. At the VVCF, for example, an 'in-breaking of the Spirit in a "Supernatural

Expectancy is heightened, as the congregation approaches certain rites, rites sometimes charged with anxious anticipation.[40] Such anticipation is stimulated by the history of the experience of the rite and the perceived presence and action of the supernatural.[41]

Pent/Char spirituality emphasizes the supernatural. The Pentecostal realm envisions a world subject to invasions by the supernatural element. Pentecostals teach adherents to expect encounters with the supernatural. For the Pentecostal the line between natural and supernatural is permeable, but the two categories are radically separate. This of course is seen in the rites, but for the Pentecostal it is extended from the Sunday communal ritual to the world at large. Even mundane elements of life are envisioned as the territory for supernatural exploits. Claims of signs, wonders and miracles are not limited to the regions of the Sunday ritual. They are to be a part of daily life.[42]

At the core of Pentecostal spirituality abides the belief in an experience characterized as a divine 'overwhelming' of the human person.[43]

---

way" ' occurs when a 'word of knowledge' reveals something that, according to the ritualist, was 'unknowable' apart from divine insight. At the Vineyard such words of knowledge normally accompany the 'ministry times'. When people ask for prayer, a ministering ritualist may receive a word of knowledge about and for the one requesting healing. This spiritual insight symbolizes to the VVCF congregants as in-breaking of the supernatural.

40. For example, the VVCF healing rites are charged with anxious anticipation, that is, congregants seem to have a very high level of expectation that there will be supernatural involvement.

41. An example of heightened anticipation of supernatural actions occur at the CCC monthly 'miracle service'. Owing to testimonies of miracles and reported healings from the previous miracles services, congregants approached the monthly service expecting to 'see God at work'. They call this heightened sense of the presence of the Spirit the 'supernatural'.

42. For Pentecostals, the term supernatural often refers to any perceived action or grace that goes beyond their understanding of 'the natural', or is believed to have a divine (supernatural) cause or source. When a Pentecostal believer perceives that God has intervened in some way in the midst of daily life, then the perceived intervention reveals the supernatural. Supernatural help, for example, comes to the believer in the form of miraculous works (e.g. dramatic healing) and in the form of divine help to do mundane tasks (e.g. accomplishing work in one's profession, work that is believed to be beyond the natural capabilities of the worker).

While such examples reveal the subjective interpretation of Pentecostal believers, the fact remains for them the 'supernatural' penetrates the natural.

43. Russell Spittler has used the term 'an overwhelming by the Holy Spirit' to

This experience of overwhelming may be identified by various terms (Spirit baptism and baptism in the Holy Spirit being among the most common) and has been understood in various ways. Yet there seems to be a general belief among Pentecostals and Charismatics that the overwhelming experience of God in the Spirit is something that they share in common.[44]

My field studies support the sense of shared experience among groups with dissimilar doctrines of charismatic operations. The VVCF, for instance, does not even claim for themselves the terms 'Pentecostal' or 'Charismatic', but congregants often speak among themselves about their experiences in the power of the Spirit. They avoid the term 'baptism in the Holy Spirit', but they pray and believe for special infusion of the power of the Spirit to work miracles, to discern spirits, to pray for healing, to pray in tongues.

On the other hand, the language of both the CCC and L&L betrays a more classical Pentecostal tinge. The central category for the experience of overwhelming of the Spirit is understood in the symbol of Spirit baptism as an event and process in the Christian life. Other experiences of the overwhelming Spirit are related, but for the most part they are understood within the baptism in the Spirit framework. Thus, Spirit baptism functions more as a boundary that defines the communities of the CCC and L&L. Spirit baptism functions less as a defining boundary among the members of the VVCF. Despite the difference in emphasis on Spirit baptism, the point remains that in all three of the churches there is a central belief in and understanding of their spirituality as one that flows from experiences of overwhelming by the supernatural. In the section to come I will consider the pragmatic function, empower-

---

describe the most fundamentally agreed upon theological experience among Pentecostals and Charismatics. Cited by Edith Blumhofer, Faculty Forum Lecture, Scotts Valley, California, Spring 1991.

44. See the Introduction for this common characteristic. Also see Kilian McDonnell and George Montague (eds.), *Fanning the Flame* (Collegeville, MN: Liturgical Press, 1991). These Roman Catholic scholars recognize this overwhelming in the Spirit as 'the later awakening of the original sacramental grace' (Christian initiation). They claim that this experience of 'baptism in the Holy Spirit' (term used by the editors) is found 'almost universally in the churches, both Protestant and Catholic, in which the Charismatic renewal' is experienced (pp. 9, 28). For a similar Roman Catholic perspective by a Catholic bishop, see Paul Josef Cordes, *Call to Holiness: Reflections on the Catholic Charismatic Renewal* (Collegeville, MN: Liturgical Press, 1997).

ment for life and service of such overwhelming. But now I turn to my second main category, the Pent/Char communal experience of God.

Experiencing God in a Communal Context
Pent/Char spirituality is rooted in a communal experience of God typified by its encouragement of democratic-participatory forms, and by its stresses on the media of biblical symbols, oral exchange and kinesthetic/music. There is truth in the characterization that Pentecostals are individualists. The essential mystical quality of their experience lends itself to a certain focus on the personal/individual dimension of spirituality. To bypass the communal characteristic of the spirituality, however, would be to miss an elemental and determinative component of Pent/Char spirituality.

Communal context. The communal context of the Pentecostal rites provides for both social and individual experiences. The findings of my field research confirm social historian Martin Marty's characterization of American Pentecostal worship as demonstrating distinctly dramatic social behavior.[45] These dramatic social behaviors I have identified and described as rites in Chapter 4. I have also pointed to the social importance of these rites as symbolic boundaries that shape the Pent/Char ethos while functioning in the process of communal and individual self-definition. Such defining occurs within the potent social dynamics of the Pent/Char ritual process.[46]

The social dynamics of the Pentecostal community are often contextualized by a liminality that facilitates moments of communitas and continued community building.[47] These communal aspects of the ritual

45. Marty, *Nation of Behavers*, pp. 106-220, and *idem*, 'Pentecostalism', pp. 193-233.

46. The religious experience of the individual is both rhetorically and practically important to the members of the three churches. Their rites allows significant 'room' to sense, experience, and express individually the divine presence within the ritual. But these personal explorations and experiences are within a highly social ritual context. A context that provides for a 'confluence of experience' where the multitude (of experiences) merge into one corporate expression (experience). The result of such a convergence of experience is the sensation of the multiplication of the power of the Spirit and an intensification of the awareness of the Spirit's presence. Marty, 'Pentecostalism', p. 211 quotes Dale Bruner.

47. See Chapter 6 for a discussion of liminality and communities. Also see Turner, *Ritual Process*.

and the extended group life are in part the secret of the Pentecostal attraction. Time and again in interviews people told us that they came to the church because of 'the worship'. The worship rite, particularly at the L&L and VVCF, is the richest in distinctive, dramatic, social expressions of worship. Social bonding is strongly reliant on these rites. The sense of community among the members of each of the three congregations to a large extent grows out of their common practice of their Pentecostal rites, so the communal aspect of the rites both attracts and retains Pentecostal worshipers. It provides the basis from which the individual may express their own personal spirituality.

Participation/Democratic. While the routinization of the Pent/Char rites tends to limit broad based ritual participation, the democratic participation persists among Pentecostals. In each of the three churches I discovered highly participatory forms of spirituality.

Lay leadership and involvement is emphasized, though in varying degrees in each of the Sea City churches.[48] The programs of all three depend heavily on lay leadership. The extensive food distribution program at the VVCF provides an example of lay leadership and involvement. Foreign service/missions trips are completely lay. Similar examples abound at the CCC and L&L.

The democratic participation involving lay persons has also to some extent been open to women of the Pent/Char tradition. From the beginning of the Pentecostal movement, women preachers, Bible teachers, evangelists and foreign missionaries have had a prominent role in the

48. Lay participation is obvious in the churches' programs and their liturgies. This too is deep in the Pentecostal tradition. As far back as the Azusa Street mission, lay participation has been a trade mark of the Pentecostal service. See Bartleman, *Azusa Street*; Robeck, Jr, 'Azusa Street Revival'; Robins, 'Rule of the Holy Spirit'. The early Azusa meetings allowed for great freedom to its attenders within its own basic structural rites. While William Seymour functioned as symbolic boundary for the service, he was not the only leader. In fact, because the Holy Spirit was the recognized Leader of the services, many and various other human leaders, lay and clergy were allowed to serve spontaneously. Extemporaneous testimonies, sometimes lasting two hours, were woven into the service. Of course, charismatic utterances and gifts were freely expressed by people moved of the Spirit. Seymour even permitted anyone to preach spontaneously, if he believed they were prompted by the Spirit. This heritage of participatory-democratic spirituality is adapted and more controlled forms persist still today. For the role and influence of women as a part of this participatory-democratic dimension see Cox, *Fire from Heaven*, ch. 7.

transmission of the group's life, doctrine and spirituality in general. The roles available to women varied among the churches of this study. This in part seems to have resulted both from the larger cultural influences and the growing impact of conservative Protestant Evangelicalism, which has maintained a more rigid perspective concerning women's roles in church leadership. Predictably then, the VVCF, the church rooted more in the Evangelical tradition, displays the least openness to women's roles in leadership. Women participate in roles of support with their husbands or work with children in Christian education.

One of the five pastors at the CCC is female. Her role is primarily that of music ministry. The importance of the musical role is obvious when one considers the prominent part the music plays in the Pentecostal ritual. Pastor Adel heads up all music programs and leads in all dimensions of the music ministry, including the congregational singing during the worship rite. The CCC also has two women on its seven-member board of deacons.[49] Similarly, the L&L employs two women as pastors, and they have five staff pastors total. None of the six 'elders'[50] (non-staff leaders) are women.

Theoretically, however, in both the CCC and L&L, no restriction limits women in leadership. Any role is open, including that of senior pastor and preacher. In practice, however, the opportunities for women in leadership ministry appear somewhat more restricted. On the other hand, within the Sunday ritual women play prominent roles by their participation and leadership in the rites. For example, women lead worship, participate on worship teams, lead dance expressions, exercise charismatic speech acts, preach, pray and perform healing rites. The Sunday rites provide a relatively free context in which women as well as men can express their spirituality within the congregational context in participatory-democratic forms. These participatory patterns that include women, laity and all groups within the Pent/Char congregation spring from a community experience of God, a spirituality that effectively encourages a participatory communal experience.

Media of the participatory communal experience. Basically, three media function as channels through which the communal experience is trans-

49. The board of deacons is the legally responsible political group of leadership for the congregation of the CCC.

50. The 'elders' of the L&L function in similar ways to the deacons of the CCC.

mitted and in which it is experienced: biblical, oral and kinesthetic/
musical. The fundamental symbols of Pent/Char spirituality are *biblical
symbols*. Pentecostals consciously attempt to understand the biblical
messages and appropriate them to their community. Biblical terms and
biblical images abound in the liturgy, the language and the lifestyles of
Pentecostals. Any doctrine, practice or innovation in the ritual or in the
community programs faces the question, 'Is it biblical?' Pentecostals
see themselves as a 'people of the Book'.[51] As such, the book, more correctly their understanding of the book, shapes their lives and their community experience. Pentecostals seek to transmit their spirituality in the
framework of biblical images. As a result they filter their experience of
God through their 'reading' of the book. In other words, the biblical
symbols provide the primary medium through which the community
understands itself and communicates that understanding; biblical images
contain and carry the Pent/Char spirituality.

Pentecostals also exploit forms of *orality* as a second main medium
of their participatory-democratic, communal experience of God.[52] Hollenweger perhaps first recognized the oral emphasis that characterizes
Pentecostal spirituality. He rightly assessed that to a great extent Pentecostal spirituality is transferred within an oral subculture. Of course, the
oral dimensions of the spirituality appear most obviously among Pentecostals in developing countries, but orality plays a major role even
within the American Pentecostal communities. For while American
Pentecostals have written tracts and cursory theological treatments (and
more recently scholarly works), to a great extent the Pent/Char liturgies,
moral codes and taboos and 'histories' remain in oral form. To a large
extent the Pent/Char spirituality persists in 'a lively oral tradition'.[53]

If it is true that Pentecostals are people of the book and people of the

51. As 'people of the book' Pentecostals have a tendency toward forms of
fundamentalism. Their emphases on the actions, gifts and words of the Spirit, however, challenge their tendency toward bibliolatry. Normally, I observed a healthy
tension existing between the two Pentecostal poles of charismata/Spirit and Bible/
literalism. In the absence of the dynamic tension between the disparate elements
inherent in the Pent/Char spirituality, Pentecostals can, however, slip into a liter-
alist-fundamentalism form of religion bordering on bibliolatry or they can move
toward the other extreme into of a form of spiritism.

52. See Hollenweger, 'Pentecostals and the Charismatic Movement', p. 551;
idem, *The Pentecostals*; Spittler, 'Spirituality', p. 805; Quebedeaux, *The New Charismatics II*, pp. 182-83; Land, 'Pentecostal Spirituality', p. 485.

53. Spittler, 'Spirituality', p. 805.

spoken word, then it is also true that they are people of music and movement.[54] The third medium through which Pentecostals transmit their spirituality is the dual dimension of *kinesthetic/musical*. The kinesthetic/musical medium for some Pentecostals claims primacy as the fundamental form of transmission. This is certainly, true among many Pentecostals of the so-called 'third world'.[55] However, in the Sea City churches I observed the significance of music and movement to the participatory nature of the communal experience. Music shapes a large part of the liturgies in each of the three churches. As described above, some Pentecostals link forms of kinesthetic movements and dance to the music, while other forms of movement connect to the spoken word or to personal spiritual impulses. Pentecostals seek to worship their God with their whole being. They have intuitively presented their bodies, their physicality, as instruments of worship. They seek to move with the Spirit, but not as incorporeal selves. Pentecostals experience God as embodied people propelled by the Spirit and by their songs. Thus, the Pent/Char communal spirituality is born in and conveyed by biblical symbols, oral exchange, and kinesthetic/musical transactions.

Experiencing God as Empowering Spirit and Commissioning Lord
Thirdly, Pentecostals experience God as empowering and commissioning. The language of power has always played a part in Pent/Char liturgy and spirituality. The language reflects a reality. Pentecostals not only see God as an all powerful Spirit, they believe that God manifests God's power in their world. The manifestation of power (e.g. in healing or other 'signs and wonders') has a sacramental quality for Pentecostals. In the manifestations of power God proves God's interest in the affairs of humankind in specific ways. The experiences of power reflect very personal experiences, an individual experiencing a personal God. For example, the event of Spirit baptism is normally experienced as profoundly personal and intimate. The sense of personal intimacy continues in the 'Spirit-filled life'. The empowerment for 'life and service'

---

54. See Chapter 3 for a discussion of kinesthetic forms of worship. For the importance of movement and gestures in ritual, see Hawthorne, 'Introduction—Method and Spirit'.

55. See Hollenweger, 'Dancing Documentaries'. For a series of essays on a related topic, see Bjorn Krondorfer (ed.), *Body and the Bible: Interpreting and Experiencing Biblical Narratives* (Valley Forge, PA: Trinity Press International, 1992).

that Pentecostals claim as a result of Spirit baptism is typically experienced as 'a closeness to Jesus'. Many speak of their Spirit empowerment as 'making Jesus more real'. They say that daily life looks and feels different because they sense a presence of Christ in them and they are confident in his ability, power to assist them in the mundane matters of life as well as the opportunities for service.

Congregants testified to us of a sense of empowerment as a result of participation in the rites. Such witnesses to empowerment did not speak only of the symbol of Spirit baptism, though that symbol remains central. Experiences of empowerment seem to occur throughout the liturgy: in the worship rite during celebrative singing, as a part of prayer times during the rites of transition and of course during the altar response. Empowering experience also seems to occur as often when a ritualist is ministering to another, as when one is being ministered unto. For example, congregants frequently noted a sense of empowerment as they prayed for someone else's needs. Charismatic phenomena often accompany such prayers. Such efficacious prayer is central to the Pent/Char understanding of 'ministry'. But the power of the Spirit seems to be experienced by both the parties in the ministry diad. Pentecostals experience God as an empowering Spirit in their rituals.

As indicated above, however, while Pentecostals experience the empowerment of the Spirit often in their corporate ritual, they move outward with a sense of the Spirit's power to serve the needs of the society, the world. Although the answers to society's ills have often been viewed simplistically by Pentecostals, nonetheless they do in their own way seek to affect the society positively by sharing good news in word and in deed. The result has been a disproportionate level of involvement in missionary, evangelistic and other service ventures. Each of these ventures emerges out of the sense of empowerment and the belief that they have been commissioned.

Pentecostals experience God as the commissioning Lord. The one who empowers, they believe, also calls and sends. Empowerment seeks more than self-edification. Instead, Pentecostals recognize in their sense of empowerment a calling to assist others. They understand the commission of Jesus to serve the world as their commission. They believe that their Lord's mission to fulfill the will of God on the earth now includes them, and they believe that the Spirit enables them to accomplish the mission not in their 'own strength' but 'in the power of the

Holy Spirit'. Thus, Pentecostals experience God as empowering Spirit and commissioning Lord.

Experiencing God as Creative
Lastly, Pentecostals experience God as creative and consequently they live out a creative spirituality. 'Exuberant creativity' seems intrinsic to Pentecostal spirituality. More than one Pentecostal observer, has been 'struck by Pentecostal self-taught inventiveness'.[56] While I have discussed such 'exuberant creativity' and 'inventiveness' as revealed in the ritualization, improvization and spontaneous inclinations within the rites of the Sea City churches, the creative impulse extends beyond the liturgy throughout the Pent/Char spirituality. Pentecostals live out a creative spirituality because they conceive of their God as creative, and their engagement with the Spirit confirms this conception experientially. Consequently, a creative and entrepreneurial form of spirituality emerges from their experience of their creative God. The emergent spirituality then displays an adaptability, a pioneering spirit, and an action orientation.

God as creative. Pentecostals conceive of God as creative. The Pentecostal God is a God who is ever creative and seeks by the Spirit to interact with and minister to humankind creatively. For Pentecostals, God's (re)creation among humanity is yet to be completed. However, this notion of God as ever creative Spirit is more than a cognitive category. Pentecostals experience God as creative. As related above, the Pentecostal interaction with the Holy Spirit is experienced as liberating, empowering and gifting. These experiences are seen as God's creative work in the individual through an engaging transaction with the Spirit. This creative, freeing endowment convinces Pentecostals that God 'has done a work *in*' them and more. Inherent in God's 'work', God's baptism, lies a sense of intimate connection to God and to the divine creativeness symbolized in the charisms for the Pentecostals, gifts are not so much possessed by the human as available divine resources. The

---

56. Grant Wacker, 'Character and the Modernization of North American Pentecostalism', in the unpublished conference papers of the Twenty-first Annual Meeting of the Society for Pentecostal Studies (Lakeland, FL: Southeastern College, November 1991), p. 15. See also Blumhofer, *Assemblies*, I, pp. 161-75; Everett A. Wilson, 'Latin American Pentecostal', *Pneuma* 9 (Spring 1987), pp. 85-90; Synan, 'Pentecostalism'.

perception of being personally attached to God and the supernatural resources converges with the Pentecostal understanding of (com)mission.

A creative entrepreneurial form of spirituality. As indicated previously, Pentecostals experience God as their commissioning Lord. That is, they believe they have been given a divine mission, a purpose in life. It is particularly within this sense of mission that Pent/Char spirituality expresses itself in its creative, entrepreneurial form. This model of Pent/Char spirituality reveals traits of pioneering innovation, adaptability and pragmatic action, among others. The history of this century's Pentecostal movement is replete with examples of Pentecostal people combining innovation, adaptability and action to produce new patterns of religious life.[57] Seventy years ago and as recently as this past decade, Sea City has witnessed the sparks of creative, entrepreneurial, Pentecostal life in the peoples of the CCC, L&L, and VVCF. The innovative actions of Willie Barrett and Tom Allen are yet unfolding. These religious entrepreneurs arrived in town armed with a message, a belief and an experience of a creative God. Their gifting, creative applications and adaptability have served in the process of creating communities that now engage in revitalizing and reappropriating symbols Pentecostals have long held dear. The resulting spirituality is authentically Pentecostal, creative and Christian.

In summary, I have characterized Pentecostal spirituality as a mystical/experiential spirituality that emphasizes encounter with the supernatural. I have asserted that it is rooted in a communal experience of God typified by its encouragement of democratic-participatory forms, which transpire in and through biblical symbols, orality, and kinesthetic/musical activity. Thirdly, this characterization presents Pentecostals as those who experience their God as an empowering Spirit who commissions through callings and giftings toward a life of service, mis-

---

57. Among the many examples of those who have noted the Pentecostal creative, adaptable, pragmatic, entrepreneurial qualities see Barrett, 'Twentieth-Century Renewal'; Blumhofer, *Restoring the Faith*; Lawson, 'The Foursquare Church; Synan, 'Pentecostalism'; Wacker, 'Function of Faith'; C. Peter Wagner, *Look Out! The Pentecostals Are Coming* (Carol Stream, IL: Creation House, 1969); Everett A. Wilson, 'Revival and Revolution in Latin America', in Edith Blumhofer and Randall Balmer (eds.), *Modern Christian Revivals* (Chicago: University of Illinois Press, 1993), pp. 180-93.

sion and evangelism. Finally Pentecostals experience God as creative and thus, as one who encourages creativity marked by an inventive and improvizational actions and an adaptable, entrepreneurial spirit.

I use the term *macro ritual* to designate an event, meeting, service or rite that may be incorporated into another event, rite or liturgy, but can stand alone as a ritual on its own.

A. Pentecostal services (liturgy)
1. Worship services
2. Evangelistic services
3. Revival meetings
4. Healing services
5. Musicals (songs, worship in song, concerts, talent nights)
6. Other special (event type) services (baptismal services)
B. Prayer meetings (in various settings)
C. Bible studies (in various settings)
D. Home/cell group meetings
E. Camp meetings
F. Retreats
G. Conferences
H. Age group and other specialized 'services'
1. Chi Alpha
2. Seniors services
3. Youth groups
4. Children's services
I. Para-church organizations
1. Full Gospel Businessmen
2. Women's Aglow
3. Mass Media
J. Christian education modes
1. Sunday school
2. Baptismal classes
3. Seminars (topical)
K. Fellowship gatherings
1. Church picnics
2. Fellowship meetings
3. Event celebrations

        4. Home groups

L. Evangelizations

M. Sending out missionaries

N. Mission trips (short term)

O. Social/humanitarian
        1. Jail visitation
        2. Feeding programs
        3. Food pantries
        4. Foreign services support
        5. Overseas trips and construction teams

P. Personal/individual rituals (personal devotions, quiet times, personal spiritual practices, disciplines)
        1. Prayer
        2. Tongues prayer
        3. Bible reading, study
        4. Other devotional practices
        5. Listening/watching religious tape recordings, radio, TV
        6. Witnessing (and/or evangelization)
        7. Ministering/Christian service
            a. In and to the world
            b. In the church community

APPENDIX B
RITES IN THE PENTECOSTAL SERVICE: LITURGICAL RITES,
FOUNDATIONAL AND MICRORITES

I.   Foundational and Primary Rites
     (the processual 'events' of the liturgy, the main processual
     liturgical rites)
     A. Gathering/greeting rites
     B. Rite of worship and praise
         1. Main transitional rites
     C. Rite of pastoral message
     D. Rite of altar/response
     E. Dispersing/farewells rites

II. Examples of Rites
     (within the categories of the foundational and primary rites,
     i.e. component parts of the foundational rites)
     A. Gathering/greeting rites (pre-service)
         1. Formal greetings at the doors
         2. Greetings and conversations
            a. Location
                (1) In the narthex
                (2) The back of the sanctuary
                (3) In the pew or chairs
                 (4) Standing or sitting
            b. Types
                (1) Shaking hands
                (2) Hugging
                (3) Embracing
                (4) Talking
            c. Clustering in conversation (gathering)
            d. Formal gathering ('call to worship'), signaled by, e.g.,
                (1) Announcement of beginning
                (2) The worship team band starting
                (3) A prayer
                (4) An introductory song
     B. Rites of worship and praise
         1. Directly connected (oriented) to music:

        a. Praise and worship songs
        b. Vocal (praise and worship) interludes
           (1) Tongues singing
        c. Special and choral music presentations
   2. Kinesthetic expressions of praise and worship
      (some corporate, others more individually oriented)
        a. Standing, kneeling, bowing, swaying
        b. Hopping, jumping
        c. Lifting hands
        d. Dancing
        e. Signing
        f. Applause ('praise offering')
        g. Applause after special music or message
        h. Clapping with music
        i. Touching
        j. Laying on of hands
        k. Anointing with oil
        l. Holding hands
        m. Reaching out toward
   3. Primarily vocal expressions
        a. Concert praise
        b. Sacred explicatives
        c. Concert intercessory/petitionary prayer
        d. Testimonies, sharing, words, ministering
        e. Charismatic utterances
   4. Transitional rites
        a. Offering (collection)
        b. Musical offertory
        c. Special musical presentations
        d. Testimonials
        e. Congregational announcements
        f. Prayer requests
        g. Prayer for needs
        h. Altar time/body life
C. Rite of preaching and and other speech acts as rites
   1. Types of preaching rites (preaching: part of a larger category
      of rites and speech acts)
        a. Evangelistic
        b. Inspirational
        c. Expository/textual
        d. Teaching/preaching
        e. Thematic
   2. Other speech acts
        a. Sermon/teaching
        b. Testimony

   c. Exhortation

   d. Prayer

   e. Praise

   f. Sacred expletive

   g. Announcements

   h. Other

  D. Altar and response rites

   1. Abbreviated or brief forms

    a. Simple benediction

    b. Pastoral prayer

    c. Congregant closing prayer

   2. Altar calls for (rites of passage and intensification):

    a. Conversion

    b. Spiritual rededication (life consecrations)

    c. Deeper life commitments

    d. Responses to callings (missions etc.)

    e. Spirit baptismal candidates

   3. Ministry

    a. Healing rites (various types)

    b. Body life (general praying for one another's needs)

    c. Deliverance and exorcisms

    d. Other ministries

   4. Times of prayer (around the altars)

    a. Individual

    b. Corporate/congregational

    c. Prayer lines

    d. Pastoral prayers for parishioners

    e. Circles of prayer and a small groups praying together

    f. Body life

  E. Dispersing/farewells rites (post-service dispersing)

   1. Formal conclusion

    a. Brief prayer or benediction

    b. Final song

    c. Brief announcement by the pastor

    d. Commissioning to the world

   2. Farewells while exiting

    a. Clustering in pews

    b. In back of sanctuary

    c. The narthex

    d. The church yard or parking lot

III. Other Categories of Rites

  (not necessarily connected to or included in a particular foundational rite category [as classified above], but potentially can emerge in and of the foundational categories. Some might be considered components of other rites, such as gestures, acts, actions, activities, social behaviors, etc.)

A. Charismatic rites
    1. Utterances (e.g. 'words', prophecy, tongues and interpretation)
    2. Discernment and knowledge (insights)
    3. Miracles, signs and wonders
    4. Other charismata
    5. Charismatic spontaneous innovations (charismatic 'ritualizing')
    6. Holy pauses
B. Categories of speech, action and music
    1. Speech acts as rites (practices)
        a. Preaching/sermons
        b. Teaching/Bible study presentation
        c. Testimonies
        d. Sharing
        e. Exhortations
        f. Word of knowledge (and other 'words')
        g. Prophetic speech
        h. Sacred expletive
        i. Shouts
        j. Quasi- or non-language 'speech'
    2. Prayer (and audible praises) as rites
        a. Concert prayer (unison prayer)
        b. Leading in prayer (pastor or other leading out often in the midst of concert congregational prayer)
        c. Ministry prayers and rites (prayers offered for and/or with another) for/with
            (1) One converting
            (2) One seeking God for deeper spiritual relationship
            (3) One seeking Spirit baptism
            (4) One seeking healing
            (5) One with specific need or concern
            (6) One in general prayer
        d. Praying in the Spirit (glossolalia prayer)
        e. Petitionary and intercessory prayer
        f. Praise prayer
    3. Kinesthetic practices (some mostly corporate, others more individually oriented)
        a. Raising (lifting) of hands
        b. Falling under the power (slain in the Spirit)
        c. Jericho march (victory march)
        d. Applause ('praise offering')
        e. Applause after special music or message
        f. Clapping with music
        g. Swaying
        h. Dancing
        i. Leaping, jumping, hopping

    j. Signing

    k. Waving

    l. Standing, bowing, kneeling

    m. Touching

    n. Laying on of hands

    o. Anointing with oil

    p. Holding hands

    q. Reaching out toward

4. Acts of response (acts normally in response to the 'word', a challenge, exhortation, sermon, prophecy and/or an inner prompting etc.)

    a. Actions/gestures of response

        (1) Altar call responses

        (2) Going forward

        (3) Raising a hand

            (a) Responding to a pastoral call

            (a) Responding to a inner 'prompting'

        (4) Crying, weeping, moaning

    b. Rites of passage and intensification

        (1) Conversion/repentance

        (2) Rededication

        (3) Deeper life commitment

        (4) Response to a calling (missions, vocational ministry etc.)

    c. Ministry acts (practices)

    d. Healing rites

    e. For special time of prayer

5. Music rites (the foundational sound for the Pentecostal liturgy is music combined together with speech acts. Music is as much a part of the fabric of the Pentecostal service and spirituality as the charismata and preaching)

    a. Singing

        (1) Congregational

        (2) Choir

        (3) Worship team/song leader

        (4) Special music (e.g. solos, ensembles)

        (5) Background

    b. Instrumentation

        (1) Pre- and post-service music

        (2) Accompaniment to congregational singing (orchestras, bands, organ and piano)

        (3) Offertory music

        (4) Special music (e.g. solos, ensembles)

        (5) Background

6. Sacraments, ordinances and ceremonies

a. Baby dedication
b. Water baptism
c. Communion
d. Ordination
    (1) Formal (clergy)
    (2) Informal (for member[s] of the congregation, often a lay member [e.g. as lay minister in the congregation or short-term ministries and missionaries])
e. Commissioning/sending out
f. Weddings
g. Funerals

BIBLIOGRAPHY

Adams, Doug, *Congregational Dancing in Christian Worship* (Austin, TX: The Sharing Company, 1971).

Albrecht, Daniel E., 'Pentecostal Spirituality: Ecumenical Potential and Challenge', *Cyberjournal for Pentecostal/Charismatic Research* 2 (1997) (http://www.pctii.org/cybertab.html/).

—'Pentecostal Spirituality: Looking through the Lens of Ritual', *Pneuma* 14.2 (Fall 1992).

—'Variations on Themes in Worship: Pentecostal Rites and Improvisations' (Geneva: World Council of Churches, forthcoming).

Alexander, Bobby C., 'Pentecostal Ritual Reconsidered: Anti-Structural Dimensions of Possession', *Journal of Ritual Studies* 3 (1985), pp. 109-28.

—*Victor Turner Revisited: Ritual as Social Change* (Academy Series, American Academy of Religion, 74; Atlanta: Scholars Press, 1991).

Alexander, Donald L. (ed.), *Christian Spirituality: Five Views of Sanctification* (Downers Grove, IL: InterVarsity Press, 1988).

Alexander, Jon, 'What Do Recent Writers Mean by Spirituality', *Spirituality Today* 32 (1980), pp. 247-57.

Alford, Delton L., 'Pentecostal and Charismatic Music', in *DPCM*, pp. 688-95.

Anderson, Robert Mapes, *Vision of the Disinherited: The Making of American Pentecostalism* (New York: Oxford University Press, 1979).

—'Pentecostal and Charismatic Christianity', in *EOR*, XI, pp. 229-35.

Baer, R.A., Jr, 'Quaker Silence, Catholic Liturgy, and Pentecostal Science: Some Functional Similarities', in Spittler (ed.), *Perspectives on the New Pentecostalism*, pp. 150-64.

Barrett, David B., 'Annual Statistical Table on Global Mission: 1997', *IBMR* 21.1 (1997), pp. 24-25.

—*World Christian Encyclopedia* (New York: Oxford University Press, 1982).

—'The Twentieth-Century Pentecostal/Charismatic Renewal in the Holy Spirit', *IBMR* 12 (July 1988), pp. 119-24.

Bartleman, Frank, *Azusa Street* (Plainfield, NJ: Logos International, 1980).

Bell, Catherine, *Ritual Theory, Ritual Practice* (New York: Oxford University Press, 1992).

Bellah, Robert N., *Beyond Belief: Essays on Religion in a Post-Traditional World* (San Francisco: Harper & Row, 1970).

—*The Broken Covenant: American Civil Religion in Time of Trial* (New York: Seabury, 1975).

—'Christian Faithfulness in a Pluralist World', in Frederic B. Burnham (ed.), *Postmodern Theology: Christian Faith in a Pluralist World* (San Francisco: HarperSanFrancisco, 1989), pp. 74-91.

—'Civil Religion in America', *Daedalus* 96.1 (Winter 1967), pp. 1-20.

—'Introduction', in Mary Douglas and Steven M. Tipton (eds.), *Religion and America: Spirituality in a Secular Age* (Boston: Beacon Press, 1983 [1982]), p. xi.

Bellah, Robert N. (ed.), *Emile Durkheim on Morality and Society* (Chicago: University of Chicago Press, 1973).

Bellah, Robert N., *et al.*, *The Good Society* (New York: Alfred A. Knopf, 1991).

—*Habits of the Heart: Individualism and Commitment in American Life* (Berkeley: University of California Press, 1985).

Bennett, Dennis J., *Nine O'Clock in the Morning* (Plainfield, NJ: Logos International, 1970).

Berger, Peter, and Thomas Luckmann, *The Social Construction of Reality* (New York: Doubleday, 1966).

Bittlinger, Arnold (ed.), *The Church Is Charismatic* (Geneva: World Council of Churches, 1981).

Bixler, Frances, 'Dancing in the Spirit', in *DPCM*, pp. 236-37.

Bloch-Hoell, Nils, *The Pentecostal Movement: Its Origins, Development, and Distinctive Character* (London: Allen & Unwin, 1964).

Blumhofer, Edith L., *Aimee Semple McPherson: Everybody's Sister* (Grand Rapids: Eerdmans, 1993).

—'Assemblies of God', in *DPCM*, pp. 23-28.

—'Assemblies of God', in *DCA*, pp. 86-88.

—*The Assemblies of God: A Chapter in the Story of American Pentecostalism* (2 vols.; Springfield, MO: Gospel Publishing, 1989).

—' "Pentecost in my Soul": Probing the Early Pentecostal Ethos', *Assemblies of God Heritage* (Spring 1989), pp. 13-14.

—*Restoring the Faith: The Assemblies of God, Pentecostalism, and American Culture* (Urbana, IL: University of Illinois Press, 1993).

Bourdieu, Pierre, *Outline of a Theory of Practice* (New York: Cambridge University Press, 1977).

Bourret, Marjorie, *et al.*, *A Citizen's Guide...* (Scotts Valley, CA: The League of Women Voters, 1984).

Bouyer, Louis, 'Some Charismatic Movements in the History of the Church', in Edward D. O'Connor (ed.), *Movement in the Catholic Church* (Notre Dame, IN: Ave Maria Press, 1971), pp. 113-31.

Boyd, James W., and Ron G. Williams, 'Ritual Spaces: An Application of Aesthetic Theory to Zoroastrian Ritual', *Journal of Ritual Studies* 3 (Winter 1989), pp. 1-43.

Bridges-Johns, Cheryl, *Pentecostal Formation: A Pedagogy among the Oppressed* (JPTSup, 2; Sheffield: Sheffield Academic Press, 1993).

Brumback, Carl, *Suddenly...from Heaven: A History of the Assemblies of God* (Springfield, MO: Gospel Publishing, 1961).

Bruner, Fredrick Dale, *A Theology of the Holy Spirit: The Pentecostal Experience and the New Testament Witness* (Grand Rapids: Eerdmans, 1970).

Byrd, Joseph, 'Formulation of a Classical Pentecostal Homiletic in Dialogue with Contemporary Protestant Homiletics' (PhD dissertation, The Southern Baptist Theological Seminary, 1990).

—'Paul Ricoeur's Hermeneutical Theory and Pentecostal Proclamation', *Pneuma* 15 (Autumn 1993).

Campolo, Tony, *How to be Pentecostal without Speaking in Tongues* (Dallas: Word Books, 1991).

Carr, Anne E., *Transforming Grace* (San Francisco: Harper & Row, 1988).

Carter, Joan Brix, 'Fresh Winds of the Spirit: Liturgy in the Free Church', *Journal of the Interfaith Forum on Religion, Art and Architecture* (Spring 1991), pp. 28-29.

Chapman, Carol A., 'Women Leading the Church into the Twenty-first Century', *Charisma* 18 (March 1993), p. 24.

Christensen, Duane, 'Reading the Bible as an Icon', *TSF Bulletin* (January–February 1985), pp. 4-6.

Christenson, Larry, *A Charismatic Approach to Social Action* (Minneapolis: Bethany Fellowship, 1974).

Coggins, James R., and Paul G. Hiebert (eds.), *Wonders and the Word: An Examination of Issues Raised by John Wimber and the Vineyard Movement* (Winnipeg, MB: Kindred Press, 1989).

Collins, Mary, 'Liturgical Methodology and the Cultural Evolution of Worship in the United States', *Worship* 49.2 (1975), pp. 85-102.

—'Ritual Symbols and Ritual Process: The Work of Victor Turner', *Worship* 50.4 (1976), pp. 336-46.

—*Worship: Renewal to Practice* (Washington, DC: Pastoral, 1987).

Conn, Charles W., *Like a Mighty Army Moves the Church of God, 1886–1995* (Cleveland, TN: Pathway Press, 1996).

Conn, Walter, *Christian Conversion* (New York: Paulist Press, 1986).

Cordes, Paul Josef, *Call to Holiness: Reflections on the Catholic Charismatic Renewal* (Collegeville, MN: Liturgical Press, 1997).

Corum, Fred T. (ed.), *Like as of Fire* (Wilmington, MA: Fred Corum, n.d.).

Cox, Harvey, *Fire from Heaven: The Rise of Pentecostal Spirituality and the Reshaping of Religion in the Twenty-first Century* (New York: Addison–Wesley, 1995).

Cucchiari, Salvatore, 'The Lords of the Culto: Transcending Time through Place in Sicilian Pentecostal Ritual', *Journal of Ritual Studies* 4 (Winter 1990), pp. 1-14.

Darrand, T.C., *Metaphors of Social Control in a Pentecostal Sect* (Lewiston, NY: E. Mellen Press, 1983).

Davis, J.G. (ed.), *Worship and Dance* (Birmingham: University of Birmingham, Institute for the Study of Worship and Religious Architecture, 1975).

Dayton, Donald W., *Theological Roots of Pentecostalism* (Grand Rapids: Zondervan, 1987).

Dayton, Donald W., and Robert K. Johnston (eds.), *The Variety of American Evangelicalism* (Knoxville: University of Tennessee Press, 1991).

Doran, Robert, *Psychic Conversion and Theological Foundations* (Chico, CA: Scholars Press, 1981).

Douglas, Mary, *Purity and Danger: An Analysis of the Concepts of Pollution and Taboo* (New York: Ark Paperbacks, 1966).

—*Natural Symbols: Explorations in Cosmology* (New York: Pantheon Books, 1982 [1970]).

Douglas, Mary, and Steven M. Tipton (eds.), *Religion and America: Spirituality in a Secular Age* (Boston: Beacon Press, 1982, 1983).

Driver, Tom F., *The Magic of Ritual: Our Need for Liberating Rites that Transform our Lives and our Communities* (San Francisco: HarperSanFrancisco, 1991).

Durkheim, Emile, *The Elementary Forms of the Religious Life* (New York: Free Press, 1965).

Dusen, Henry P. van, 'The Third Force in Christendom', *Life* 44 (2 June 1958), pp. 113-24.

Eliade, Mircea, *The Sacred and the Profane: The Nature of Religion* (trans. Willard R. Trask; New York: Harcourt Brace Jovanovich, 1957, 1987).

Encyclopedia of California (St Clair Shores, MI: Somerset Publications, 1980).

Epstein, Daniel Mark, *Sister Aimee: The Life of Aimee Semple McPherson* (New York: Harcourt Brace Jovanovich, 1993).

Ervin, Howard, *Spirit Baptism: A Biblical Investigation* (Peabody, MA: Hendrickson, 1987).

Evdokimov, Paul, *The Art of the Icon: A Theology of Beauty* (Torrance, CA: Oakwood Publications, 1990).

Farah, Charles, 'America's Pentecostals: What They Believe', *CT* (16 October 1987), pp. 22, 24-26.

—'Differences within the Family', *Christianity Today* (16 October 16 1987), p. 25.

Faupel, David W., *The American Pentecostal Movement: A Bibliographic Essay* (Willmore, KY: B.L. Fisher Library, Asbury Theological Seminary, 1972).

—*The Gospel of the Kingdom: The Significance of Eschatology in the Development of Pentecostal Theology* (PhD dissertation; University of Birmingham, England, 1989).

Fenwick, John, and Bryan Spinks, *Worship in Transition: The Liturgical Movement in the Twentieth Century* (New York: Continuum, 1995).

Fernandez, James W., 'The Performance of Ritual Metaphors', in J. David Sapir and J. Christopher Crocker (eds.), *The Social Use of Metaphor: Essays on the Anthropology of Rhetoric* (Philadelphia: University of Pennsylvania Press, 1977), pp. 100-31.

Flora, C.B., 'Social Dislocation and Pentecostalism: A Multivariate Analysis', *Sociological Analysis* 34 (1973).

Gadamer, Hans-Georg, *Truth and Method* (trans. Joel Weinsheimer and Donald G. Marshall; New York: Crossroad, 2nd rev. edn, 1989).

Gee, Donald, *Concerning Spiritual Gifts* (Springfield, MO: Gospel Publishing, 1972 [1937]).

Geertz, Clifford, *The Interpretation of Cultures: Selected Essays* (New York: Basic Books, 1973).

—'The Balinese Cockfight', in Clifford Geertz (ed.), *Myth, Symbol and Culture* (New York: Norton, 1971).

Geertz, Clifford (ed.), *Myth, Symbol and Culture* (New York: Norton, 1971).

Gelpi, Donald L., *Charism and Sacrament: A Theology of Christian Conversion* (New York: Paulist Press, 1976).

—*Committed Worship: A Sacramental Theology for Converting Christians* (2 vols.; Collegeville, MN: Liturgical Press, 1993).

—*The Divine Mother: A Trinitarian Theology of the Holy Spirit* (Lanham, MD: University Press of America, 1984).

—*Experiencing God: A Theology of Human Emergence* (New York: University Press of America, 1987).

—*Grace as Transmuted Experience and Social Process, and Other Essays in North American Theology* (Lanham, MD: University Press of America, 1988).

—*Inculturating North American Theology: An Experiment in Foundational Method* (Atlanta: Scholars Press, 1988).

—*Pentecostalism: A Theological Viewpoint* (New York: Paulist Press, 1971).

—*Pentecostal Piety* (New York: Paulist Press, 1972).

—'Pentecostal Theology: A Roman Catholic Viewpoint', in Spittler (ed.), *Perspectives on the New Pentecostalism*, pp. 86-103.

—*The Turn to Experience in Contemporary Theology* (New York: Paulist Press, 1994).

Gerlach, Luther, 'Pentecostalism: Revolution or Counter-Revolution?', in I.I. Zaretsky and M.P. Leone (eds.), *Religious Movements in Contemporary America* (Princeton, NJ: Princeton University Press, 1974), pp. 669-99.

Gerlach, Luther, and Virginia Hine, *People, Power, Change: Movements of Social Transformation* (Indianapolis: Bobbs–Merril, 1970).

—'Five Factors Crucial to the Growth and Spread of a Modern Religious Movement', *JSSR* (Spring 1968), pp. 23-40.

Glock, Charles Y., and Robert N. Bellah (eds.), *The New Religious Consciousness* (Berkeley: University of California Press, 1976).

Gluckman, Max (ed.), 'Les rites de passage', in *idem*, *The Ritual of Social Relations* (Manchester: Manchester University Press, 1962), pp. 1-52.

Goffman, Erving, *Frame Analysis: An Essay on Face-to-Face Behavior* (Garden City, NY: Doubleday, 1974).

—*The Presentation of Self in Everyday Life* (New York: Anchor Books, 1959).

Grandy, Lee, 'Wimber Plots New Course for Vineyard', *Charisma* (22 February 1993), p. 64.

Grimes, Ronald L., *Beginnings in Ritual Studies* (Lanham, MD: University Press of America, 1982).

—*Research in Ritual Studies* (Metuchen, NJ: Scarecrow Press and the American Theological Library Association, 1985).

—*Ritual Criticism: Case Studies in its Practice, Essays on its Theory* (Columbia, SC: University of South Carolina Press, 1990).

—'Ritual Studies', in *EOR*, XII, pp. 422-25.

Hamilton, Michael P. (ed.), *The Charismatic Movement* (Grand Rapids: Eerdmans, 1975).

Hanson, Bradley C. (ed.), *Modern Christian Spirituality: Methodological and Historical Essays* (Atlanta: Scholars Press, 1990).

Hargrove, Barbara, *The Sociology of Religion: Classical and Contemporary Approaches* (Arlington Heights, IL: Harlan Davidson, 1979).

Harrell, David Edwin, Jr, *All Things Are Possible: The Healing and Charismatic Revivals in Modern America* (Bloomington, IN: University Press 1987 [1975]).

Hart, James D., *A Companion to California* (New York: Oxford University Press, 1978).

Haslam, Donald, 'Spiritual and Religious: Introduction', in *A...Compendium: People's Yellow Pages* (Santa Cruz, CA: Bootstrap Press, 4th edn, 1980), pp. 54-55.

Hawthorne, Ann, 'Introduction—Method and Spirit: Studying the Diversity of Gestures in Religion...', in Tyson, Peacock and Patterson (eds.), *Diversities of Gifts*, pp. 3-20.

Hocken, Peter D., 'Charismatic Movement', in *DPCM*, pp. 130-60.

—*One Lord One Spirit One Body* (Gaitherburg, MD: Word among Us Press, 1987).

Hocken, Peter D., *et al.*, *New Heaven? New Earth? An Encounter with Pentecostalism* (Springfield, IL: Templegate, 1977).

Hollenweger, W.J. ,'Dancing Documentaries: The Theological and Political Significance of Pentecostal Dancing', in Davis (ed.), *Worship and Dance*, pp. 76-82.

—*Pentecostalism: Origins and Developments Worldwide* (Peabody, MA: Hendrickson, 1997).

—*The Pentecostals* (ET; London: SCM Press, 1972; Minneapolis: Augsburg, 1976; Peabody, MA: Hendrickson, 1988).

—*Pentecostals between Black and White: Five Case Studies on Pentecost and Politics* (Belfast: Christian Journals, 1974).

—'Pentecostal Research: Problems and Promises', in C.E. Jones (ed.), *A Guide to the Study of the Pentecostal Movement*, I (Metuchen, NJ: Scarecrow Press, 1983), pp.vii-ix.

—'The Pentecostals and the Charismatic Movement', in Cheslyn Jones *et al.*, *The Study of Spirituality* (New York: Oxford University Press, 1986), pp. 549-51.

Hughes, Ray H., 'Preaching: A Pentecostal Perspective', in *DPCM*, pp. 722-24.

Hunter, Harold D., *Spirit-Baptism: A Pentecostal Alternative* (Lanham, MD: University Press of America, 1983).

—'Charismatic Movement', in *DCA*, pp. 241-44.

Jacobs, Louis, *Hasidic Prayer* (Oxford: Oxford University Press, 1972).

James, William, *The Varieties of Religious Experience* (New York: New American Library, 1958).

Jennings, Theodore, 'On Ritual Knowledge', *JR* 62.1 (1982), pp. 111-27.

—'Ritual Studies and Liturgical Theology: An Invitation to Dialogue', *Journal of Ritual Studies* 1.1 (1987), pp. 35-56.

Johns, Cheryl Bridges, *Pentecostal Formation: A Pedagogy among the Oppressed* (JPTSup, 2; Sheffield: Sheffield Academic Press, 1993).

Johns, Donald A., 'Singing in Tongues', in *DPCM*, p. 788.

Jones, Charles, *A Guide to the Study of the Pentecostal Movement* (2 vols.; Metuchen, NJ: Scarecrow Press, 1983).

—*A Guide to the Study of the Charismatic Movement* (Metuchen, NJ: Scarecrow Press, 1987).

Jones, Cheslyn, Geoffrey Wainwright and Edward Yarnold (eds.), *The Study of Spirituality* (New York: Oxford University Press, 1986).

—*The Study of Liturgy*. New York: Oxford University Press, 1978.

Kantzer, S., 'The Charismatics among Us', *Christianity Today* (22 February 1980).

Kearney, Michael, *World View* (Novato, CA: Chandler & Sharp, 1984).

Kelleher, Margaret Mary, 'The Communion Rite: A Study of Roman Catholic Liturgical Performance', *Journal of Ritual Studies* 5.2 (Summer 1991), pp. 99-122.

—'Liturgical Theology: A Task and a Method', *Worship* 62.1 (January 1988), pp. 2-25.

—'Liturgy: An Ecclesial Act of Meaning', *Worship* 59.6 (November 1985), pp. 482-97.

Kelsey, Morton, *Dreams: The Dark Speech of the Spirit* (Garden City, NY: Doubleday, 1968).

—*Tongue Speaking* (New York: Crossroad, 1981).

Kendrick, Klaude, *The Promise Fulfilled: A History of the Modern Pentecostal Movement* (Springfield, MO: Gospel Publishing, 1961).

Kraft, Charles H., *Christianity with Power: Discovering the Truth about Signs and Wonders* (Ann Arbor, MI: Servant Publications, 1989).

Kraiss, Wayne, and Barbara Kraiss, 'The Changing Face of Worship', *Theology, News and Notes* (March 1991), pp. 7-11.

Krondorfer, Bjorn (ed.), *Body and Bible: Interpreting and Experiencing Biblical Narratives* (Valley Forge, PA: Trinity Press International, 1992).

Ladd, George Eldon, *Crucial Questions about the Kingdom of God* (Grand Rapids: Eerdmans, 1952).

—*The Gospel of the Kingdom* (Grand Rapids: Eerdmans, 1959).

—*The Presence of the Future* (Grand Rapids: Eerdmans, 1974).

—*A Theology of the New Testament* (Grand Rapids: Eerdmans, 1974).

Land, Steven J., *Pentecostal Spirituality: A Passion for the Kingdom* (JPTSup, 1; Sheffield: Sheffield Academic Press, 1993).

—'Pentecostal Spirituality: Living in the Spirit', in Louis Dupre and Don Saliers (eds.), *Christian Spirituality*. III. *Post-Reformation and Modern* (World Spirituality Series; New York: Crossroad, 1989), pp. 479-99.

Lane, Ralph, Jr, 'Catholic Charismatic Renewal', in Charles Y. Glock and Robert N. Bellah (eds.), *The New Religious Consciousness* (Berkeley: University of California Press, 1976), pp. 162-79.

Lawson, Steve, 'The Foursquare Church Faces the Twenty-first Century: A Pentecostal Denomination Reshapes its Message and its Methods so It Can Reach Contemporary Society', *Charisma* 18 (March 1993), pp. 16-26.

—'Preparing to Solve Twenty-first Century Urban Problems', *Charisma* 18 (March 1993), p. 26.

Lederle, Henry, *Treasures Old and New* (Peabody, MA: Hendrickson Publishers, 1988).

Lee, Jae Bum, 'Pentecostal Type distinctives and Korean Protestant Church Growth' (PhD dissertation, Fuller Theological Seminary, 1986).

Leach, Edmund, *Political Systems of Highland Burma* (Boston: Beacon Press, 1964).

Leech, Kenneth, *Soul Friend: The Practice of Christian Spirituality* (San Francisco: Harper & Row, 1977).

Lewis, I.M., *Ecstatic Religion: An Anthropological Study of Spirit Possession and Shamanism* (Baltimore: Penguin Books, 1971).

LIFE, 'History of Foursquaredom' (Unpublished mimeographed manuscript prepared by LIFE Bible College, n.d.), p. 266.

Lonergan, Bernard F., *Method in Theology* (New York: Herder, 1972).

Luecke, David S., 'Introduction, the Changing Face of Worship', *Theology, News and Notes* 37 (March 1991), pp. 3-4.

Ma, Wonsuk, and Robert P. Menzies (eds.), *Pentecostalism in Context: Essays in Honor of William Menzies* (JPTSup, 11; Sheffield: Sheffield Academic Press, 1997).

Malinowski, Bronislaw, 'Magic, Science, and Religion', in James Needham (ed.), *Science, Religion and Reality* (New York: Macmillan, 1925), pp. 17-29.

Maloney, H. Newton, and A. Adams Lovekin, *Glossolalia: Behavioral Science Perspectives on Speaking in Tongues* (New York: Oxford University Press, 1985).

Marcus, George E., and Michael M.J. Fischer, *Anthropology as Cultural Critique* (Chicago: University of Chicago Press, 1986).

Martin, David, *Tongues of Fire: The Explosion of Protestantism in Latin America* (Oxford: Basil Blackwell, 1990).

Marty, Martin E., *A Nation of Behavers* (Chicago: University of Chicago Press, 1976).

—'Pentecostalism in the Context of American Piety and Practice', in Vinson Synan (ed.), *Aspects of Pentecostal-Charismatic Origins* (Plainfield, NJ: Logos International, 1975), pp. 193-233.

—*Pilgrims in their Own Land* (Boston: Little, Brown & Co., 1984).

McClung, L.G., Jr, 'Evangelism', in *DPCM*, pp. 248-88.

—'Missiology', in *DPCM*, pp. 607-609.

McDonnell, Kilian, 'The Ideology of Pentecostal Conversion', *JES* (Winter 1968), pp. 114-15.

—*Charismatic Renewal and the Churches* (New York: Seabury, 1976).

McDonnell, Kilian (ed.), *Presence, Power, Praise: Documents on the Charismatic Renewal* (3 vols.; Collegeville, MN: Liturgical Press, 1980).

McDonnell, Kilian, and Arnold Bittlinger, *The Baptism in the Holy Spirit as an Ecumenical Problem* (South Bend, IN: Charismatic Renewal Services, 1972).

McDonnell, Kilian, and George Montague (eds.), *Fanning the Flame* (Collegeville, MN: Liturgical Press, 1991).

—*Christian Initiation and Baptism in the Holy Spirit* (Collegeville, MN: Liturgical Press, 1991).

McGee, Gary B., 'The Azusa Street Revival and 20th Century Missions', *IBMR* 12 (April 1988), pp. 58-61.

—'Leaving Room for Sacred Pauses', *Advance* 28 (January 1992), pp. 8-9.

—'Missions, Overseas, (North American)', in *DPCM*, pp. 610-25.

McGuire, Meredith B., *Pentecostal Catholics: Power, Charisma, and Order in a Religious Movement* (Philadelphia: Temple University Press, 1982).

—*Ritual Healing in Suburban America* (New Brunswick, NJ: Rutgers University Press, 1988).

McNally, Randal G., *Community as Social Text: A Critical Hermeneutic of Select Asian and North American Colleges and Universities* (PhD dissertation, University of San Francisco, 1991).

McPherson, Aimee Semple, *Declaration of Faith* (Los Angeles: International Church of the Foursquare Gospel, n.d.).

—*The Foursquare Gospel* (n.p.: Echo Park Evangelistic Association, 1946).

—*The Story of my Life* (Hollywood, CA: International Correspondents, 1951).

—*This Is That: Personal Experiences, Sermons and Writings* (Los Angeles: Echo Park Evangelistic Association, 1923).

Menzies, William W., *Anointed to Serve: The Story of the Assemblies of God* (Springfield, MO: Gospel Publishing, 1971).

Meyer, John W., and Brian Ravan, 'Institutionalized Organizations'. Formal Structure as Myth and Ceremony', American Journal of Sociology 83 (1977), pp. 340-63.

Michaels, J. Ramsey, 'Gifts of the Spirit', in *DPCM*, pp. 332-34.

Mills, Watson E., *Charismatic Religion in Modern Research: A Bibliography*) Macon, GA: Mercer University Press, 1985).

Mol, Hans, *Identity and the Sacred* (New York: Free Press, 1976).

Moore, Sally F., and Barbara G. Myerhoff (eds.), *Secular Ritual* (Assun/Amsterdam: Van Gorcum, 1977).

Myerhoff, Barbara G., 'A Death in Due Time: Construction of Self and Culture in Ritual Drama', in John J. MacAloon (ed.), *Rites, Drama, Festival, Spectacle: Rehearsals toward a Theory of Cultural Performance* (Philadelphia: Institute for the Study of Human Issues, 1984), pp. 149-78.

—*Number our Days* (New York: Simon & Schuster, 1978).

Myerhoff, Barbara G., *et al.*, 'Rites of Passage, an Overview', in *EOR*, XII, pp. 380-86.

Nichol, J.T., *Pentecostalism* (New York: Harper & Row, 1966).

Nouwen, Henri J.M., *Behold the Beauty of the Lord: Praying with Icons* (Notre Dame, IN: Ave Maria Press, 1987).

Numbers, Ronald L., and Darrel W. Amundsen (eds.), *Caring and Curing: Health and Medicine in the Western Religious Traditions* (New York: Macmillan, 1986).

O'Connor, Edward D., *The Pentecostal Movement in the Catholic Church* (Notre Dame, IN: Ave Maria Press, 1971).

Obeyesekere, Gananath, *Medusa's Hair: An Essay on Personal Symbols and Religious Experience* (Chicago: University of Chicago Press, 1981).

Oesterley, W.O.E., *The Sacred Dance: A Study in Comparative Folklore* (Cambridge: Cambridge University Press, 1923).

Ong, Walter J., *The Barbarian within and Other Fugitive Essays and Studies* (New York: Macmillan, 1962).

—*Their Presence of the Word: Some Prolegomena for Cultural and Religious History* (New Haven: Yale University Press, 1967).

Otto, Rudolf, *The Idea of the Holy: An Inquiry into the Non-Rational Factor in the Idea of the Divine and its Relation to the Rational* (London: Oxford University Press, 2nd edn 1950 [1923]).

Parker, Stephen E., *Led by the Spirit: Toward a Practical Theology of Pentecostal Discernment and Decision Making* (JPTSup, 7; Sheffield: Sheffield Academic Press, 1997).

Patterson, Ben, 'Cause for Concern', *CT* 30 (8 August 1986), p. 20.

Pierce, T.B., 'The Dance and Corporate Worship', *The Pentecost Evangel* (2 November 1986), pp. 8-10.

Pike, K., *Language in Relation to a Unified Theory of the Structure of Human Behavior*, I (Glendale: Summer Institute of Linguistics, 1954).

Poloma, Margaret M., *The Charismatic Movement: Is There a New Pentecost?* (Boston: Twayne Publishers, 1982).

—*The Assemblies of God at the Crossroads: Charisma and Institutional Dilemmas* (Knoxville: University of Tennessee Press, 1989).

Pratt, Thomas D., 'The Need to Dialogue: A Review of the Debate on the Controversy of Signs, Wonders, Miracles and Spiritual Warfare Raised in the Literature of the Third Wave Movement', *Pneuma* 13 (Spring 1991), pp. 7-32.

Quebedeaux, Richard, *The New Charismatics*. II.4 *How a Christian Renewal Movement Became Part of the American Religious Mainstream* (San Francisco: HarperSanFrancisco, 1983).

Radcliff-Brown, A.R., *Taboo* (Cambridge: Cambridge University Press, 1939).

Ranaghan, Kevin, and Dorothy Ranaghan, *Catholic Pentecostals* (New York: Paulist Press, 1969).

Rapoport-Albert, Ada, 'God and the Zaddik as the Two Focal Points of Hasidic Worship', *HR* 18 (1978), pp. 269-325.

Reid, Daniel G., Robert Linder, Bruce Shelley and Harry Stout (eds.), *The Dictionary of Christianity in America* (Downers Grove, IL: InterVarsity Press, 1990).

Religion and the Dance: A Report of the Consultation on the Dance (New York: Department of Worship and the Arts, National Council of Churches, 1960).

Ricoeur, P., *Hermeneutics and the Human Sciences* (ed. and trans. John B. Thompson; Cambridge: Cambridge University Press, 1981).

—The Model of the Text: Meaningful Action Considered as Text', in *idem* (ed.), *Hermeneutics*, pp. 197-221.

—*The Symbolism of Evil* (trans. Emerson Buchanan; Boston: Beacon Press, 1967).

Riggs, Ralph M., *The Spirit Himself* (Springfield, MO: Gospel Publishing House, 1949).

Robeck, Cecil M., Jr, 'The Assemblies of God and Ecumenical Cooperation: 1920–1965', in Ma and Menzies (eds.), *Pentecostalism in Context*, pp. 107-150.

—'Azusa Street Revival', in *DPCM*, pp. 31-36.

—'International Church of the Foursquare Gospel', in *DPCM*, pp. 461-63.

—Introduction, in Frank Bartleman, *Witness to Pentecost* (New York: Garland Publishing, 1985).

—'McPherson, Aimee Semple', in *DPCM*, pp. 568-71.

—'McPherson, Rolf Kennedy', in *DPCM*, pp. 571-72.

—'Pentecostals and the Apostolic Faith: Implications for Ecumenism', *Pneuma* 9 (1987), pp. 61-84.

—'The Pentecostal Movements in the U.S.: Recent Historical Bibliography', *Evangelical Studies* 3 (March 1986), pp. 7-9.

Robins, Roger G., 'Pentecostal Movement', in *DCA*, pp. 885-91.

—'Pentecostals and the Apostolic Faith: Implications for Ecumenism', *Pneuma* 9 (1987), pp. 61-84.

—'The Rule of the Holy Spirit in Early Pentecostalism: Order in the Courts' (unpublished paper presented to the Sixteenth Annual Meeting of the Society for Pentecostal Studies, 13–15 November 1986, at Southern California College, Costa Mesa, California).

Roozen, David A., William McKinney and Jackson W. Carroll, *Varieties of Religious Presence: Mission in Public Life* (New York: Pilgrim Press, 1984).

Salier, Don E., *The Soul in Paraphrase: Prayer and the Religious Affections* (New York: Seabury, 1980).

Salitore, Edward V., *California: Past, Present, Future* (Lakewood, CA: Edward Salitore, 1973).

Samarin, W.J., *Tongues of Men and Angels: The Religious Language of Pentecostalism* (New York: Macmillan, 1972).

Sarles, Ken L., 'An Appraisal of the Signs and Wonders Movement', *BSac* 145 (January–March 1988), pp. 57-82.

Schechner, Richard, *Essays on Performance Theory 1970–1976* (New York: Drama Book Specialists, 1977).

—'The Future of Ritual', *Journal of Ritual Studies* 1 (1987), pp. 5-33.

Schechner, Richard, and Willa Appel (eds.), *By Means of Performance: Intercultural Studies of Theater and Ritual* (Cambridge: Cambridge University Press, 1989).

Schmidt, John P., 'New Wine from the Vineyard', *Direction* 17 (Fall 1988), pp. 42-56.

Schneiders, Sandra, 'Spirituality in the Academy', *Theological Studies* 50 (1989), pp. 676-97.

—'The Study of Christian Spirituality', *CSB* 6.1 (1998), pp. 1-12.

—'Theology and Spirituality: Strangers, Rivals, or Partners?', *Horizons* 13 (1986), pp. 253-74.

Scholem, Gershom G., *Major Trends in Jewish Mysticism* (New York: Schocken Books, 1941), Ch. 9.

Schultz, Lee, *Biennial Report of the Assemblies of God* (Springfield, MO: Executive Presbytery for the 44th General Council, 1991).

Sheldrake, Philip, *Spirituality and History: Questions of Interpretation and Method* (New York: Crossroad, 1992).

Shememann, Alexander, *Introduction to Liturgical Theology* (New York: St Vladimir's Seminary Press, 1975.

Shepperd, Jerry W., 'Sociology of Pentecostalism', in *DPCM*, pp. 794-99.

—'Worship', in *DPCM*, pp. 903-905.

Smelser, N.J., *Theory of Collective Behavior* (New York: Free Press, 1962).

Smith, H.B., 'America's Pentecostals: Where They Are Going', *CT* (16 October 1987), pp. 27-30.

Smith, Jonathan Z., *Imagining Religion: From Babylon to Jonestown* (Chicago: University of Chicago Press, 1982).

Spittler, Russell P., 'The Pentecostal View', in Donald L. Alexander (ed.), *Christian Spirituality: Five Views of Sanctification* (Downers Grove, IL: InterVarsity Press, 1988), pp. 133-54.

—'Spirituality: Pentecostal and Charismatic', in *DPCM*, pp. 800-809.

—'Suggested Areas for Further Research in Pentecostal Studies', *Pneuma* 5 (1983), pp. 40-43.

Spittler, Russell P. (ed.), *Perspectives on the New Pentecostalism* (Grand Rapids: Baker Book House, 1976).

—'Scripture and the Theological Enterprise: View from a Big Canoe', in Robert K. Johnson (ed.), *The Use of the Bible in Theology: Evangelical Options* (Atlanta: John Knox Press, 1985).

Spradley, James P., *Participant Observation* (San Francisco: Holt, Rinehart & Winston, 1980).

Springer, Kevin (ed.), *Power Encounters among Christians in the Western World* (San Francisco: HarperSanFrancisco, 1988).

Stafford, Tim, 'Testing the Wine from John Wimber's Vineyard', *CT* 30.11 (8 August 1986), pp. 17-22.

Steindl-Rast, David, *A Listening Heart: The Art of Contemplative Living* (New York: Crossroad, 1988).

Stevenson, Geoffrey, and Judith Stevenson, *Steps of Faith: A Practical Introduction to Mime and Dance* (Eastbourne, Sussex: Kingsway, 1984).

Suenens, Leon Joseph Cardinal, *A New Pentecost?* (New York: Seabury, 1974).

Sullivan, Francis A., 'Catholic Charismatic Renewal', in *DPCM*, pp. 110-26.

Sullivan, Lawrence E., 'Body Works: Knowledge of the Body in the Study of Religion', *History of Religions* 30.1 (1990), pp. 86-99.

—'Sound and Senses: Toward a Hermeneutics of Performance', *HR* 26.1 (1986), pp. 1-33.

Synan, Vinson, *The Holiness–Pentecostal Movement in the United States* (Grand Rapids: Eerdmans, 1971).

—*In the Latter Days* (Ann Arbor, MI: Servant Books, 1984).

—'Fulfilling Sister Aimee's Dream: The Foursquare Church Is Alive Today', *Charism* (July 1987), pp. 53-54.

—'Pentecostalism: Varieties and Contributions', *Pneuma* 8 (Fall 1986), pp. 31-49.

—*The Twentieth-Century Pentecostal Explosion* (Altamonte Springs, FL: Creation House, 1987).

—'The Third Force in Christendom', *Life* 9 (June 1958), p. 124.

Synan, Vinson (ed.), *Aspects of Pentecostal–Charismatic Origins* (Plainfield, NJ: Logos International, 1975).

Tambiah, Stanley J., 'A Performative Approach to Ritual', *Proceedings of the British Academy* 65 (1979), pp. 113-69.

Taylor, Margaret, *Look up and Live* (North Aurora, IL: The Sharing Company, 1953).

Thomas, Lately, *Storming Heaven: The Lives and Turmoils of Minnie Kennedy and Aimee Semple McPherson* (New York: William Morrow, 1970).

Tinlin, Paul B., and Edith L. Blumhofer, 'Decade of Decline or Harvest? Dilemmas of the Assemblies of God', *The Christian Century* (10–17 July 1991), pp. 684-87.

Tipton, Steven M., *Getting Saved from the Sixties: Moral Meaning in Conversion and Cultural Change* (Berkeley: University of California Press, 1982).

Troeltsch, Ernst, *The Social Teachings of the Christian Church* (trans. Olive Wyon; London: George Allen, 1931).

Turner, Victor, *Dramas, Fields, and Metaphors: Symbolic Action in Human Society* (Ithaca, NY: Cornell University Press, 1974).

—*The Forest of Symbols: Aspects of Ndembu Ritual* (Ithaca, NY: Cornell University Press, 1967).

—*From Ritual to Theater: The Human Seriousness of Play* (New York: Performing Arts Journal Publications, 1982).

—*The Ritual Process: Structure and Anti-Structure* (Ithaca, NY: Cornell University Press, 1977).

—'Variations on a Theme of Liminality', in Sally F. Moore and Barbara G. Myerhoff (eds.), *Secular Ritual* (Assen: Van Gorcum, 1977), pp. 36-52.

Tyrrell, Bernard J., *Christotherapy II* (New York: Paulist Press, 1982).

Tyson, Ruel, Jr, James L. Peacock and Daniel W. Patterson (eds.), *Diversities of Gifts: Field Studies in Southern Religion* (Chicago: University of Illinois Press, 1988).

Underhill, Evelyn, *The Essentials of Mysticism and Other Essays* (New York: E.P. Dutton, 1960 [1920]).

—*Mysticism* (New York: New American Library, 12th edn, 1974 [1911]).

—*Mystics of the Church* (Wilton, CN: Morehouse–Barlow, 1925).

—*Practical Mysticism* (New York: E.P. Dutton, 1915).

US Bureau of the Census, *State and Metropolitan Area Data Book* (Washington, DC: US Government Printing Office, 1986).

Van Gennep, Arnold, *The Rites of Passage* (trans. Monika B. Vizedom and Gabrielle L. Caffee; Chicago: University of Chicago Press, 1960).

Wacker, Grant, 'America's Pentecostals: Who They Are', *CT* (16 October 1987), pp. 16-21.

—'Bibliography and Historiography of Pentecostalism (U.S.)', in *DPCM*, pp. 65-76.

—'Character and the Modernization of North American Pentecostalism', in the unpublished conference papers of the Twenty-first Annual Meeting of the Society for Pentecostal Studies, (Lakeland, FL: Southeastern College, November 1991), p. 15.

—'The Function of Faith in Primitive Pentecostalism', *HTR* 77.3-4 (1984), pp. 353-75.

—'Marching to Zion', *Church History* 54 (December 1985), pp. 496-511.

—'Pentecostalism', in Charles H. Lippy and Peter W. Williams (eds.), *The Encyclopedia of American Religious Experience*, II (New York: Charles Scribner's Sons, 1988), pp. 933-45.

—'The Pentecostal Tradition', in Ronald L. Numbers and Darrel W. Amundsen (eds.), *Caring and Curing: Health and Medicine in the Western Religious Traditions* (New York: Macmillan, 1986), pp. 514-38.

Wagner, C. Peter, 'Church Growth', in *DPCM*, pp. 180-95.

—*Look Out! The Pentecostals Are Coming* (Carol Stream, IL: Creation House, 1969).

—'Third Wave', in *DPCM*, pp. 843-44.

—'Vineyard Christian Fellowship', in *DPCM*, pp. 871-72.

—'Wimber, John', in *DPCM*, p. 889.

Wallace, Anthony F.C., *Religion: An Anthropological View* (New York: Random House, 1966).

—'Revitalization Movements', *American Anthropologist* 58 (1956), pp. 264-81.

Ware, Kallistos, 'The Spirituality of the Icon', in Cheslyn Jones, Geoffrey Wainwright and

Edward Y. Arnold (eds.), *The Study of Spirituality* (New York: Oxford University Press, 1986), pp. 195-98.

Warner, Wayne E., 'International Church of the Foursquare Gospel', in *DCA*, p. 578.

Weber, Max, *The Protestant Ethic and the Spirit of Capitalism* (New York: Charles Scribner's Sons, 1958).

—*The Sociology of Religion* (trans. Ephraim Fischoff; Boston: Beacon Press, 4th edn, 1963).

—*The Theory of Social and Economic Organization* (New York: Free Press, 1947).

Whalin, W. Terry, 'Breaking the Rules to Build a Twenty-first Century Church', *Charisma* 18 (March 1993), p. 22.

White, Charles E., 'Phoebe Worrall Palmer', in *DCA*, pp. 860-61.

White, James F., *Introduction to Christian Worship* (Nashville: Abingdon Press, rev. edn, 1990).

—*Protestant Worship and Church Architecture* (New York: Oxford University Press, 1964).

—*Protestant Worship: Traditions in Transition* (Louisville, KY: Westminster/John Knox Press, 1989).

White, John, *When the Spirit Comes with Power: Signs and Wonders among God's People* (Downers Grove, IL: InterVarsity Press, 1988).

Williams, C.G., *Tongues of the Spirit: A Study of Pentecostal Glossolalia and Related Phenomena* (Cardiff: University of Wales, 1991).

Williams, Don, *Signs, Wonders, and the Kingdom of God: A Biblical Guide for the Reluctant Skeptic* (Ann Arbor, MI: Servant Publications, 1989).

Williams, J. Rodman, *The Gift of the Holy Spirit Today* (Plainfield, NJ: Logos International, 1980).

—*The Pentecostal Reality* (Plainfield, NJ: Logos International, 1972).

Williams, Peter W., *Popular Religion in America: Symbolic Change and the Modernization Process in Historical Perspective* (Urbana, IL: University of Illinois Press, 1989).

Wilson, Bryan R., 'An Analysis of Sect Development', *American Sociological Review* 24 (1959).

—*Sects and Society: A Sociological Study of the Elim Tabernacle, Christian Science, and Christadelphians* (Berkeley: University of California Press, 1961).

Wilson, Everett A., 'Identity, Community, and Status: The Legacy of the Central American Pentecostal Pioneers', in Joel A. Carenter and Wilbert R. Shenk (eds.), *Earthen Vessels: American Evangelicals and Foreign Missions, 1880–1980* (Grand Rapids: Eerdmans, 1990), pp. 133-51.

—'Latin American Pentecostal', *Pneuma* 9 (Spring 1987), pp. 85-90.

—'Revival and Revolution in Latin America', in Edith Blumhofer and Randall Balmer (eds.), *Modern Christian Revivals* (Urbana: University of Illinois Press, 1993), pp. 180-93.

—*Strategy of the Spirit: J. Philip Hogan and the Growth of the Assemblies of God Worldwide, 1960–1990* (Carlisle: Paternoster Press, 1997).

Wilson, Everett A., and Darlene Little (compilers), *Seventy-Five Years of Dreams, of Destiny... A Narrative and Pictorial History* (n.p., 1994).

Wimber, Carol, 'A Hunger for God: A Reflective Look at the Vineyard's Beginnings', *The Vineyard Newsletter* 2 (Fall 1987), pp. 1-3, 7.

Wimber, John, *Power Healing* (San Francisco: Harper & Row, 1987).

—*Power Points: A Basic Primer for Christians* (Anaheim, CA: Vineyard Ministries International, 1985).

—*Power Points: Seven Steps to Christian Growth* (San Francisco: HarperCollins, 1991).

Wimber, John, with Kevin Springer, *Power Evangelism* (San Francisco: Harper & Row, 1986).

Worsely, Peter, *The Trumpet Shall Sound* (New York: Schocken Books, 2nd edn, 1968).

Wosien, Maria-Gabriele, *Sacred Dance: Encounter with the Gods* (New York: Avon Books, 1974).

Wuthnow, Robert, *The Consciousness Reformation* (Berkeley: University of California Press, 1976).

—*Meaning and Moral Order: Explorations in Cultural Analysis* (Berkeley: University of California Press, 1987).

Wuthnow, Robert *et al.*, *Cultural Analysis* (New York: Routledge & Kegan Paul, 1984).

Zaehner, R.C., *Mysticism, Sacred and Profane: An Inquiry into Some Varieties of Praeternatural Experience* (Oxford: Clarendon Press, 1957).

—*Zen, Drugs, and Mysticism* (New York: Pantheon Books, 1972).

Zuesse, Evan M., 'Ritual', in *EOR*, XII, pp. 405-22.

INDEX OF AUTHORS

JOURNAL OF PENTECOSTAL THEOLOGY

Supplement Series

1 PENTECOSTAL SPIRITUALITY: A PASSION FOR THE KINGDOM
Steven J. Land
pa £15.95/$21.95
ISBN 1 85075 442 X

2 PENTECOSTAL FORMATION:
A PEDAGOGY AMONG THE OPPRESSED
Cheryl Bridges-Johns
pa £10.95/$13.95
ISBN 1 85075 438 1

3 ON THE CESSATION OF THE CHARISMATA:
THE PROTESTANT POLEMIC ON MIRACLES
Jon Ruthven
pa £15.95/$21.95
ISBN 1 85075 405 5

4 ALL TOGETHER IN ONE PLACE:
THEOLOGICAL PAPERS FROM THE BRIGHTON CONFERENCE
ON WORLD EVANGELIZATION
Harold D. Hunter and Peter D. Hocken (eds.)
pa £15.95/$21.95
ISBN 1 85075 406 3

5 SPIRIT AND RENEWAL:
ESSAYS IN HONOR OF J. RODMAN WILLIAMS
Mark Wilson (ed.)
pa £15.95/$21.95
ISBN 1 85075 471 3